30119 026 404 01 4

WA

D1357144

GUIDE TO ECONOMIC INDICATORS

OTHER ECONOMIST BOOKS

Guide to Analysing Companies
Guide to Business Modelling
Guide to Business Planning
Guide to the European Union
Guide to Financial Management
Guide to Financial Markets
Guide to Hedge Funds
Guide to Investment Strategy
Guide to Management Ideas and Gurus
Guide to Organisation Design
Guide to Project Management
Guide to Supply Chain Management
Numbers Guide
Style Guide

Book of Obituaries
Brands and Branding
Business Consulting
Buying Professional Services
The City
Coaching and Mentoring
Dealing with Financial Risk
Doing Business in China
Economics
Emerging Markets
The Future of Technology
Headhunters and How to Use Them
Mapping the Markets
Marketing
Organisation Culture
Successful Strategy Execution
The World of Business

Directors: an A–Z Guide
Economics: an A–Z Guide
Investment: an A–Z Guide
Negotiation: an A–Z Guide

Pocket World in Figures

GUIDE TO ECONOMIC INDICATORS

Making Sense of Economics

THE ECONOMIST IN ASSOCIATION WITH
PROFILE BOOKS LTD

Published by Profile Books Ltd
3A Exmouth House, Pine Street, London EC1R 0JH
www.profilebooks.com

Additional research Lisa Davies, James Fransham, Carol Howard, David McKelvey,
Jane Shaw, Christopher Wilson

Typeset in EcoType by MacGuru Ltd
info@macguru.org.uk

Printed in Great Britain by
Clays, Bungay, Suffolk

A CIP catalogue record for this book is available
from the British Library

ISBN 978 1 84668 176 9

The paper this book is printed on is certified by the © 1996 Forest Stewardship
Council A.C. (FSC). It is ancient-forest friendly. The printer holds FSC chain of
custody SGS-COC-2061

Contents

Gross domestic product (GDP) and gross national product (GNP) or gross national income (GNI), as it is sometimes referred to now, are similar measures of total economic activity. GDP has slightly wider international usage and the term is used in this book to mean either GDP or GNP/GNI unless the context makes it clear that the reference is to one in particular. Precise definitions are given on pages 28–29.

List of tables

List of charts

1 Interpreting economic indicators

An economist is an expert who will know tomorrow why the things he predicted yesterday didn't happen today.

Dr Laurence J. Peter

All politicians seem able to demonstrate that their party presided over the fastest economic growth, the biggest fall in unemployment or the lowest inflation. Common sense suggests that they cannot all be correct. How can you interpret such claims?

This book shows how economic figures can be manipulated to demonstrate almost anything. More important, it explains how to read them, cut through any media hype and make up your mind about what they show, requiring no prior knowledge of economics or statistics. It deals with all the most important economic indicators and answers questions such as the following.

- **What are they?** What are GDP, the invisibles balance, the terms of trade, the labour force?
- **What do they cover?** What is included in retail sales data, what is not in GDP, who is in the labour force?
- **What is their significance?** What do GDP, capacity utilisation or the terms of trade tell us?
- **Where and when are they are published?** Should you look for weekly figures from the central bank, monthly information from a private organisation, quarterly numbers from the Department of Commerce, and so on?
- **How reliable are they?** Reasonably reliable in the case of spending by a particular government department, reasonably unreliable in the case of the size of the labour force. Who knows how many people not registered as unemployed would come forward if jobs were suddenly available?
- **Will they be revised or are the first-reported figures set in stone?** For example, GDP data are revised endlessly, consumer-price data rarely.
- **How should they be interpreted?** The most important question.

Why interpret economic figures?

There are as many reasons for interpreting economic indicators as there are published statistics. You may want to:

- get the best return on investing your money;
- measure companies and their products;
- judge if the time is right to give the go-ahead to a new capital investment project, to launch a takeover or to move into new markets;
- get a better understanding of how an economy is performing;
- judge the government's economic policies;
- obtain a feel for an unfamiliar economy;
- compare several countries;
- make a forecast; or
- simply obtain a better understanding of the news.

The countries

This book takes a global view and is intended as a guide to interpreting economic indicators worldwide.

Since it would be cumbersome if not impossible to list figures for all countries, the tables generally show data for the largest industrial countries and the leading developing countries. Where appropriate, totals or averages are also shown for the OECD and the euro area (see definitions below).

The Economist includes over 40 countries each week, with more on its website, www.economist.com. This book therefore provides the background to these figures and the historical data behind the up-to-the-minute information.

America. If at times undue attention seems to be given to America, it is because the American economy occupies such a dominant position, accounting as it does for about one-fifth of world output and over one-third of the output of the industrialised countries.

Bankers, financiers and politicians worldwide depend on economic events in America. For example, apart from the direct effects on the major financial markets, a change in the dollar's exchange rate affects the prices of many internationally traded commodities such as oil, and influences trade balances worldwide, especially those of the 40 or so countries with currencies directly pegged to the dollar.

Table 1.1 **World output**

	Countries no.	*World GDP* 1998 %	2008 %
Advanced countries			
US		23.5	20.6
Japan		8.1	6.3
Germany		5.3	4.2
UK		3.6	3.2
France		3.7	3.1
Italy		3.4	2.6
Canada		2.1	1.9
Other advanced countries	26	13.6	13.2
Total advanced countries	**33**	**63.3**	**55.1**
Developing countries			
Africa	50	2.8	3.1
Asia	26	14.5	21.0
Middle East and Turkey	14	3.5	4.0
Latin America and Caribbean	32	9.2	8.6
Total developing countries	**122**	**30.0**	**36.7**
Countries in transition			
Central and Eastern Europe	15	3.3	3.6
CIS, Georgia and Mongolia	13	3.4	4.6
Total world	183	100.0	100.0
Miscellaneous groups			
G7	7	49.8	42.0
EU	27	25.5	22.0
Euro area	16	18.7	15.7
Sub-Saharan Africa	47	2.2	2.4
Newly industrialised Asian economies	4	3.3	3.7

Note: The GDP shares are based on the purchasing-power-parity valuation of country GDPs.
Source: IMF

Country groups. In 2008 total world economic output was around $60,000 billion a year at market exchange rates and $70,000 billion a year at purchasing power parity. Table 1.1 shows how this was split among advanced and developing countries, and various other groups which are sometimes used as a basis for analysis. The terminology and definitions are internationally accepted and are used by the World Bank (IBRD) and the International Monetary Fund (IMF), among others.

Developing countries. Of the 183 countries in Table 1.1, the 122 developing countries account for over one-third of world output. Of these the 47 sub-Saharan African states account for less than one-fortieth of world output. Many of them are debt-laden, with slow economic growth and low income per head. They are used in this book as an example of one of the extremes of economic performance.

Asia. At the other extreme, the four Asian newly industrialised countries (NICs) – Hong Kong, Singapore, South Korea and Taiwan – account for 3.7% of world output. Their economic growth rates – and those of China (the world's third largest economy), Indonesia, Malaysia and Thailand – were among the highest in the world in the 1980s and 1990s, up to the Asian crisis of 1997.

Key regional and economic groups

Group of Seven (G7)
Canada, France, Germany, Italy, Japan, the UK and the United States, which together accounted for over 50% of world GDP in 2008, measured at market exchange rates; over 40% using purchasing-power parity exchange rates. The G8 includes Russia.

European Union (EU – 27 countries)
Austria, Belgium, Bulgaria, Cyprus, Czech Republic, Denmark, Estonia, Finland, France, Germany, Greece, Hungary, Ireland, Italy, Latvia, Lithuania, Luxembourg, Malta, the Netherlands, Poland, Portugal, Romania, Slovakia, Slovenia, Spain, Sweden and the UK.

Euro area (16 countries)
Eleven of the EU's member states (Austria, Belgium, Finland, France, Germany, Ireland, Italy, Luxembourg, the Netherlands, Portugal and Spain) adopted a single currency, the euro, on January 1st 1999. Greece joined on January 1st 2001, Slovenia on January 1st 2007, Cyprus and Malta on

January 1st 2008 and Slovakia on January 1st 2009. Economic statistics for the euro area, as well as national economies, are published in *The Economist* each week. Table 1.2 gives some key data on the euro area countries.

Advanced countries (IMF definition – 33)
Euro area members plus Australia, Canada, Czech Republic, Denmark, Iceland, Israel, Japan, New Zealand, Norway, Sweden, Switzerland, the UK and the United States, plus the four newly industrialised Asian economies.

Organisation for Economic Co-operation and Development (OECD – 31)
As at May 2010, the euro area (without Cyprus, Malta or Slovenia) and other G7 countries plus Australia, Chile, Czech Republic, Denmark, Hungary, Iceland, Mexico, New Zealand, Norway, Poland, South Korea, Sweden, Switzerland and Turkey. The term industrial countries is used in this book to refer to the OECD. Strictly speaking the two are not quite the same since the OECD includes some emerging countries but they account for only a small amount of OECD economic output.

Sub-Saharan Africa
African countries without a Mediterranean coastline.

Organisation of Petroleum Exporting Countries (OPEC – 12)
Algeria, Angola, Ecuador, Iran, Iraq, Kuwait, Libya, Nigeria, Qatar, Saudi Arabia, United Arab Emirates and Venezuela.

Newly industrialised Asian economies (4)
Hong Kong, Singapore, South Korea and Taiwan.

Visegrad four
Czech Republic, Hungary, Poland and Slovakia.

Commonwealth of Independent States (CIS – 11)
Armenia, Azerbaijan, Belarus, Kazakhstan, Kyrgyzstan, Moldova, Russia, Tajikistan, Turkmenistan, Ukraine, Uzbekistan.

The indicators

This book groups the major economic indicators together in chapters to highlight linkages and aid interpretation. These groups, which are not mutually exclusive, cover the economy and economic growth, population and employment, government fiscal policies, consumers,

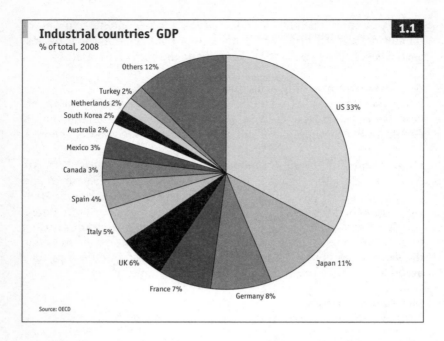

1.1

Industrial countries' GDP
% of total, 2008

- Others 12%
- Turkey 2%
- Netherlands 2%
- South Korea 2%
- Australia 2%
- Mexico 3%
- Canada 3%
- Spain 4%
- Italy 5%
- UK 6%
- France 7%
- Germany 8%
- Japan 11%
- US 33%

Source: OECD

investment and savings, industry and commerce, external flows, exchange rates, money and interest rates, and prices and wages.

The briefs. Each chapter begins with a short introduction followed by a series of briefs covering the key indicators. Each brief begins with a few lines summarising the indicator, its significance, what to look for, the source, and so on. These summaries, which are necessarily general, focus on what might be expected from a major industrialised country, such as the United States, Britain, Germany or Japan, when the economy is in relatively good shape.

Time periods. To aid interpretation, most of the tables show average rates of growth or another appropriate average over various time periods. These cover a 30-year period and provide useful yardsticks for judging future trends.

Germany. Unification took place in October 1990 but it was only in 1993 that a wide range of consolidated figures was produced.

Table 1.2 **Selected countries compared, 2008**

	Population m	Density population per sq km	GDP $bn	GDP per head $ at purchasing-power-parities	Exports of goods and services % of GDP
Australia	21.5	3	1,013.5	36,918	23.3
Austria	8.4	100	414.8	39,887	59.4
Belgium	10.7	350	506.2	36,416	92.1
Brazil	195.4	23	1,572.8	10,466	14.3
Canada	33.9	3	1,499.6	39,098	35.1
China	1,354.1	141	4,327.4	5,970	35.8
Finland	5.3	16	271.9	36,320	47.0
France	62.6	114	2,867.0	34,205	26.4
Germany	82.1	230	3,673.1	35,539	47.3
India	1,214.5	369	1,206.7	2,780	22.7
Ireland	4.6	65	267.6	42,110	83.5
Italy	60.1	199	2,313.9	30,631	28.8
Japan	127.0	336	4,910.7	34,116	17.5
Mexico	110.6	57	1,088.1	14,534	28.3
Netherlands	16.7	401	877.0	40,558	76.8
Russia	140.4	8	1,676.6	15,948	31.4
South Korea	48.5	487	929.1	27,692	52.9
Spain	45.3	90	1,602.0	30,589	26.5
Sweden	9.3	21	479.0	37,334	54.2
Switzerland	7.6	184	500.3	43,196	56.4
UK	61.9	255	2,680.0	36,358	29.2
US	317.6	33	14,441.4	47,440	12.7

Sources: IMF; UN

Sources of information

Countless economic figures are published every day in the news media and in various special reports, such as those circulated by investment advisers and financial institutions. The information is necessarily selective, so that readers may wish to go back to the original source of the statistics.

National sources. Apart from the various trade organisations such as the US Institute for Supply Management or the Confederation of British Industry (CBI), each country has its own sources of official statistics.

Sometimes the appropriate government department is self-evident; for example, labour statistics generally come from the department of employment or labour. For data which affect more than one department, such as GDP or balance of payments figures, good sources include the central bank or a central statistical agency, such as Germany's Federal Statistics Office or France's National Institute of Statistics and Economic Studies (INSEE). In America the Commerce Department is the most comprehensive source of data.

Key statistical publications produced by official bodies in the countries focused on are listed below. In general central bank sources contain monetary data and the other sources cover more general figures, but there is usually some overlap between the two. These official sources frequently include a summary of the major private-sector figures.

International sources. International organisations publish various national and international data, frequently in standardised or semi-standardised form, within a few weeks of their original release. Key sources include the following. Website details are given in the Appendix on page 240.

- **OECD.** The monthly *Main Economic Indicators* includes output, prices and trade in the OECD's 31 member and a dozen non-member countries. The numbers are often rebased (for example, to 2005 = 100), but are derived from the original national data. Periodic *Economic Surveys* and special reports provide data and analysis relating to economic developments in one member country or to one group of indicators such as employment data.

- **IMF.** The monthly *International Financial Statistics* covers monetary data and many other figures such as GDP and trade for the 183 IMF member countries.

- **UN (United Nations).** The *Monthly Bulletin of Statistics* includes some production and trade figures for a wide range of countries in more detail than IMF figures. Data on the production of various commodities are interesting.

- **European Commission.** The monthly *Eurostatistics* contains comparative data for EU member countries, while the quarterly *European Economy* includes statistics and ad hoc reports.

Useful national statistical publications

Australia
Reserve Bank: *Report and Financial Statements; Statistical Bulletin*
Australian Bureau of Statistics: *Monthly Review of Business Statistics; Digest of Current Economic Statistics*

Austria
National Bank: *Annual Report; Mitteilungen*
Statistical Office: *Statistische Nachrichten*

Belgium
National Bank: *Annual Report; Statistical Bulletin*
National Institute of Statistics: *Bulletin of Statistics*

Canada
Bank of Canada: *Review*
Statistics Canada: *Canadian Economic Observer*

Denmark
National Bank: *Reports and Accounts; Monetary Review*
Statistics Denmark: *Statistical Bulletin*

France
Bank of France: *Statistiques Monétaires Définitives; Statistiques Monétaires Provisoires; Quarterly Bulletin*
National Institute of Statistics and Economic Research (INSEE): *Monthly Statistics Bulletin; Informations Rapides*
Ministry of Economics, Finance and Budget: *Les Notes Bleues; Statistics and Financial Studies*

Germany
Bundesbank: *Monthly Report; Supplements to the Monthly Reports*
Federal Statistical Office: *Aussenhandel, Reihe 1, Wirtschaft und Statistik*

Italy
Bank of Italy: *Annual Report; Economic Bulletin; Statistical Bulletin*
Central Institute of Statistics: *Monthly Bulletin*

Japan
Bank of Japan: *Economics Statistics Monthly*
Bureau of Statistics: *Monthly Statistics of Japan*

Netherlands
Netherlands Bank: *Annual Report; Quarterly Bulletin*
Central Bureau of Statistics: *Statistical Bulletin; Monthly Financial Statistics (Financiele Maandstatistiek); Social-economisch Maandstatistiek; Maandschrift (Monthly Bulletin)*

Spain
Bank of Spain: *Annual Report; Statistical Bulletin*

National Statistical Institute: *Monthly Bulletin of Statistics*; *National Accounts of Spain*
Sweden
Bank of Sweden: *Yearbook; Quarterly Review*
National Institute of Economic Research: *The Swedish Economy*
Central Bureau of Statistics: *Monthly Digest of Swedish Statistics*; *Statistical Reports*
Switzerland
Swiss National Bank: *Annual Report; The Swiss Banking System; Monthly Bulletin*
Message of the Federal Council to the Federal Assembly
United Kingdom
Bank of England: *Monetary and Financial Statistics*
Office for National Statistics: *Monthly Digest of Statistics; Economic Trends; Financial Statistics*
United States
Board of Governors of the Federal Reserve System: *Federal Reserve Bulletin*
US Department of Commerce: *Survey of Current Business*
US Treasury Department: *Treasury Bulletin*

Interpretation

These are the first questions to ask when you come across any economic indicators.

- **Who produced the figures?** Was it a reliable government agency such as Statistics Canada or a recently established market research company?
- **Will the data be revised?** If so by how much? For example, America's GDP growth in the first quarter of 2006 was revised upwards from 4.8% to 5.3%.
- **To what period do the figures relate?** For example, American retail sales of $320 billion would be excellent for a month, appalling for a year.
- **Are the data seasonally adjusted?** If so is the adjustment reliable? For example, an increase in sales of umbrellas in the wettest month on record will not necessarily indicate a lasting improvement in the fortunes of umbrella companies.
- **What were the start and end points for changes?** For example, the change in unemployment between a recession and a boom

will look much more impressive than the change between boom and slump.

◪ **What about inflation?** For example, a 2% increase in spending is rather disappointing if prices rose by 5% over the same period.

◪ **What other yardsticks will aid interpretation?** For example, total population, employment or GDP. A 5% rise in the number of jobs is not such good news if the working-age population expanded by 10% over the same period.

Chapter 2 runs through some critical ideas about numbers and their interpretation. Chapter 3 describes how economic activity is measured and comments on yardsticks and reliability. Chapters 4–13 cover the indicators themselves, as previewed above.

2 Essential mechanics

Please find me a one-armed economist so we will not always hear "On the other hand ..."

Herbert Hoover, US president

This chapter looks at some basic methods of interpreting numbers and some of the common associated problems. It also lays the groundwork for analysing any kind of economic data.

Volume, value and price

When interpreting economic figures it is important to distinguish between the effects of inflation and changes in the real level of economic activity. Indicators measure one of three things:

- **volume,** such as tonnes of steel or barrels of oil;
- **value,** such as the market value of steel or oil produced in one month or year; or
- **price,** such as the market price of 1 tonne of steel or 1 barrel of oil.

The relationship between these three is simple. *Volume* times *price* equals *value* (see Table 2.1).

There is one possible complication. If the volume of oil or steel produced each year is valued in the prices ruling in, say, 2005, the result is an indicator of output in "2005 price terms". Such a series is in money units, but it is a volume indicator because it provides information about changes in volumes not prices. This is known also as output in constant prices, real prices or real terms.

The value of oil output measured in actual selling prices is known as a current price or nominal price series or a series in nominal terms. Thus:

- **values, current prices, nominal prices and nominal terms** include the effects of inflation; while
- **volumes, constant prices, real prices and real terms** exclude any inflationary influences.

Table 2.1 **OPEC crude oil production and prices**

	volume	×	price	=	value
	Production m barrels		Price $/barrel		Value of production $bn
2003	11,730		28.10		329.6
2004	12,685		36.05		457.3
2005	13,044		50.64		660.5
2006	13,143		61.08		802.7
2007	13,036		69.08		900.5
2008	13,434		94.45		1,268.8

Sources: BP Statistical Review of World Energy; OPEC

In Table 2.2 column A shows the money value of annual US economic output (gross domestic product or GDP, see page 28), which reflects changes in both output and prices. The next two columns disentangle these factors. Column B shows the volume of output with all goods and services measured in 2005 prices. Column C indicates the path of inflation (but see the comment on chained-weighted index numbers below).

The value of output rose in 2004–05 (from $11,868 billion to $12,638 billion), yet in terms of the prices ruling in 2005, real output moved much less over the same period (from $12,264 billion to $12,638 billion).

Price indicators used to convert between current and constant prices (to deflate) are sometimes called price deflators.

- Current price series divided by constant price series (× 100) equals the price deflator.
- Current price series divided by price deflator (× 100) equals the constant price series.
- Constant price series times the price deflator (÷ 100) equals current price series.

Any series of numbers can be converted into index numbers, as described below for the constant price series in Table 2.2 column E.

Step 1 A reference base is selected, 2005 in this case.

Step 2 The value in the reference base is divided by 100 (12,638 ÷ 100 = 126.38).

Table 2.2 **US GDP**

	Current prices $bn A	Constant 2005 chained dollars $bn B	Price deflator index 2005 = 100 C	Current prices index 2005 = 100 D	Constant prices index 2005 = 100 E
1999	9,353.5	10,779.8	86.8	74.0	85.3
2000	9,951.5	11,226.0	88.6	78.7	88.8
2001	10,286.2	11,347.2	90.7	81.4	89.8
2002	10,642.3	11,553.0	92.1	84.2	91.4
2003	11,142.1	11,840.7	94.1	88.2	93.7
2004	11,867.8	12,263.8	96.8	93.9	97.0
2005	12,638.4	12,638.4	100.0	100.0	100.0
2006	13,398.9	12,976.2	103.3	106.0	102.7
2007	14,077.6	13,254.1	106.2	111.4	104.9
2008	14,441.4	13,312.2	108.5	114.3	105.3

Source: US Commerce Department, Bureau of Economic Analysis

Step 3 All numbers in the original series are divided by the result of step 2.

For example, the index value for 2007 is 14,077.6 ÷ 126.38 = 111.4

Index numbers

Index numbers are values expressed as a percentage of a single base figure. For example, if annual production of a particular chemical rose by 35%, output in the second year was 135% of that in the first year. In index terms, output in the two years was 100 and 135 respectively.

Index numbers have no units. Chemical production in the second year is referred to as 135, not 135 tonnes or 135%. The advantages are that distracting units are avoided and changes are easier to assess by eye. The arithmetic is straightforward, as shown in Table 2.2.

Composite indices and weighting. Frequently two or more indices are combined to form one composite index. For example, indices of consumer spending on food and on all other items might be combined into one index of total spending.

Base weighting. The most straightforward way of combining indices is to calculate a weighted average using the same weights throughout. This is known as a base-weighted index, or sometimes a Laspeyres index after the German economist who developed the first one. The following is an example of a base-weighted price index for single-person household consumption of wine and cheese each week.

Base data

Item	—— Price ——		Quantity consumed	
	2005	2010	2005	2010
Wine	9.00	10.50	5	6
Cheese	5.00	8.00	2	3

Where prices are in, say, dollars and quantities are litres of wine/kilos of cheese:

Weekly expenditure in 2005
= (2005 quantity of wine × 2005 price of wine)
+ (2005 quantity of cheese × 2005 price of cheese)
= (5 × 9.00) + (2 × 5.00)
= 45.00 + 10.00 = 55.00

Weekly expenditure in 2010, based on 2005 quantities
= (2005 quantity of wine × 2010 price of wine)
+ (2005 quantity of cheese × 2010 price of cheese)
= (5 × 10.50) + (2 × 8.00)
= 52.50 + 16.00 = 68.50

Index number for 2005 = 55.00/55.00 × 100 = 100.0
Index number for 2010 = 68.50/55.00 × 100 = 124.5

Current weighting. The problem with weighted averages is that weights usually need revising from time to time. With the consumer prices index, spending habits change because of variations in relative cost, quality, availability, and so on. One way to proceed is to calculate a new set of current weights at regular intervals, and use these to derive a single long-term index. This is known as a current-weighted index, or occasionally a Paasche index, again after its founder. The following is an example of a current-weighted price index for single-person household consumption of wine and cheese each week.

Base data

Item	—— Price ——		Quantity consumed	
	2005	2010	2005	2010
Wine	9.00	10.50	5	6
Cheese	5.00	8.00	2	3

Where prices are in, say, dollars and quantities are litres of wine/kilos of cheese:

Weekly expenditure in 2005, based on 2010 quantities
= (2010 quantity of wine × 2005 price of wine)
+ (2010 quantity of cheese × 2005 price of cheese)
= (6 × 9.00) + (3 × 5.00)
= 54.00 + 15.00 = 69.00

Weekly expenditure in 2010
= (2010 quantity of wine × 2010 price of wine)
+ (2010 quantity of cheese × 2010 price of cheese)
= (6 × 10.50) + (3 × 8.00)
= 63.00 + 24.00 = 87.00

Index number for 2005 = 69.00/69.00 × 100 = 100.0
Index number for 2010 = 87.00/69.00 × 100 = 126.1

Neither base weighting nor current weighting is perfect. Base-weighted indices are simple to calculate but they tend to overstate changes over time. Current-weighted indices are more complex to produce and they understate long-term changes.

Current-weighted price indices reflect changes in both prices and relative volumes, while base-weighted versions record price changes only. The price deflator in Table 2.2 is actually chain-weighted, ie the weights are adjusted each year and the indices are linked.

Mathematically, there is no ideal method for weighting indices; expediency usually rules. Most commonly indices are a combination of base-weighted and current-weighted. A new set of weights might be introduced every five years or so and the new index then spliced or chained to the old index. Table 2.3 shows how two indices are joined.

It is essential to know the basis for the weighting, as illustrated above.

Table 2.3 **Chaining index numbers**

	Old index A	New index B	Old index rebased C	Chained index D
2003	100		62	62
2004	110		69	69
2005	121		76	76
2006	133	83	83	83
2007		91		91
2008		100		100
2009		110		110

Chaining index numbers

Step 1 Identify one period when there are figures for both indices; 2006 in Table 2.3.

Step 2 For this period, divide the new figure by old figure; $83 \div 133 = 0.62$.

Step 3 Multiply all old figures by the result; each figure in column C = figure in column A $\times$ 0.62.

Step 4 Put the rebased data with the new figures to create one long run of data.

Effects of reweighting/out-of-date weights. To show the effects of reweighting, consider GDP (total output) based on 2000 weights when, say, manufacturing accounted for half of all economic activity. If in 2000 manufacturing grew by 6% while all other activity was static, initial 2000 figures showed total GDP rising by $6 \times 0.50 = 3\%$. By 2005 the results of a major survey were available and GDP from 1998 was reweighted to take account of the fact that the manufacturing sector had shrunk to a mere 10% of total GDP. As a result the revised figure for total growth in 2000 was $6 \times 0.10 = 0.6\%$.

This is obviously an extreme example, but index numbers can easily become distorted if one item is much less or much more significant than the others. For example, demand tends to grow most rapidly for goods and services which increase least in price, and so on rebasing these items are allocated larger relative weights. In order to be able to track economic changes more accurately, most countries and organisations calculate real GDP growth using chain-weighted methods.

When looking at index numbers it is a good idea to check when they

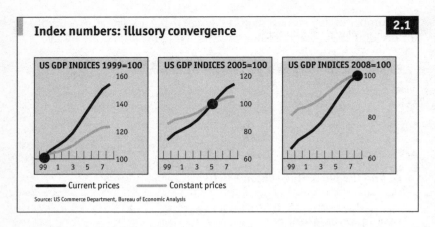

Index numbers: illusory convergence `2.1`

US GDP INDICES 1999=100 | US GDP INDICES 2005=100 | US GDP INDICES 2008=100

— Current prices   — Constant prices

Source: US Commerce Department, Bureau of Economic Analysis

were last rebased and ask whether any component is increasing or decreasing in relative importance. The same approach should be taken to constant price series, such as the GDP data in 2005 dollars in Table 2.2, because these are essentially index numbers with a base value other than 100.

Convergence. Look out also for illusory convergence on the base. Two or more series will always meet at the base period because that is where they both equal 100 (see Chart 2.1, using data from Table 2.2). This can be highly misleading. When you encounter indices on a graph, the first thing to do is check where the base is located.

Measuring changes

If an index of stockmarket prices rose from 1,200 to 1,260, you could say either that it rose by 60 points or, alternatively, that it increased by 5%.

Stating the increase as 60 points (an absolute measure) is simple and straightforward. Yet to interpret the figure it must be judged against another figure, such as the starting level. A rise of 60 points in an index standing at 120 is much more dramatic than an increase of 60 points in an index which started at 12,000.

The percentage change (a relative measure) is easy to interpret. It indicates the size of a change when the starting level is 100. Percentages therefore provide a consistent yardstick for interpreting changes.

Calculating percentages. This is a matter of simple arithmetic. Basic rules for calculating percentage changes are given below. The various operations in the examples are similar. They are designed to minimise the number of key strokes required when using a calculator. Multiplying or dividing by 100 and adding or subtracting 1 can be done by eye.

1 To find one number as a percentage of another

	General procedure	Example 1	Example 2
	Y as % of X	150 as % of 120	120 as % of 150
Step 1	Divide Y by X	$150 \div 120 = 1.25$	$120 \div 150 = 0.80$
Step 2	Multiply by 100	$1.25 \times 100 = 125$	$0.80 \times 100 = 80.0$
		>150 is 125% of 120	>120 is 80% of 150

2 To find the percentage change between two amounts

	General procedure	Example 1	Example 2
	Change between X	change between 120	change between 150
	and Y as % of X	and 150 as % of 120	and 120 as % of 150
Step 1	Divide Y by X	$150 \div 120 = 1.25$	$120 \div 150 = 0.80$
Step 2	Subtract 1	$1.25 - 1 = 0.25$	$0.80 - 1 = -0.20$
Step 3	Multiply by 100	$0.25 \times 100 = 25.0$	$-0.20 \times 100 = -20.0$
		>150 is 25% greater than 120	>120 is 20% smaller than 150

3 To find a given percentage of an amount

	General procedure	Example 1	Example 2
	X% of Y	125% of 120	80% of 150
Step 1	Divide X by 100	$125 \div 100 = 1.25$	$80 \div 100 = 0.8$
Step 2	Multiply by Y	$1.25 \times 120 = 150$	$0.8 \times 150 = 120$
		>150 is 125% of 120	>120 is 80% of 150

4 To find an amount after a given percentage increase or decrease

	General procedure	Example 1	Example 2
	Y increased by X%	120 increased by 25%	150 reduced by 20%
Step 1	Divide X by 100	$25 \div 100 = 0.25$	$20 \div 100 = -0.2$
Step 2	Add 1	$0.25 + 1 = 1.25$	$-0.2 + 1 = 0.8$
Step 3	Multiply by Y	$1.25 \times 120 = 150$	$0.8 \times 150 = 120$
		>150 is 25% greater than 120	>120 is 20% less than 150

Basis points. Financiers deal in very small changes in interest or exchange rates. For convenience one unit, say 1% (that is, 1 percentage point), is often divided into 100 basis points.

$$1 \text{ basis point} = 0.01 \text{ percentage point}$$
$$10 \text{ basis points} = 0.10 \text{ percentage point}$$
$$25 \text{ basis points} = 0.25 \text{ percentage point}$$
$$100 \text{ basis points} = 1.00 \text{ percentage point}$$

Common traps

Units and changes. Do not confuse percentage points with percentage changes. If an interest rate or inflation rate increases from 10% to 13%, it has risen by three units, or 3 percentage points, but the percentage increase is 30% (3 ÷ 10 × 100).

Up and back. A percentage increase followed by the same percentage decrease results in a figure below the starting level. For example, a 50% rise followed by a 50% cut leaves you 25% worse off.

- $1,000 increased by 50% is $1,500.
- 50% of $1,500 is $750.

Starting levels. A 10% pay rise for chief executives earning $500,000 a year puts an extra $50,000 in their annual pay packets. The same percentage increase for cleaners on $10,000 a year gives them a mere $1,000 extra.

The importance of the base from which changes are calculated is also illustrated in Tables 2.4 and 2.5.

Using Table 2.4, it could be claimed that in February 2006 the 12-month rate of inflation fell from 10% to 0%. In fact all that happened is that the increase a year earlier fell out of the 12-month comparison. In this example, shop prices changed just once during the period January 2004–February 2006, perhaps owing to an increase in the rate of sales tax or VAT.

Table 2.5 shows that orders in the third quarter of 2006 were down from the previous quarter. However, the figure for the previous quarter was unusually high, and the third-quarter figures were better than the first quarter's and any quarter of 2005. When comparing data over several years it is easy to overlook the distortion that can arise from using an unusually high or low starting or ending value.

Table 2.4 **When did inflation fall?**

Consumer prices index		—— % change over ——	
		1 month	12 months
2008			
January	100	0	0
February	100	0	0
2009			
January	100	0	0
February	110	10	10
March	110	0	10
2010			
January	110	0	10
February	110	0	0

Table 2.5 **Choosing the period for comparison**

	Orders £bn	Over four quarters	—— % change from fourth quarter 2000 —— actual	annualised
2008				
1st quarter	33.3			
2nd quarter	33.8			
3rd quarter	34.3			
4th quarter	33.6			
Average for year	**33.7**			
2009				
1st quarter	34.3	3.0	2.1	8.6
2nd quarter	36.0	6.5	7.1	14.8
3rd quarter	35.2	2.6	4.8	6.4
4th quarter	32.9	-2.1	-2.1	-2.1
Average for year	**34.6**	**2.7**		

Growth rates

If consumer spending rises by 1% a month, by how much will it increase over a full year? Not 12%, but 12.7%. Each month expenditure is 1% greater than the month before and each percentage increase is calculated (compounded) from a higher base. Thus 12.7% a year is the same as

1% a month annualised. It is important to distinguish between the following terminology (numerical examples from Table 2.5).

◼ **12-month or 4-quarter change.** This compares one month or quarter with the same one in the previous year. For example, orders rose 2.6% between the third quarters of 2008 and 2009.

◼ **Change this year.** This compares the latest figure with the very end of the previous year. For example, when third-quarter figures for 2009 were published, commentators might have said that orders had risen by 4.8% over the three quarters to the third quarter of 2009.

◼ **Annualised change.** This is the change which would occur if the movement observed in any period were to continue for exactly 12 months. For example, orders rose 6.4% annualised during the first three quarters of 2009.

◼ **Annual change.** This compares the total or average for one calendar or fiscal year with the previous one. For example, orders in 2009 were 2.7% higher than in 2008.

◼ **Change to end-year.** This compares end-year with end-year: for example, orders fell by 2.1% over the four quarters to end-2009.

How to use Table 2.6. Locate in column 1 any observed rate, say a 1% monthly increase in consumer prices. If this rate continues, prices will double after almost 70 months (column 2) and increase by 12.7% in a year (final column). If the 1% change took place over one quarter (three months), the doubling time is 70 quarters (column 2) and the annual rate of increase is 4.1% (column 3).

Table 2.6 shows annualised rates for a selection of simple rates. US commentators tend to focus on annualised rates. This makes it easy to compare monthly or quarterly changes with annual rates, but it can be misleading. Many economic figures bump around from month to month, and annualised rates exaggerate erratic fluctuations. A mere 0.1% change in a month adds 1.2% to the annualised figure. Columns C and D of Table 2.7 (see page 26) compare simple and annualised changes and show how annualising can emphasise erratic fluctuations.

Each week *The Economist* shows changes in indicators such as industrial production and consumer prices as the percentage change over 12 months.

Table 2.6 **Annualised and doubling rates**

Observed % rate	Doubling time	— Annualised rate if the observed rate is —	
		quarterly	monthly
0.1	693.5	0.4	1.2
0.2	346.9	0.8	2.4
0.3	231.4	1.2	3.7
0.4	173.6	1.6	4.9
0.5	139.0	2.0	6.2
0.6	115.9	2.4	7.4
0.7	99.4	2.8	8.7
0.8	87.0	3.2	10.0
0.9	77.4	3.6	11.4
1.0	69.7	4.1	12.7
1.1	63.4	4.5	14.0
1.2	58.1	4.9	15.4
1.3	53.7	5.3	16.8
1.4	49.9	5.7	18.2
1.5	46.6	6.1	19.6
1.6	43.7	6.6	21.0
1.7	41.1	7.0	22.4
1.8	38.9	7.4	23.9
1.9	36.8	7.8	25.3
2.0	35.0	8.2	26.8
2.5	28.1	10.4	34.5
3.0	23.4	12.6	42.6
3.5	20.1	14.8	51.1
4.0	17.7	17.0	60.1
4.5	15.7	19.3	69.6
5.0	14.2	21.6	79.6
5.5	12.9	23.9	90.1
6.0	11.9	26.2	101.2
6.5	11.0	28.6	112.9
7.0	10.2	31.1	125.2
7.5	9.6	33.5	138.2
8.0	9.0	36.0	151.8
8.5	8.5	38.6	166.2
9.0	8.0	41.2	181.3
10.0	7.3	46.4	213.8
11.0	6.6	51.8	249.8
12.0	6.1	57.4	289.6
13.0	5.7	63.0	333.5
14.0	5.3	68.9	381.8
15.0	5.0	74.9	435.0
16.0	4.7	81.1	493.6
18.0	4.2	93.9	628.8
20.0	3.8	107.4	791.6

The arithmetic for dealing with growth rates

1 To find the growth rate over several periods when the rate over one period is known.

	General procedure	Example 1	Example 2
	r% per period	0.3% per month	7.5% per year
	over n periods	for 12 months	for 10 years
Step 1	Divide r by 100	$0.3 \div 100 = 0.003$	$7.5 \div 100 = 0.075$
Step 2	Add 1	$0.003 + 1 = 1.003$	$0.075 + 1 = 1.075$
Step 3	Raise to power of n	$1.003^{12} = 1.037$	$1.075^{10} = 2.061$
Step 4	Subtract 1	$1.037 - 1 = 0.037$	$2.061 - 1 = 1.061$
Step 5	Multiply by 100	$0.037 \times 100 = 3.7$	$1.061 \times 100 = 106.1$
		>Growth of 0.3% per month annualises to 3.7% a year	>Growth of 7.5% per year equals a 106.1% increase over 10 years

Note on step 3. Raising a number to the power of n is a shorthand way of saying multiply it by itself n times. For example, $2^3 = 2 \times 2 \times 2 = 8$. Use the calculator key marked x^y (the letters might be slightly different) to perform this operation. If there is no x^y key use logarithms (the LOG and 10^x or LN and e^x keys). Replace step 3 with the following.

Step 3a	Take the log	$\text{Log } 1.003 = 0.0013$	$\text{Log } 1.075 = 0.0314$
Step 3b	Multiply by n	$0.0013 \times 12 = 0.0156$	$0.0314 \times 10 = 0.314$
Step 3c	Take the antilog	$\text{Antilog } 0.0156 = 1.037$	$\text{Antilog } 0.314 = 2.061$

The formula for these calculations is $[(1 + {}^r/_{100})^n - 1] \times 100$ or, for PC spreadsheet users, $= ((1 + r/100)^{\wedge}(n) - 1)^*100$.

2 To find the growth rate over one period when the rate over several periods is known.

	General procedure	Example 1	Example 2
	r% over n periods	3.7% over 12 months	106.1% over 10 years
Step 1	Divide r by 100	$3.7 \div 100 = 0.037$	$106.1 \div 100 = 1.061$
Step 2	Add 1	$0.037 + 1 = 1.037$	$1.061 + 1 = 2.061$
Step 3	Raise to power of 1/n	$1.037^{1/12} = 1.003$	$2.061^{1/10} = 1.075$
Step 4	Subtract 1	$1.003 - 1 = 0.003$	$1.075 - 1 = 0.075$
Step 5	Multiply by 100	$0.003 \times 100 = 0.3$	$0.075 \times 100 = 7.5$
		>Growth of 3.7% per year equals 0.3% per month	>Growth of 106.1% over 10 years equals 7.5% per year

Note on step 3. If your calculator does not have an $x^{1/y}$ key, use logarithms (the LOG and 10^x or LN and e^x keys). Replace step 3 with the following.

Step 3a	Take the log	Log 1.037 = 0.0158	Log 2.061 = 0.314
Step 3b	Divide by n	0.0158 ÷ 12 = 0.0013	0.314 ÷ 10 = 0.0314
Step 3c	Take the antilog	Antilog 0.0013 = 1.003	Antilog 0.0314 = 1.075

The formula for these calculations is $[(1 + r/100)^{1/n} - 1] \times 100$ or, for PC spreadsheet users, $= ((1 + r/100)\wedge(1/n) -1)*100$.

Moving averages

One way to smooth out erratic fluctuations is to look at an average. When reviewing, say, total high street sales in June, you might take an average of figures for May, June and July. A sequence of such averages is called a moving average. Column E of Table 2.7 (page 26) and the footnote show the calculation of a three-month moving average for a short run of data.

The moving average can average any number of periods. A five-year moving average helps to smooth out the economic cycle described on pages 55–59, although a lot of data would be needed to calculate it. Moreover, the more periods covered by a moving average, the slower it will be to show changes in trend.

Seasonality

Most economic figures show a seasonal pattern that repeats itself every year. For example, prices of seasonal foods rise in the winter, sales of beachwear increase with the onset of summer, and industrial production falls in the months when factories close for annual holidays.

Seasonal adjustment. There is a simple numerical process called seasonal adjustment which adjusts raw data for the observed seasonal pattern. Briefly, if sales or output in February are typically 85% of the monthly average, the seasonal adjustment process divides all observations for February by 85%.

Many published figures are seasonally adjusted to aid interpretation, but it is important to remember that seasonal adjustment is not infallible. For example, in a particularly cold month energy use increases by more than the amount expected by seasonal adjustment, while more building workers than usual are temporarily laid off. The

Table 2.7 **Analysing seasonal and erratic influences**

	Retail sales index *A*	*1 month B*	% change over 1 month annualised *C*	12 months *D*	3-month moving average Index *E*	% change from 12 months ago *F*
2008						
Oct	119.2					
Nov	120.2	0.8				
Dec	121.8	1.3			120.4	
2009						
Jan	121.6	-0.2			121.2	
Oct	130.7	-0.5	-5.8	9.6		
Nov	133.4	2.1	27.8	11.0		
Dec	134.4	0.7	9.3	10.3	132.8	10.3
2010						
Jan	129.2	-3.9	-37.7	6.2	132.3	9.2

Note: Calculations for January 2010:
Column B: $[(129.2 \div 134.4) - 1] \times 100 = -3.9\%$
Column C: $[(129.2 \div 134.4)^{12} - 1] \times 100 = -37.7\%$
Column D: $[(129.2 \div 121.6) - 1] \times 100 = 6.2\%$
Column E: $(133.4 + 134.4 + 129.2) \div 3 = 132.3$
Column F: $[(132.3 \div 121.2) - 1] \times 100 = 9.2\%$

adjusted figures might be erroneously taken to suggest that energy use or unemployment was rising when the underlying situation was very different. Climatic and other influences might be overlooked when viewing the economy from the comfort of seasonally adjusted data.

Coping with seasonality and blips. Table 2.7 indicates some problems of interpreting data which are subject to erratic or seasonal influences.

- The figures in column A are an index of retail sales. At first glance it appears that sales in January 2010 were very poor, since there was a 4% decline from the previous month (column B). It seems that this interpretation is confirmed because the 4% fall is worse than the 0.2% decline in the same month a year earlier.
- The percentage changes over 12 months (column D) give some

encouragement. They indicate that the trend in sales is upward, though growth over the 12 months to January 2010 (6.2%) was slacker than in the previous few months (around 10%).

☑ Column F smooths out short-term erratic influences by comparing sales in the latest three months with sales in the same three months a year earlier. This suggests that the fall in January was not as severe as it appeared at first glance, with the 12-month growth rate remaining at close to 10%.

This final interpretation is the correct one. Indeed, a full run of figures would show that sales fell in January only because this was a correction to an exceptionally steep rise in the earlier few months.

Commentators are inclined to interpret blips as changes in trend. In general you should examine a run of data, form a view about the trend, and stick to it until there is clear evidence that the trend has changed.

3 Measuring economic activity

GDP should really stand for grossly distorted picture.

The Economist

Total economic activity may be measured in three different but equivalent ways.

Perhaps the most obvious approach is to add up the value of all goods and services produced in a given period of time, such as one year. Money values may be imputed for services such as health care which do not change hands for cash. Since the output of one business (for example, steel) can be the input of another (for example, automobiles), double counting is avoided by combining only "value added", which for any one activity is the total value of production less the cost of inputs such as raw materials and components valued elsewhere.

A second approach is to add up the expenditure which takes place when the output is sold. Since all spending is received as incomes, a third option is to value producers' incomes.

Thus output = expenditure = incomes.

The precise definition of economic activity varies. The three main concepts are gross domestic product, gross national product and net national product.

Gross domestic product. GDP is the total of all economic activity in one country, regardless of who owns the productive assets. For example, Britain's GDP includes the profits of a foreign firm located in Britain even if they are remitted to the firm's parent company in another country.

Gross national income or gross national product. GNI, a term which has replaced GNP in national accounts, is the total of incomes earned by residents of a country, regardless of where the assets are located. For example, Britain's GNI includes profits from British-owned businesses located in other countries.

Net national income. The "gross" in GDP and GNI indicates that there is no allowance for depreciation (capital consumption), the amount of capital resources used up in the production process due to wear and tear, accidental damage, obsolescence or retirement of capital assets. Net national income is GNI less depreciation.

The relationship between the three measures is straightforward:

GDP (gross domestic product)
+ net property income from abroad
(rent, interest, profits and dividends)
= GNI (gross national income)
– capital consumption (depreciation)
= NNI (net national income)

Capital consumption. Capital consumption is not identifiable from a set of transactions; it can only be imputed by a system of conventions. For example, when investment spending of $1m on a new machine is included in GDP figures, national accounts statisticians pencil in depreciation of, say, $100,000 a year for each of the next ten years. This gives a stinted view of productive capacity. After five years the machine might still be producing at full capacity, but the national accounts would show it as capable of producing only half the volume that it could when new.

Choosing between GDP, GNI and NNI

Net national income (NNI) is the most comprehensive measure of economic activity, but it is of little practical value due to the problems of accounting for depreciation. Gross concepts are more useful.

All the major industrial countries now use GDP as their main measure of national economic activity. America, Germany and Japan, which had until the early 1990s focused on GNP, now use GDP. The difference between GDP and GNI or GNP is usually relatively small, perhaps 1% of GDP, but there are a few exceptions; for example, in 2007 Ireland's GDP was 19% bigger than its GNI, owing to the profits earned by foreign investors in the country. In the short term a large change in total net property income has only a minor effect on GDP. When reviewing longer-term trends, it is advisable to check net property income to see if it is making GNI grow faster than GDP.

Net material product

Some countries in the past, mainly centrally planned economies, used net material product (NMP) to measure overall economic activity. NMP was less comprehensive than GDP because it excluded "non-productive services", such as banking, government administration, health and education, and was quoted net of capital consumption (depreciation). As a rule of thumb, NMP was roughly 80–90% of GDP.

Omissions
Deliberate omissions
There are many things which are not in GDP, including the following.

- **Transfer payments.** For example, social security and pensions.
- **Gifts.** For example, $10 from Aunt Agatha on your birthday.
- **Unpaid and domestic activities.** If you cut your grass or paint your house the value of this productive activity is not recorded in GDP, but it is if you pay someone to do it for you.
- **Barter transactions.** For example, the exchange of a sack of wheat for a can of petrol.
- **Second-hand transactions.** For example, the sale of a used car (where the production was recorded in an earlier year).
- **Intermediate transactions.** For example, a lump of metal may be sold several times, perhaps as ore, pig iron, part of a component and, finally, part of a washing machine (the metal is included in GDP once at the net total of the value added between the initial production of the ore and its final sale as a finished item).
- **Leisure.** An improved production process which creates the same output but gives more recreational time is recorded in the national accounts at exactly the same value as the old process.
- **Depletion of resources.** For example, oil production is recorded at sale price minus production costs and no allowance is made for the fact that an irreplaceable part of the nation's capital stock of resources has been consumed.
- **Environmental costs.** GDP figures do not distinguish between green and polluting industries.
- **Allowance for non-profit-making and inefficient activities.** The civil service and police force are valued according to expenditure on salaries, equipment, and so on (the appropriate price for these services might be judged to be very different if they were provided by private companies).
- **Allowance for changes in quality.** You can buy very different electronic goods for the same inflation-adjusted outlay than you could a few years ago, but GDP data do not take account of such technological improvements.

Some of the exclusions can be identified elsewhere. For example, environmental costs are seen in statistics on pollution and most countries report known oil or coal reserves (although these estimates may be over-optimistic or clouded by genuine ignorance about the size of underground reserves).

One other point to note is that the more advanced government statistical agencies include in GDP an allowance for the imputed rent paid by home owner-occupiers. This avoids an apparent change in national output because of any switch between owner-occupation and renting.

Surveys and sampling

Many of the figures which go into GDP are collected by surveys. For example, governments ask selected manufacturing or retailing companies for details of their output or sales each month. This information is used to make inferences about all manufacturers or all retailers. Such estimates may not be correct, especially as the most dynamic parts of the economy are small firms constantly coming into and going out of existence, which may never be surveyed.

Sample evidence is supplemented by other information, including documentation required initially for bureaucratic purposes such as customs clearance or tax assessment. Such data take a long time to collect and analyse, which is why economic figures are frequently revised even when they are several years old.

Unrecorded transactions

GDP may under-record economic activity, not least because of the difficulties of keeping track of new small businesses and because of tax avoidance or evasion.

Deliberately concealed transactions form the black, grey, hidden or shadow economy. This is largest at times when, and in countries where, taxes are high and bureaucracy is smothering. Estimates of the size of the shadow economy vary enormously. For example, differing studies put America's at 4–33%, Germany's at 3–28% and Britain's at 2–15%. What is agreed, though, is that among the industrial countries the shadow economy is largest in Greece, at perhaps 30% of GDP, followed by Italy, Portugal and Spain, while the smallest black economies are in Japan, Switzerland and America at around 10% of GDP.

The only industrial countries that adjust their GDP figures for the shadow economy are Italy and America and they may well underestimate its size.

World GDP

The Great Recession is receding, according to our measure of global GDP, based on data from 52 countries. World output fell by 1.2% in the year to the third quarter, around half the rate of decline recorded in the year to the second quarter. In most of the countries that have published third-quarter figures, GDP was lower than a year earlier. The exceptions were mostly in Asia: China and India recorded the fastest growth, followed by Indonesia. Only one European country, Poland, reported higher GDP in the third quarter than a year earlier. But some of the world's most troubled economies are in eastern Europe. The three Baltic countries – Estonia, Latvia and Lithuania – suffered the biggest falls in GDP.

World GDP*
% change on a year earlier

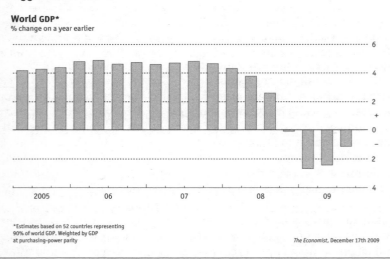

*Estimates based on 52 countries representing
90% of world GDP. Weighted by GDP
at purchasing-power parity

The Economist, December 17th 2009

Output, expenditure and income
Output

The output measure of GDP is obtained by combining value added (value of production less cost of inputs) by all businesses: agriculture, mining, manufacturing and services. Output data are usually presented in index form (that is, with a base year such as 2005 = 100).

Sectors. In general countries have larger agricultural sectors in the early stages of economic development. The manufacturing sector's share of

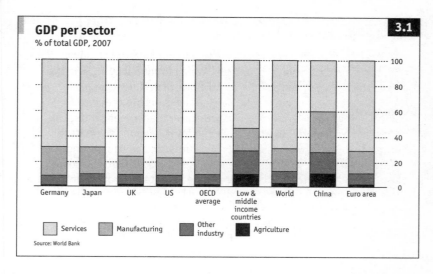

GDP per sector `3.1`
% of total GDP, 2007

Germany · Japan · UK · US · OECD average · Low & middle income countries · World · China · Euro area

☐ Services ☐ Manufacturing ☐ Other industry ■ Agriculture

Source: World Bank

output increases as the economy develops and services take the largest share of output in mature economies.

Highly detailed data are often available. The production of tens or hundreds of goods and services industries may be recorded separately. For example, there will probably be an appropriate index in the GDP output breakdown to allow you to compare the performance of, say, a furniture manufacturing company with that of the industry as a whole. The industrialised countries generally publish more detailed (and more up-to-date) statistics than less developed countries.

Classifications. Economic information has to be categorised, but the correct classification is not always self-evident. For example, should the production of man-made fibres from petroleum be recorded under textiles (as they generally used to be) or chemicals (as they are now)?

Standards have been introduced to deal with these problems and provide consistency. Industrial production, retail trade, imports and exports are classified according to standard themes. Many countries now follow the United Nations' international standard industrial classification (ISIC), while European countries tend to use the similar EU *Nomenclature statistique des Activités économiques dans les Communautés Européennes* (NACE). These are fairly detailed and they need revision from time to time.

For example, if the standard industrial classification (SIC), which was introduced in the UK in 1948, had not been revised several times, computer manufacturing would be classified under office equipment, which is part of non-electrical engineering.

When making sectoral comparisons between two or more countries, try to find out if the sectors are made up of the same industries, otherwise there may be inconsistencies in the comparison.

Expenditure

The expenditure measure of GDP is obtained by adding up all spending:

consumption (spending on items such as food and clothing)
+ investment (spending on houses, factories, and so on)
= total domestic expenditure
+ exports of goods and services (foreigners' spending)
= total final expenditure
− imports of goods and services (spending abroad)
= GDP

Government consumption. The level of government spending reflects the role of the state. Government consumption is generally 10–20% of GDP, although it is higher in countries such as Denmark and Sweden where the state provides many services. Changes in government spending tend to reflect political decisions rather than market forces.

Private consumption. This is also called personal consumption or consumer expenditure. It is generally the largest individual category of spending (but see exports, page 36). In the industrialised countries consumption is around 60% of GDP. The ratio is higher in poor countries which invest less and consume more.

Investment. Investment is perhaps the key structural component of spending since it lays down the basis for future production. It covers spending on factories, machinery, equipment, dwellings and inventories of raw materials and other items. Investment averages about 20% of GDP in the industrialised countries (see Chart 3.2), but is over 30% of GDP in East Asian countries, and over 40% in China.

Consumption or investment? There are some anomalies in the identification of consumption and investment. Government spending on roads, defence and education is generally scored as consumption rather than investment. Consumer spending on cars and other durable goods

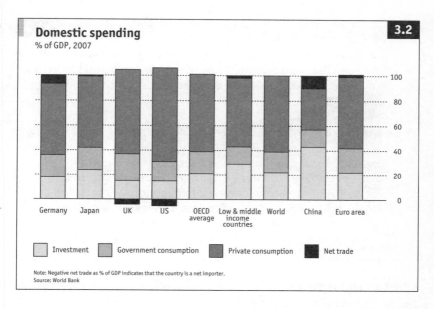

Domestic spending
% of GDP, 2007
`3.2`

Germany | Japan | UK | US | OECD average | Low & middle income countries | World | China | Euro area

☐ Investment   ☐ Government consumption   ☐ Private consumption   ■ Net trade

Note: Negative net trade as % of GDP indicates that the country is a net importer.
Source: World Bank

(items with a life of over one year) is considered to be consumption. Capital goods purchased by a financial institution and leased to an industrial company are also usually classified as consumption. Thus consumption tends to be overstated and investment under-recorded.

Total domestic expenditure (TDE). Consumption plus investment is known as total domestic expenditure. This is a useful concept because it measures domestic spending, some of which goes on imported goods and services. It under-records sales because it does not include those goods and services sold abroad (exports).

Total final expenditure/output (TFE/TFO). Consumption and investment plus exports of goods and services is known as total final expenditure. This takes account of the fact that some consumer and investment goods and services are purchased by foreigners.

Another way of looking at this is as total final output: the value of home-produced and imported goods and services available for consumption, investment or export.

TFE and TFO are identical in coverage. The difference is in the terminology, which depends on whether the emphasis is on output or spending. Since some expenditure goes on goods and services originating

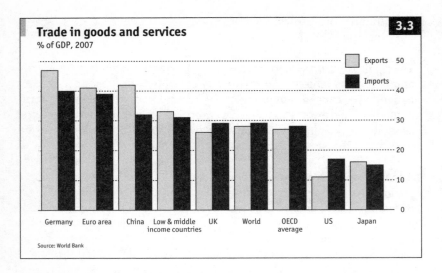

Trade in goods and services
% of GDP, 2007

3.3

Exports 50
Imports

Germany | Euro area | China | Low & middle income countries | UK | World | OECD average | US | Japan

Source: World Bank

overseas, TFE/TFO has to be reduced by the amount of imports of goods and services to give total output.

Exports and imports. Exports generate foreign currency income, while imports are a leakage of domestic spending into another country's production. These external transactions can have an important effect on GDP.

Some countries have a low dependence on external trade. American imports are about 17% of GDP and exports over 11%. Other countries, especially those on the Pacific rim, are heavily dependent on external flows. Hong Kong and Singapore, both trading economies, have imports and exports each of which are around 200% of GDP (many imports are re-exported). These are open economies, while America and Japan are relatively closed (see Chart 3.3). Open economies have greater opportunity for export-led growth but are also more vulnerable to external shocks.

Income

The income measure of GDP is based on total incomes from production. It is essentially the total of:

- ◪ wages and salaries of employees;
- ◪ income from self-employment;
- ◪ trading profits of companies;

- trading surpluses of government corporations and enterprises; and
- income from rents.

These are known as factor incomes. GDP does not include transfer payments such as interest and dividends, pensions, or other social security benefits. The breakdown of incomes sheds additional light on economic behaviour because it is the counterpart to expenditure in what economists call the circular flow of money. It also provides a useful basis for forecasting inflation.

Accounting conventions. Incomes data are collected from figures which are based on common accounting conventions, rather than the principles of national accounting. One result is that reported company profits include any increase or decrease in the value of inventories. A value (as opposed to a volume) change does not represent any real economic activity, so this stock appreciation is deducted from total domestic income to arrive at GDP. Britain's Office for National Statistics uses a definition of profits that excludes the change in the value of stocks, so no stock-appreciation adjustment is shown in national accounts.

Discrepancies
In a perfect world, the output, expenditure and income measures would be identical. In practice there are discrepancies owing to inevitable shortcomings in data collection, differences in the reported timing of transactions and the shadow economy. The discrepancy between any pair of measures is typically up to 1–2% of GDP. It can be much larger than this, as it was in many countries in the mid-1970s when data collection was complicated by sharp oil price increases and rapid inflation.

Since output, expenditure and income data are, by and large, collected independently, the safest approach is to take the average of the three as indicative of overall economic trends. Not many governments, however, publish such averages and it may not be practical to calculate them. Consequently it is usually necessary to focus on one.

The output measure is usually the most reliable indicator of short-term developments (that is, up to one year) as the survey data are fairly concrete. For longer periods the expenditure measure is probably better, mainly because the weights used to aggregate the output indicators are updated at infrequent intervals and they become out of date. The income measure is usually the last available and least reliable.

Prices

Market prices, factor cost and basic prices

Many transactions are subject to taxes and subsidies. Sales tax or value-added tax (VAT) and subsidised housing are obvious examples. The expenditure measure of GDP records market prices, which includes these taxes and subsidies. The income and output measures are generally reported at factor cost (that is, they exclude taxes and subsidies). The relationship is simple:

$$\begin{array}{l} \text{GDP at market prices} \\ \left. \begin{array}{l} - \text{ indirect taxes} \\ + \text{ subsidies} \end{array} \right\} \text{factor cost adjustment} \\ = \text{GDP at factor cost} \end{array}$$

The factor cost adjustment. The factor cost adjustment (the net total of taxes and subsidies) enables the income, expenditure and output measures to be converted freely between factor cost and market prices. This allows consistent comparisons and highlights the effect of government intervention.

Basic prices. Britain's official statisticians now call the basic output measure of GDP "gross value added (GVA) at basic prices". This includes subsidies and excludes taxes (such as VAT) on products only. GVA or GDP at factor cost also excludes taxes on production, such as business property taxes. The statisticians consider GVA at basic prices to be a better measure of short-term movements in the economy than the old factor-cost measure.

National conventions. Americans tend to measure economic activity at market prices right through to the net national product stage. They then adjust for taxes and subsidies to reach national income at factor cost. Thus a reference to American GDP probably means GDP at market prices. In Britain, the "headline" measure of GDP is at market prices. However, GVA at basic prices is also reported. The only way to be sure is to check the basis of the figures in question.

Current and constant prices

GDP figures are reported in current and constant prices.

◼ Output data are generally collected in both current and constant prices. The constant price figures for each industry are obtained by valuing current output in the prices applicable in a given base year; say, 2000 or 2005.

◪ Expenditure data are mostly collected in current prices. They are converted into constant prices by the same adjustment process used with output data, or – slightly differently – by deflating each component by an estimated price indicator. Once the current and constant price versions of the expenditure measure are available, they are used to calculate an overall deflator (that is, the price index) which is used with the income measure.

◪ Income data are collected in current prices and converted into constant prices using deflators derived from the expenditure measure.

The deflator. The GDP deflator calculated from expenditure data at factor cost is also known as the implicit price deflator. This is a handy measure of economy-wide inflation trends, but it is affected by changes in the composition of GDP (see page 226).

Adjusting for inflation is less reliable at times when prices are changing rapidly. Small errors in the measurements of current values and prices can combine to create large errors in the constant price series. Make it a rule to question the accuracy of price deflators. For example, 12% nominal GDP growth with inflation of 10% results in approximately 2% real growth in GDP. If inflation is actually slightly higher, at 11%, real GDP growth is halved to a mere 1%.

Putting it in context
Population

The notes on omissions (pages 30–32) suggest that output figures are a dubious guide to the quality of life. Nevertheless, total output per head (that is, GDP divided by the size of the population) is used as a broad indicator of living standards. A rise in real GDP that is greater than any increase in population is taken to indicate an improvement in economic well-being. However, if, for example, real GDP increases by 3% while the population expands by 5%, the economy is "worse off" (that is, real GDP per head has declined).

Purchasing power

Output per head in current prices is a useful guide to levels of economic activity when making snapshot comparisons between countries. Since it is necessary, however, to convert the figures into a common currency, the underlying message can be distorted by exchange-rate effects.

The best solution is to use output per head on a purchasing power parity (PPP) basis, which adjusts for national variations in the prices paid for goods and services. This is not easy to calculate accurately, but some intergovernmental agencies such as the World Bank, IMF and OECD produce estimates. Their figures show, for example, that although Finland's GDP per head is higher than that of Canada if converted into dollars at current exchange rates, after adjusting for variations in prices the spending power of the Finnish is below that of Canadians (see Table 4.2).

Employment

Another way of measuring relative activity is with output per person employed. This is an important measure of productivity which is discussed extensively in Chapter 4.

Reliability

Some problems of obtaining information by surveys and samples are outlined above. In addition, the rush to publish information often means that figures are revised several times as new information comes to hand, perhaps causing major changes in interpretation. For example, industrial production figures may be based initially on sales and output data and adjusted later to take account of changes in inventories not caught in the sales figures.

Statisticians go to great lengths to account for these and other problems. The techniques employed are reasonably reliable, at least in the more developed countries. It is important to remember, however, that published figures for GDP, average earnings, prices, and so on are only estimates.

Moreover, the basis on which some figures are calculated by less scrupulous governments does not stand up to close examination. Consumer-price indices are particularly vulnerable. They may include only selected subsidised goods and services and omit those which increase in price too rapidly.

4 Growth: trends and cycles

When your neighbour loses his job, it's a slowdown; when you lose your job, it's a recession; when an economist loses his job, it's a depression.

Anon

Chapter 3 focused on national income as a snapshot of economic activity. This chapter considers the changes in economic activity over time. The introduction outlines the basic issues which affect growth. The GDP briefs explain how to interpret indicators of overall activity. The productivity brief shows how employment and investment lay down the basis for long-term growth. Finally the brief on cyclical indicators indicates the way that many economic series fluctuate around the trend.

Trends and cycles

Economic developments should be judged in the context of trends and cycles.

Trends. The trend is the long-term rate of economic expansion. The industrial economies have enjoyed a growth trend for decades or even centuries. Since the second world war the volume of goods and services that they produce has grown by 3–4% a year in general. Chart 4.1 shows the 1990–2009 trend for the American economy.

Cycles. The cycle reflects short-term fluctuations around the trend. There are always a few months or years when growth is above trend, followed by a period when the economy contracts or grows below trend (see Chart 4.1).

Sources of growth

Long-term growth. In the long term the growth in economic output depends on the number of people working and output per worker (productivity).

Clearly there are limits to changes in the size of the population and the number of people in employment. But only an extreme pessimist can see an end to long-term productivity improvements. Output per worker

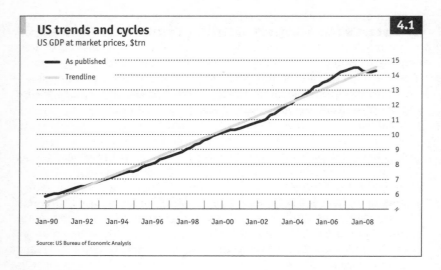

US trends and cycles   4.1
US GDP at market prices, $trn

— As published
— Trendline

Jan-90   Jan-92   Jan-94   Jan-96   Jan-98   Jan-00   Jan-02   Jan-04   Jan-06   Jan-08

Source: US Bureau of Economic Analysis

grows through technical progress and investment in new plant, machinery and equipment. Investment and productivity are therefore the basis for continued and sustained economic expansion.

The Productivity brief (page 52) quantifies the relationship between employment, investment and growth. It is important to distinguish between economic growth, which may reflect nothing more than an expanding population, and overall economic welfare which, if measured by the volume of goods and services produced per person, improves only if output grows faster than the population.

See GDP and GDP per head, pages 43–52.

Short-term cycles. The brief on Cyclical indicators (page 55) explains the way that economic growth fluctuates around the trend. The brief is important because it lays the basis for interpreting many economic indicators. For example, a downturn in housing starts or an increase in inventories may signal a recession perhaps 12 months hence.

The circular flow of incomes. Firms and households are the backbone of an economy. Firms employ people to make goods and provide services. This gives households their incomes. Household spending provides the rationale for the existence of firms. Thus the circular flow continues; in short, output = income = expenditure.

There are leakages from and injections into the circular flow. Money is taken out of circulation when people buy imports, save or pay taxes. This means less spending, so firms sell fewer goods and services. Money is put into circulation when people run down their savings or borrow, when governments spend their taxes and when foreigners buy exports. These actions boost spending, so firms sell more goods and services.

All leakages and injections affect spending power and influence savings and investment decisions. These may be thought of as causing cyclical variations while productivity determines long-term growth. Life is never simple, of course, and productivity depends on investment, which in turn depends on many factors including the cycle itself.

Inflation and volumes

Higher demand can easily result in inflation. For example, if employers increase wages without raising output, and if the extra incomes are spent in full, prices will be pulled up (demand-pull inflation) but there will be no increase in real welfare.

The effects of inflation are wide and far-reaching. They are particularly relevant when analysing small parts of the economy in great detail, such as when projecting earnings and share prices for one company. For assessing the economy as a whole it is better to focus on the volume of output rather than its nominal money value, and to think in volume or inflation-adjusted constant price terms. These concepts are discussed in Chapter 2; Chapter 13 reviews inflation in detail.

Nominal GDP

Measures:	Total economic activity in current prices.
Significance:	Describes the total level of production. Use as a yardstick for measuring "economic achievement" or other indicators (such as the current-account balance as a percentage of GDP).
Presented as:	Quarterly and annual totals – more rarely, monthly.
Focus on:	Totals. Use factor cost when reviewing output or incomes, market prices if looking at expenditure patterns.
Yardstick:	The world world total was $60.56 billion in 2008.
Released:	Quarterly, 1–3 months in arrears; frequently revised.

Interpretation

Nominal GDP or GNI (GNP) is used to measure total economic activity. The choice between the two depends largely on national conventions (see page 29). Where GNI/GNP is higher than GDP it indicates net investment income from abroad.

Table 4.1 **Nominal GDP, 2008**

	% of total	$bn	$PPP[a]	GDP bn[b]	GNI bn[b]	GNI as % of GDP
Australia	1.7	1,013	799	1,185	1,232	104.0
Austria	0.7	415	331	282	282	100.0
Belgium	0.8	506	390	344	344	100.0
Brazil	2.6	1,573	1,984	2,890	2,890	100.0
Canada	2.5	1,500	1,300	1,600	1,602	100.1
China	7.1	4,327	7,926	30,067	30,067	100.0
Finland	0.4	272	191	185	186	100.5
France	4.7	2,867	2,130	1,948	1,950	100.1
Germany	6.1	3,673	2,918	2,496	2,491	99.8
India	2.0	1,207	3,298	52,525	53,218	101.3
Ireland	0.4	268	186	182	183	100.5
Italy	3.8	2,314	1,818	1,572	1,572	100.0
Japan	8.1	4,911	4,356	507,567	507,584	100.0
Mexico	1.8	1,088	1,551	12,111	12,111	100.0
Netherlands	1.4	877	677	596	595	99.8
Russia	2.8	1,677	2,265	41,668	41,668	100.0
South Korea	1.5	929	1,345	1,023,938	1,023,938	100.0
Spain	2.6	1,602	1,395	1,089	1,095	100.6
Sweden	0.8	479	343	3,157	3,157	100.0
Switzerland	0.8	500	316	542	533	98.3
UK	4.4	2,680	2,228	1,446	1,443	99.8
US	23.8	14,441	14,441	14,441	14,093	97.6
Euro area	22.4	13,582	10,907	9,272	9,212	99.3
OECD	67.5	40,899	36,659	40,899	41,033	100.3
World	100.0	60,557	69,609	60,557	60,355	99.7

a Purchasing power parity.   b Local currency.
Sources: IMF; World Bank

The annual total GDP ranges from under $1 billion in some small African countries to over $14,000 billion in America. For countries at similar stages of development, magnitude depends largely on population size. (See GDP per head below and Real GDP, page 47.)

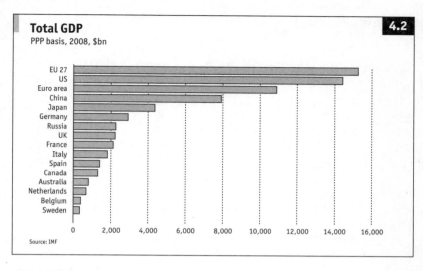

Total GDP
PPP basis, 2008, $bn

4.2

Source: IMF

GDP per head

Measures:	Output per person; GDP divided by population size.
Significance:	Used as an indicator of overall economic welfare.
Presented as:	Quarterly and annual totals.
Focus on:	Nominal totals; changes in real terms.
Yardstick:	The OECD average was $36,575 per head in 2008.
Released:	Annually, sometimes quarterly; well in arrears; frequently revised.

What to look for

Output per head is a good guide to living standards. It implicitly allows for qualitative factors such as literacy or health although these are not covered directly.

In 2008, annual output per head was below $400 in some African states, and a mere $138 in Burundi, while the world average was around $8,300. The output per head of the rich industrial countries was nearly three times greater than the average. After adjusting for variations in purchasing power, the gap between the richest and poorest countries looks narrower. Even so, the richest countries' output per head was nearly three times the world average (nearly $30,000). Zimbabwe's was a mere $8.

If real GDP per head increases it indicates an improvement in overall economic well-being. Seeking to provide a better indicator of human development, the United Nations Development Programme, the UN's

45

Table 4.2 **GDP per head, 2008**

	$	$, PPP	National currency	Real GDP annual % change 1998–2008	2008
Australia	46,824	36,918	54,748	1.8	0.4
Austria	50,039	39,887	34,001	2.0	1.9
Belgium	47,289	36,416	32,132	1.7	0.6
Brazil	8,295	10,466	15,240	2.0	4.0
Canada	45,085	39,098	48,108	1.9	-0.7
China	3,259	5,970	22,647	9.1	8.5
Finland	51,588	36,320	35,053	2.9	0.8
France	46,037	34,205	31,281	1.4	-0.2
Germany	44,729	35,539	30,392	1.5	1.4
India	1,017	2,780	44,276	5.4	5.8
Ireland	60,510	42,110	41,115	3.7	-4.9
Italy	38,996	30,631	26,497	0.8	-1.8
Japan	38,457	34,116	3,974,918	1.2	-0.7
Mexico	10,200	14,534	113,519	1.8	0.5
Netherlands	52,500	40,558	35,672	1.8	1.5
Russia	11,807	15,948	293,437	7.3	5.7
South Korea	19,136	27,692	21,088,949	4.8	2.0
Spain	35,117	30,589	23,861	2.0	-0.8
Sweden	52,181	37,334	343,928	2.5	-0.5
Switzerland	68,433	43,196	74,119	1.8	1.6
UK	43,734	36,358	23,598	2.1	0.2
US	47,440	47,440	47,440	1.6	-0.5
Euro area	35,118	39,947	24,000	1.3	nil
EU 27	31,606	36,728	–	1.9	0.5
OECD	25,696	27,627	–	1.7	-0.1

Sources: Eurostat; IMF

global development network, has been publishing its Human Development Index since 1990. It is a composite index using data on life expectancy, adult literacy, education enrolment rates and GDP per head. The 2009 rankings for over 180 countries showed Norway and Australia at the top and Afghanistan and Niger at the bottom. Newly industrialising countries such as South Korea and Singapore have moved rapidly up the rankings.

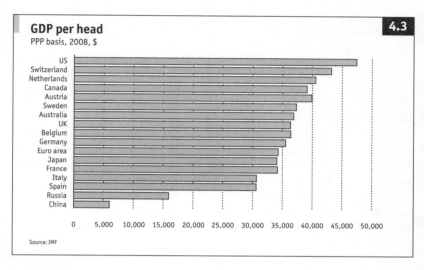

GDP per head
PPP basis, 2008, $

US
Switzerland
Netherlands
Canada
Austria
Sweden
Australia
UK
Belgium
Germany
Euro area
Japan
France
Italy
Spain
Russia
China

0   5,000 10,000 15,000 20,000 25,000 30,000 35,000 40,000 45,000 50,000

Source: IMF

Real GDP

Measures:	Total economic activity in constant prices.
Significance:	Most useful for tracking developments over time.
Presented as:	Quarterly and annual totals.
Focus on:	Percentage changes, annual or over four quarters.
Yardstick:	The Euro-area average was 1.3% a year growth during the period 1998–2008.
Released:	Quarterly, 1–3 months in arrears; frequently revised.

What to look for

Real (constant price) GDP or GDP figures reveal changes in economic output after adjusting for inflation. These should be put in the context of the cycle (see Cyclical indicators, page 55). Strong economic growth following a recession may simply indicate that slack capacity is being put back into use (see Unemployment and Capacity use, pages 68 and 118).

Strong growth when the economy is already buoyant may indicate the installation of new capacity which will add still more to future output (see Investment, Chapter 8). However, excess growth at the top of the cycle may bubble over into inflation and/or imports (see Chapter 13).

Developing countries have the capacity for faster GDP growth than more mature industrial economies. Real growth of around 3% per year is good for America and Europe. The newly industrialising countries of

Table 4.3 **Four world cycles**
Average annual % change in real GDP

	Four cycles				Cycles disaggregated					
	1980–90	1990–2000	2000–04	2004–08	down 1980–83	up 1983–90	down 1990–92	up 1992–2000	down 2000–02	up 2002–08
Australia	3.2	3.4	1.3	1.2	1.2	4.1	0.4	4.2	3.2	3.1
Austria	2.0	2.5	0.5	1.1	1.5	2.2	2.6	2.5	1.1	2.5
Belgium	2.0	2.3	0.6	0.9	0.4	2.8	1.6	2.5	1.1	2.1
Brazil	1.5	2.5	1.1	1.8	-2.4	3.3	0.2	3.1	2.0	4.1
Canada	2.8	2.9	1.0	0.9	1.1	3.6	-0.6	3.8	2.4	2.3
China	9.3	10.4	3.7	4.3	8.4	9.7	11.7	10.1	8.7	10.7
Finland	3.0	2.0	1.0	1.3	2.4	3.3	-5.0	3.8	2.1	3.1
France	2.4	2.0	0.6	0.7	1.5	2.8	1.1	2.2	1.4	1.7
Germany	2.3	2.1	0.2	0.8	0.3	3.2	3.6	1.7	0.6	1.4
India	5.6	5.6	2.3	3.5	5.5	5.6	3.3	6.2	4.2	8.4
Ireland	2.9	7.1	2.1	1.4	1.1	3.6	2.6	8.2	6.1	3.9
Italy	2.4	1.6	0.4	0.3	0.8	3.1	1.2	1.7	1.1	0.8
Japan	4.6	1.2	0.5	0.6	3.5	5.1	2.1	1.0	0.2	1.6
Mexico	1.9	3.5	0.6	1.3	1.4	2.1	3.9	3.4	0.3	3.1
Netherlands	2.2	3.1	0.5	1.1	0.0	3.2	1.9	3.3	1.0	2.3
South Korea	8.7	6.1	1.8	1.6	8.1	9.0	7.6	5.7	5.5	4.0
Spain	3.0	2.9	1.3	1.2	0.8	3.9	1.7	3.2	3.2	3.1
Sweden	2.2	2.0	0.9	1.0	0.9	2.7	-1.2	2.8	1.7	2.7
Switzerland	2.3	1.1	0.4	1.2	0.7	3.1	-0.4	1.4	0.8	2.3
UK	2.7	2.5	1.0	0.8	1.4	3.3	-0.6	3.3	2.3	2.3
US	3.2	3.4	0.9	0.8	1.7	3.9	1.6	3.9	1.4	2.4
EU 27	2.3	2.2	1.9	2.4	0.9	2.9	0.7	2.5	1.7	2.3
OECD	3.3	2.8	0.8	0.9	0.8	4.2	1.5	3.7	1.8	3.0
World	3.3	3.1	3.4	4.4	2.1	3.8	1.7	3.4	2.6	4.4

Note: These peaks and troughs identified may differ from those identified by national authorities.
Sources: IMF; OECD

the Pacific rim, for instance, achieved much higher rates in 1999 and 2000. Before the Asian crisis of 1997, they even managed at least double that. China's real GDP per head has averaged 9.1% between 1998 and 2008.

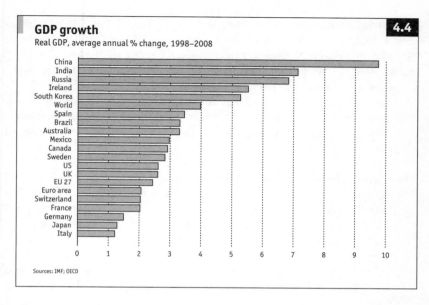

GDP growth `4.4`

Real GDP, average annual % change, 1998–2008

China
India
Russia
Ireland
South Korea
World
Spain
Brazil
Australia
Mexico
Canada
Sweden
US
UK
EU 27
Euro area
Switzerland
France
Germany
Japan
Italy

0   1   2   3   4   5   6   7   8   9   10

Sources: IMF; OECD

The inflation/output trade-off

The change in real GDP plus the change in the deflator (see page 39) approximately equals the change in nominal GDP. For example, if real output rises by 3% and inflation is 5%, nominal output has risen by about 8%. Some economists argue that aggregate demand determines nominal GDP and that there is a trade-off between real output and inflation: each can rise by any amount so long as the total equals the change in nominal output. Higher inflation therefore means lower growth in output.

World cycles

For the industrialised world, 1960, 1968, 1973 and 1979 were peak years for economic activity. There was another peak around the start of the 1990s, but it was unusual in that it was staggered across countries (see Cyclical indicators, page 55). The financial crisis of 2008 saw the first truly global recession since the 1930s, but with many large developing countries, such as China and India, bouncing back into growth rapidly, developed European countries such as Britain and Spain were slower to climb out of recession. Table 4.3 shows examples of economic growth rates within each cycle, which provide useful yardsticks for judging future growth rates.

Industrial economies. The 1960s were a period of rapid expansion, due at least in part to technological advances and freedom from external shocks. The 1973 and 1979 oil price rises caused temporary setbacks. Japan was perhaps more badly hit by the first; Europe and America suffered more from the second. Growth was rapid again in the mid–late 1980s and 1990s. The financial crisis of 2008 impacted all industrial economies, particularly those heavily exposed to financial markets and property bubbles such as the United States, United Kingdom, Ireland and Spain.

Developing countries. The oil producers enjoyed rapid growth rates in the 1970s and suffered the greatest setbacks in the 1980s. Broadly similar patterns were recorded by many Latin American and African countries, with the slowdown in the 1980s reflecting the debt crisis, a lack of inward investment and shortages of foreign exchange. East European countries also had feeble growth in the 1980s, reflecting the shortcomings of their planned economies. Export-orientated economies such as China, India and Brazil continued to grow rapidly once the financial crisis abated.

GDP: output

Measures:	GDP according to sector (agriculture, mining, manufacturing and service industries).
Significance:	Provides analysis of total output at a high level of detail.
Presented as:	Quarterly and annual totals.
Focus on:	Real growth rates.
Yardstick:	Overall real growth in the GDP total.
Released:	Quarterly, 1–3 months in arrears; frequently revised.

What to look for

Compare the percentage change in each sector with the overall percentage change in GDP. A sector which is growing faster than the average is making a very positive contribution to growth. A sector which is growing less rapidly than the average is clawing it down.

A change in a dominant sector has a larger effect on total activity than a change in a smaller sector. For example, in the industrial economies a 1% rise in services boosts GDP by more than a similar increase in agriculture. Indeed, the mature industrialised countries have been undergoing a shift from manufacturing to services. In the OECD countries, services' share of output rose from 45% in 1960 to 72% in 2007.

Table 4.4 **Dominant sectors**
Output as % of GDP, 2007

		General trend
Agriculture		
Guinea-Bissau	64	less developed
Central African Rep.	54	⬇
Manufacturing		
Swaziland	44	developing
China	32	⬇
Services		
US	77	developed
UK	76	

Source: World Bank

In general developing countries depend more on agriculture or, if they are at a later stage of development, manufacturing.

Chapter 9 reviews individual indicators of output.

GDP: expenditure

Measures:	GDP according to category of spending (consumption, investment and net exports).
Significance:	Provides detailed analysis of total spending.
Presented as:	Quarterly and annual totals.
Focus on:	Real growth rates.
Yardstick:	Overall real growth in the GDP total.
Released:	Quarterly, 1–3 months in arrears; frequently revised.

What to look for

As with the GDP output breakdown, compare the percentage change in each category of spending with the overall percentage growth in GDP in the same period.

Personal consumption. Growth in this category often leads a general recovery from recession, encouraging manufacturers to invest more. However, if consumption grows faster than the productive capacity of an economy, imports are sucked in and inflation rises. Personal

consumption typically accounts for 60% of GDP in industrial countries, so a change in consumption has a big effect on total output.

Government spending. This reflects, to some extent, politics rather than
market forces. Its share in GDP is higher in countries where the state
provides many services. A short-term increase in government spending
can provide a stabilising boost to the economy, but in general it diverts
resources from productive growth.

Investment. This is a key component, contributing to current growth
and laying down the foundation for future expansion. Look for spending
on machinery (which produces more output) rather than, say, dwellings.

Changes in stocks. These can be erratic. They decline when demand is
growing more rapidly than production (a good sign at the beginning of
a recovery, potentially inflationary at the end) or when manufacturers
and distributors are squeezed and are trying to cut the cost of holding
stocks. Inventories tend to rise when demand slows.

Exports and imports. Exports contribute to overall GDP growth; higher
imports reduce the increase in output relative to the growth in demand.
A sudden increase in import penetration (imports divided by GDP) suggests that consumer demand is growing faster than the domestic economy can cope with (overheating). A longer-term increase in imports
relative to exports may imply a decline in the competitiveness of
domestic producers. Imports that are substantially larger than exports
may point to exchange-rate problems.

Productivity

Measures:	Output for one unit of labour or capital.
Significance:	Indicator of efficiency and potential total economic output.
Presented as:	Index numbers.
Focus on:	Trend, especially relative to other countries.
Yardstick:	OECD average growth in real GDP per hour worked was 1.4% a year during 2004–08.
Released:	Sometimes monthly, often two months in arrears; frequently revised.

Overview
Productivity measures the amount of output that is produced with given

amounts of factor inputs (mainly land, labour and capital). Land is basically fixed and capital is very difficult to measure, so attention tends to focus on labour productivity. This can be defined in various ways. The most common are as follows.

- Output per worker = total output divided by total employment.
- Output per man hour = total output divided by hours worked.

Labour productivity reflects capital investment and offers a guide to capital productivity. A company using high-tech machinery will probably produce more per person than a company using 19th-century steam technology. Other factors which affect labour productivity include social attitudes, work ethics, unionisation and, perhaps most important, training. These are not measured directly by economic statistics.

The arithmetic of growth

Economic growth reflects growth of the labour force plus growth of labour productivity.

Labour productivity in turn depends on new investment (which raises the capital:labour ratio, which is known as factor substitution in economic jargon) and technological progress (which increases output for a given capital:labour ratio).

Interpretation

Productivity figures can be calculated in money terms, but they are generally produced as index numbers. As a result, analysts often look at changes over time and disregard the important question of the base from which the index numbers are calculated. If this was a period of high or low productivity, changes will be distorted.

Nevertheless, trends are important. If output per person increases by 5%, an identical increase in wage rates may leave profitability unchanged. Indeed, since total labour costs (including, for example, the cost of providing recreational facilities for workers) may increase less rapidly than wages, profitability may actually improve. (See Wages and Unit labour costs, pages 214 and 217.)

Cycles. Productivity is highly cyclical since employment and capital are less flexible than demand and output. When production falls after a peak in economic activity, employment declines less rapidly and output per head plummets.

Table 4.5 **Productivity**
Average annual % change in real GDP per worker

	Four cycles				Cycles disaggregated					
	1979– 90	1990– 2000	2000– 04	2004– 08	down 1979– 83	up 1983– 90	down 1990– 92	up 1992– 2000	down 2000– 02	up 2002– 08
Australia	1.2	2.3	2.3	0.4	2.0	0.7	3.3	2.0	2.9	0.8
Belgium	2.4	2.2	0.9	0.3	3.2	2.0	3.4	2.0	-0.6	1.0
Canada	1.0	1.9	0.8	0.7	1.1	0.9	1.3	2.0	1.2	0.6
Finland	2.9	2.9	2.1	1.8	2.2	3.4	2.0	3.1	1.5	2.1
France	3.1	2.0	1.4	1.1	2.1	3.6	1.8	2.1	2.0	1.0
Germany	2.2	2.5	1.2	1.2	1.7	2.5	3.9	2.1	1.7	1.1
Ireland	3.8	4.6	3.6	1.6	3.8	3.9	4.7	4.6	4.4	2.0
Italy	1.8	1.5	0.0	0.1	0.7	2.4	0.6	1.7	0.2	0.0
Japan	3.3	2.2	2.3	1.4	1.9	4.2	2.2	2.2	2.0	1.8
Netherlands	2.1	2.1	1.1	0.6	2.1	2.1	2.3	2.1	0.7	0.9
South Korea	–	5.1	4.2	4.6	–	6.9	5.8	4.9	4.2	4.4
Spain	3.2	1.4	0.7	1.1	4.0	2.7	2.3	1.2	0.7	0.9
Sweden	1.1	2.3	2.7	0.9	0.5	1.4	1.8	2.4	2.1	1.7
Switzerland	1.1	0.5	0.6	1.5	0.9	1.2	-3.0	1.4	1.5	0.9
UK	1.9	2.7	2.2	1.5	3.5	1.0	3.1	2.6	1.9	1.8
US	1.3	1.8	2.7	1.3	1.1	1.5	2.1	1.7	2.8	1.8

Source: OECD

When demand for goods and services increases after a recession, slack capacity is called into use and productivity rises rapidly.

Comparisons

When comparing absolute levels of productivity (rather than trends) remember that productivity also depends on technology and costs. Companies in Asia have a lower dollar value of output per person, but can still be more profitable than European or American companies because labour costs are cheaper in Asia.

Exchange-rate changes are also important for international comparisons of competitiveness (see page 166).

Cyclical or leading indicators

Measures: The economic cycle.
Significance: Useful tool for short-term predictions of economic activity.
Presented as: Index numbers.
Focus on: Trends.
Yardstick: Look for turning points.
Released: Monthly, at least one month in arrears; frequently revised.

Overview

In developed economies at least, GDP progresses erratically around its long-term growth trend. There are periods when growth spurts ahead, followed by periods of recession. This variation is known as the economic, business or trade cycle. It repeats every five years or so, although no two cycles are ever of the same magnitude or duration.

The cycle has four phases: expansion, peak, recession and trough.

Expansion. When demand first increases, for whatever reason, it gathers momentum automatically. The first sign is often a rundown in inventories. Output then rises faster than demand while these are rebuilt (see Stocks or inventories, page 107). Companies take on unemployed workers, who spend their new income on postponed purchases of consumer goods. This creates more demand and so companies employ more people, and so the process continues (the multiplier). Before long producers come up against capacity constraints. If they are confident that demand will remain buoyant (expectations), they invest more in new plant and machinery, which generates even more demand (the accelerator).

Peak. The upward momentum cannot continue indefinitely. Eventually output hits a ceiling owing to bottlenecks and supply constraints. Demand for investment funds may push up interest rates to the point where new investment is not profitable, or at full employment there may be no more workers to take on. Consumer demand may be steady, but the fall in investment demand pulls back the level of total output.

Recession. With investment demand falling, producers of capital goods start to cut back on labour. Higher unemployment reduces consumer demand. The inventories, multiplier, expectations and accelerator principles work in reverse and so the economic contraction gathers momentum.

Not much of a party

How the most recent recessions in rich countries compare

GDP growth of 0.1% in the three months to December 2009 means that Britain, where output fell for six successive quarters, is now officially out of its longest post-war recession. This leaves Spain, whose fourth-quarter GDP figures are not yet published, as the only big, rich country where growth may still not have resumed. Britain's slump was not nearly as deep as Japan's, where GDP contracted by 8.6% from peak to trough. Canada's recession was the least severe of any country in the G7: output fell by a relatively modest 3.3% between its peak and the bottom of the cycle.

GDP
Percentage fall from peak in 2008 to trough in 2009, %

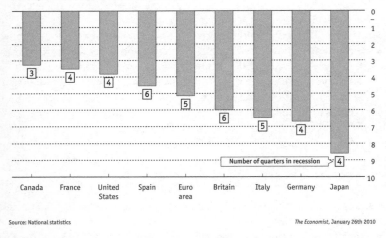

Source: National statistics

The Economist, January 26th 2010

Trough. Output will not fall indefinitely. It will stop at some minimum level (a trough or depression) because employees retain jobs and spending power where they work in government or in industries supplying food, basic essentials and perhaps export goods. Unemployment and welfare payments, past saving and new borrowing enable other consumers to buy essentials.

Slack demand for investment funds may pull back interest rates making new or replacement investment attractive, at least for the industries providing basic essentials. And with consumer demand steady,

Table 4.6 **Implied peaks and troughs in GDP**
Month/year

	Peak	Trough	Peak	Trough	Peak	Trough	Peak	Trough
Australia	11/88	12/90	02/94	02/96	11/99	03/01	10/07	05/09
Austria	05/90	03/93	10/94	03/96	04/00	10/01	05/07	02/09
Belgium	12/91	04/93	12/94	01/96	03/00	03/03	07/07	02/09
Brazil	05/89	04/90	10/94	01/99	12/00	04/03	05/08	03/09
Canada	07/87	12/90	07/94	11/95	07/97	07/01	08/07	02/09
China	12/87	07/90	12/96	–	–	11/01	01/08	12/08
France	12/88	03/93	10/94	12/96	12/99	04/03	07/07	12/08
Germany	07/90	02/93	11/94	03/96	04/00	10/01	04/07	02/09
India	–	–	07/95	09/98	02/00	12/01	11/07	12/08
Italy	11/88	12/92	10/94	08/96	11/99	09/01	02/07	12/08
Japan	11/87	11/92	09/96	08/98	03/00	11/01	01/07	03/09
Mexico	01/89	11/92	02/94	03/95	10/97	02/01	05/06	12/08
Netherlands	07/89	02/93	11/94	03/96	08/00	05/03	12/07	03/09
Russia	–	–	06/97	07/98	07/00	12/01	03/08	02/09
South Korea	01/91	07/92	09/94	01/98	05/99	03/01	03/07	11/08
Spain	09/88	01/93	06/94	01/96	02/99	11/01	11/07	01/09
Sweden	04/89	10/92	02/94	05/96	06/00	10/01	04/07	04/09
Switzerland	06/89	11/92	03/94	07/96	03/98	11/01	12/06	02/09
UK	10/87	02/91	01/94	11/98	11/99	04/03	08/07	01/09
US	07/87	12/90	06/94	11/95	01/00	02/03	07/07	02/09
Euro area	11/98	02/93	10/94	05/96	02/00	10/01	04/07	01/09
OECD	11/98	11/92	09/94	10/98	02/00	09/01	05/07	02/09

Note: These peaks and troughs identified by the OECD may differ from those identified by national authorities.
Source: OECD Composite Leading Indicators

investment demand begins to lift the economy again.

In America a recession is technically defined as two consecutive quarters of falling GDP. The snag with this is that if GDP plunges steeply in the first and third quarters of a year, but rises slightly in the second and fourth quarters, then officially an economy has escaped a recession, even though output may end the year sharply lower. Some economists prefer to define a recession as a year-on-year fall in output. Others talk about a "growth recession" when a country's GDP growth rate falls below its long-term productive potential. In Japan, for example, annual growth of less than 3% has often been called a recession.

Table 4.6 shows dates for peaks and troughs in selected countries.

Causes

There is no general consensus about what causes cycles or even about what is a cause and what is an effect. Major influences include fixed investment and inventory cycles, external shocks and well-meaning or perhaps self-interested government policies. It is not unknown for the government of the day to engineer an economic boom just before an election, thus setting the cycle in motion. Expansionary policies aimed at reducing unemployment followed by contractionary policies to limit the inflationary consequences can cause severe cyclical swings. More-over, measures to cool a boom may be imposed when automatic con-tractionary forces are already in motion, thus hastening the downhill slide.

Cyclical patterns in economic indicators

Cyclical patterns can be detected in many economic series. Peaks and troughs do not fall in step. This means that indicators which turn in advance of GDP can be used to predict economic developments. The following timings indicate roughly what might be expected in a stan-dard cycle in an industrial economy.

(Some economists argue that interest rates are a lagging indicator. They are included here as a leading indicator since most people are familiar with the idea of, say, lowering interest rates to boost a flagging economy.)

Leading indicators. Interest rates pass their low point and begin to rise about 18 months ahead of a peak in output.

Business confidence, share prices, housing starts and companies' financial surpluses peak 8–16 months ahead of output. Consumer credit, car sales and manufacturing orders peak about six months ahead. Retail sales peak 2–3 months in advance.

Coincident indicators. GDP establishes the reference point for the overall cycle, while other indicators which peak within a month or two of GDP are used to confirm that the economy is turning.

Lagging indicators. Manufacturing capacity utilisation peaks about a month after total output. Job vacancies peak about three months later, growth in average earnings after four months and growth in unit labour costs after five months. Productivity and unemployment stop falling and turn upwards six months after the peak in overall activity, and inflation peaks at about that time also. Investment, order backlogs and stocks peak around 12 months after output.

The cyclical indicators

Several countries and OECD statisticians have combined groups of economic indicators into composite cyclical indicators. Generally trends are removed, erratic fluctuations are smoothed, and the series are combined into weighted averages in index form.

The components of the indices vary, reflecting changes in economic habits and analysts' understanding of the economy. For example, in the early 1990s America downgraded the role of share prices after it was found that an increase in stockmarket values was taken as an indicator of an upturn, which prompted share buying and pushed up the leading indicator still further.

Interpretation. Use composite indicators as a guide to the cycle. Leading indicators turn 6–12 months ahead of GDP; coincident indicators turn with it; lagging indicators turn perhaps six months later.

Watch mainly for changes in direction in leading indicators and use coincident indicators to confirm the change. Most composite indicators are used only to identify turning points. However, American indicators are scaled so that percentage changes are broadly suggestive of the magnitude of fluctuations in the overall level of economic activity.

Composite indicators are frequently published when only a few components are available and are revised in subsequent months as more information comes to hand and as component indicators are themselves revised. The composites should be interpreted with care and supplemented by examination of individual economic series.

5 Population, employment and unemployment

Work is the refuge of people who have nothing better to do.

Oscar Wilde

This chapter contains a series of population and employment briefs. Among other things, they highlight the following points.

Trends. The first things to check when assessing longer-term economic trends are employment, productivity and investment. The brief on Productivity (page 52) shows their relationship to growth.

The size and age structure of the population provides an indicator of long-term pressures on the economy. GDP must grow at least as fast as the population if output per head is not to decline, while an increasing number of people of working age may signal enhanced productive potential, or higher unemployment.

Cycles. Unemployment is an excellent indicator of the state of the economic cycle. High unemployment (compared with the average over the past few years) suggests a recessionary gap. Low unemployment at the top of the cycle is broadly indicative of inflationary pressures. Note, however, that unemployment lags behind the cycle by perhaps 6–12 months (see Cyclical indicators, page 55).

Services. The services sector accounts for 65–75% of output in the major industrialised countries, but it is relatively neglected among the commonly followed indicators of output. Employment provides a useful guide to activity in the sector.

Incomes. Employment data provide guides to personal incomes, wages and unit labour costs (see pages 89, 214 and 217). These are the basis for measuring GDP on an incomes basis and they help when assessing inflationary pressures.

Table 5.1 **Population**

	Total 1997 m	Total 2007 m	Annual change[a] 2007–25, %	Area '000 km^2	Population, per km^2
Australia	18,518	21,072	0.9	7,692,024	2.7
Austria	7,968	8,315	0.2	83,871	99.1
Belgium	10,181	10,623	0.3	30,528	348.0
Brazil	163,780	187,642	0.7	8,514,877	22.0
Canada	29,907	32,976	0.9	9,984,670	3.3
China	1,230,075	1,324,655	0.5	9,596,961	138.0
France	58,207	61,707	0.4	551,500	111.9
Germany	82,052	82,263	-0.2	357,114	230.4
India	960,497	1,134,023	1.3	3,287,263	345.0
Italy	56,890	59,375	0.1	301,336	197.0
Japan	126,057	127,772	-0.3	377,930	338.1
Mexico	94,478	105,791	0.9	1,964,375	53.9
Netherlands	15,611	16,382	0.3	37,354	438.5
Russia	147,915	142,115	-0.4	17,098,242	8.3
South Korea	45,954	48,456	0.1	99,678	486.1
Spain	39,583	44,874	0.5	505,992	88.7
Sweden	8,846	9,148	0.4	441,370	20.7
Switzerland	7,089	7,551	0.3	41,277	182.9
UK	58,314	60,975	0.5	242,900	251.0
US	272,647	301,621	1.0	9,629,091	31.3
Euro area	303,281	319,803	0.2	2,581,895	8.1
EU 27	478,630	495,305	0.2	4,318,195	8.7
World	5,840,000	6,671,000	1.0	136,127,000	49.0

a Forecast.
Sources: Eurostat; UN

Old story

Which countries have most elderly people?

As the world gets healthier and wealthier, people are living longer. And with fertility rates declining in many rich countries, the number of elderly people as a share of those of working age is projected to rise sharply over the next 40 years, according to the European Commission. The biggest absolute increase in the old-age dependency ratio will be in Japan, which will jump from 35.1% in 2010, already the world's highest, to 73.8% by 2050. At that point, the number of pensioners in China will be equivalent to 38.8% of its labour force, up from 11.6% in 2010. The European Union, which had 84.6m elderly people last year, will have 148.4m in 2050. And the ratio for the world as a whole will more than double to over 25%.

Old-age dependency ratios
Number of people aged 65 and over
As % of labour force (aged 15-64), forecasts

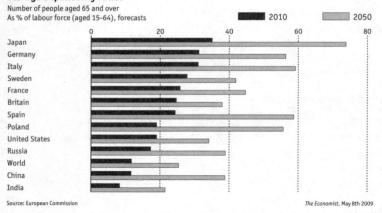

Source: European Commission

The Economist, May 8th 2009

Population

Measures:	Total number of people in a country.
Significance:	Yardstick for minimum GDP growth.
Presented as:	Total number.
Focus on:	Age structure and changes.
Yardstick:	The Euro area population grew by 0.5% a year between 1997 and 2007. Average annual growth of 0.2% was forecast for the period 2007–25.
Released:	Annually.

Overview

Real GDP must grow as least as fast as the population if living standards are not to fall. This may not be too hard in the industrial countries, where populations are expected to grow by less than 1% a year or even fall in 2007–25. It will be more difficult in sub-Saharan Africa, where populations are forecast to increase by around 2.2% a year over the same period. Developing countries elsewhere are likely to expand a little less rapidly, except for some Arab states and China. The population of China is projected to grow by 0.5% a year in 2007–25.

Migration and the age structure have important effects on output (see Labour or workforce below).

Labour or workforce

Measures:	Employees plus self-employed plus the unemployed.
Significance:	Indicator of maximum potential output.
Presented as:	Total number.
Focus on:	Structure and changes.
Yardstick:	Average annual growth in the OECD labour force was 0.9% in 1998–2008.
Released:	Monthly, at least one month in arrears; see Employment, page 66.

Definitions

The labour force or workforce is the number of people employed and self-employed plus those unemployed but ready and able to work. The grand total is sometimes known as the economically active population. The components of the labour force are notoriously difficult to measure (see also Employment and Unemployment, pages 66 and 68).

The labour force is defined variously to include, for example, people whose age in years is over 15 (Italy, Canada), 16 (America), or in the range 15–74 (Norway, Sweden).

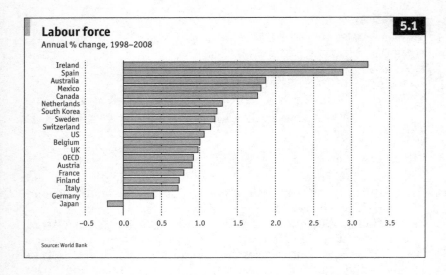

5.1

Labour force
Annual % change, 1998–2008

Ireland
Spain
Australia
Mexico
Canada
Netherlands
South Korea
Sweden
Switzerland
US
Belgium
UK
OECD
Austria
France
Finland
Italy
Germany
Japan

−0.5   0.0   0.5   1.0   1.5   2.0   2.5   3.0   3.5

Source: World Bank

There is a tendency to focus on the civilian labour force (that is, excluding the armed forces). Spain includes professional military personnel but excludes conscripts from its regular figures.

Changes in the labour force

The things to watch for are the three factors which affect the size of the labour force: population, migration and the proportion participating in economic activity.

Population. Birth rates in most industrial countries fell to replacement levels or lower in the 1980s. Meanwhile, earlier population growth boosted to record levels the number of 15–24 year-olds entering the labour force (exceptions include Japan and Switzerland). This implies an older workforce and higher old-age dependency rates (the number of retired people as a percentage of the population of working age) in the future. Output per employee must grow for GDP per head to remain constant. By 2025 20% of the population in industrial economies will be over 65 years of age.

Developing countries have young populations with around 30% under 15 years. This suggests an expanding working-age population with potential problems for housing and job creation.

Table 5.2 **Labour force** (including armed forces)

| | Size | — Annual average % change — | | | | – Female particip. rate – | |
	2008 m	1980–89	1990–99	2000–08	2008	1998	2008
Australia	11.3	2.3	1.2	2.0	2.1	65.1	70.8
Austria	4.3	1.1	1.2	1.0	0.9	61.9	69.3
Belgium	4.8	0.2	0.5	1.0	1.0	57.7	61.3
Canada	18.3	1.9	1.0	1.8	1.7	68.6	74.6
Finland	2.7	0.6	-0.1	0.6	1.2	69.9	74.5
France	28.4	0.5	0.9	0.7	0.0	63.1	65.3
Germany	41.8	0.6	2.8	0.7	0.2	63.1	70.3
Ireland	2.2	0.5	2.7	3.1	1.0	52.7	63.7
Italy	25.1	0.8	-0.5	0.7	1.5	45.1	52.1
Japan	66.5	1.2	0.7	-0.2	-0.3	63.9	67.5
Netherlands	8.9	2.4	1.6	1.1	1.1	62.7	73.5
South Korea	24.2	2.5	1.7	1.1	0.0	52.6	59.0
Spain	22.8	1.3	1.2	3.0	3.0	48.9	63.4
Sweden	4.9	0.5	-0.5	1.3	1.2	74.2	78.1
Switzerland	4.6	1.8	0.9	1.3	1.7	75.9	81.3
UK	31.1	0.8	-0.2	1.0	1.3	67.0	70.0
US	154.3	1.6	1.1	0.9	0.8	69.8	70.4

Sources: OECD; ILO

Migration. In the industrial countries inflows of foreign workers increased since the late 1980s and a substantial number of illegal immigrants were granted amnesty in America, France, Italy and Spain. The expansion of the EU to include eastern European countries has resulted in an increase in flows of legal migrants to rich European countries, and America's less welcoming policy towards migrant labour hasn't prevented large numbers of Mexicans from working illegally in the country.

Inward migration may be a bonus for some economies. For example, the unification of east and west Germany boosted that country's productive potential. However, large numbers of refugees seeking asylum can have significant adverse effects on income per head.

Wealthier developing countries, especially oil producers, have large proportions of foreigners in their labour forces. Workers frequently make a substantial contribution to the balance of payments in their home countries by remitting savings from their salaries.

Participation. Participation rates (the labour force as a percentage of the total population) generally increased in the 1980s and 1990s with earlier retirement for men, especially in France, Finland and the Netherlands, generally offset by more married women entering the labour force, especially in America, Australia, Britain, New Zealand and Scandinavia.

Women account for a smaller proportion of the workforce in predominantly Muslim countries (30%) and a greater proportion in Africa (around 40%) where they traditionally work on the land.

Employment

Measures: Total employment = employees in employment plus the self-employed.
Significance: Indicator of current output potential.
Presented as: Totals.
Focus on: Structure and changes.
Yardstick: OECD employment grew by 1.0% a year between 1998 and 2008.
Released: Monthly, at least one month in arrears.

Data collection

Measuring employment is tricky. The main sources of data are censuses and surveys of population and employment. Household surveys are generally the most reliable since surveys of employers tend to double count people with more than one job.

Most countries conduct household surveys; some monthly (Australia, Britain, Japan, the United States and Canada), some quarterly (Israel, Italy, New Zealand) and some less frequently still (China, India). Figures for months between main surveys are based on employment surveys or are estimates or interpolation.

Apart from the definitional problems mentioned in the previous brief, other distortions and international inconsistencies arise owing to factors such as the method of counting home workers and domestic servants, part-time staff, people with more than one job and those temporarily ill or laid off. Full employment is usually defined as the workforce less the natural rate of unemployment. (See also Unemployment, page 68.)

Basic analysis

The level of production depends on the number of people employed, hours worked, education, training and the quality of capital equipment. (See also Productivity, page 52.)

Table 5.3 **Total employment**

	Total	Annual average % change						
	2008 m	1960–69	1970–79	1980–89	1990–99	2000–08	2007	2008
Australia	10.8	2.7	1.3	2.3	1.2	2.3	2.8	2.3
Austria	4.1	-0.8	0.3	0.9	1.1	1.0	2.5	1.5
Belgium	4.5	0.7	0.2	0.0	0.7	1.0	2.7	1.5
Canada	17.2	3.0	3.3	1.9	1.1	1.9	2.3	1.5
China	774.8	–	–	3.2	1.2	0.9	0.8	0.6
Finland	2.6	0.0	0.7	0.8	-1.0	1.0	1.9	1.6
France	26.3	0.5	0.6	0.2	0.7	0.8	1.4	0.6
Germany	38.6	0.0	0.0	0.4	2.4	0.7	2.2	1.5
Ireland	2.1	0.1	1.1	-0.4	3.6	3.0	4.0	0.3
Italy	23.4	-0.6	0.4	0.3	-0.5	1.2	1.0	0.8
Japan	63.9	1.4	0.8	1.1	0.4	-0.1	0.5	-0.4
Mexico	43.5	–	–	–	5.1	1.8	1.7	2.3
Netherlands	8.6	1.1	0.3	2.2	2.1	1.1	2.4	1.5
Russia	71.0	–	–	–	-1.8	1.1	2.5	0.6
South Korea	23.6	–	3.9	2.8	1.3	1.4	1.2	0.6
Spain	20.3	0.7	-0.3	0.6	1.3	3.3	3.1	-0.5
Sweden	4.6	0.6	0.9	0.5	-1.1	1.2	4.6	1.1
Switzerland	4.5	1.5	-0.2	1.8	0.6	1.2	2.5	1.9
UK	29.5	0.3	0.3	0.6	-0.1	1.0	0.6	1.3
US	145.4	1.9	2.4	1.9	1.3	0.6	1.1	-0.5

Sources: OECD; ILO
a 2007

Hours worked consists of core hours and overtime. There is a tendency for core hours to decline as economies mature and workers demand more leisure.

Interpretation

Employment and unemployment are highly cyclical. When demand increases, companies first tend to increase overtime. They take on more employees only when higher demand is perceived to be strong and durable. When demand turns down, hours are cut before jobs.

Watch hours worked and overtime for early signals, and employment for confirmation. Survey evidence (see Business conditions, page

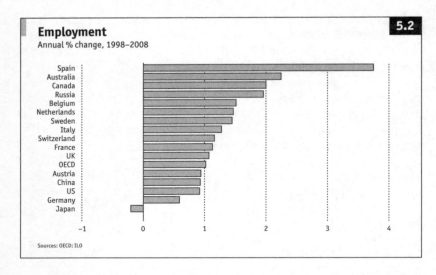

Employment
Annual % change, 1998–2008

5.2

Sources: OECD; ILO

115) indicating plans to take on or lay off workers may also provide early warning of changes in employment.

Try to identify to what extent an increase in payrolls represents second jobs. These limit employers' ability to increase output. A high number of second jobs with low unemployment suggests that any increase in consumer demand may be inflationary.

Sectoral trends. Where employment figures are available by sector, they provide a rough-and-ready guide to output trends in parts of the economy. Employment in services is an imperfect but useful indicator for that sector since output data for service industries are hard to find.

Unemployment and vacancies

Measures: Total = people out of work but ready and able to work. Rate = unemployment as a percentage of the labour force.

Significance: Indicator of spare labour capacity (and wasted resources).

Presented as: Total number, percentage.

Focus on: Structure and changes.

Yardstick: The OECD standardised rate of unemployment averaged 6.6% between 1998 and 2008.

Released: Monthly, at least one month in arrears.

Total unemployment. Based on people registered as unemployed (Austria, Switzerland) or claiming benefit (Belgium, Britain) or on survey evidence (Britain again, and many other countries). Surveys tend to make better indicators because they catch people who would take employment if work was available but who are not registered as unemployed.

Distortions and international inconsistencies arise owing to factors such as students claiming benefits during vacations, the treatment of people temporarily laid off, discouraged workers who do not declare themselves available for work and people who have part-time jobs but who are looking for full-time employment.

The unemployment rate. Usually defined as unemployment as a percentage of the labour force (the employed plus the unemployed). National variations are rife: Germany excludes the self-employed from the labour force; Belgium produces two unemployment rates expressing unemployment as a percentage of both the total and the insured labour force.

By changing the definition, which governments are inclined to do, the unemployment rate can be moved up or, more usually, down by several percentage points.

The International Labour Organisation (ILO) and other international organisations produce standardised unemployment rates which differ from national figures but which provide a consistent basis for cross-country comparisons. The 2008 figures in Table 5.4 show some slight differences between standardised and national rates.

Total unemployment

Unemployment never drops to zero for various reasons.

- **Frictional unemployment.** There are always people changing jobs and temporarily recorded as unemployed. Their number might be reduced by better information flows (bringing together vacancies and the unemployed) and training.
- **Structural unemployment.** This indicates people whose skills and locations do not match job opportunities, usually because they were trained for industries which are collapsing under competition from modern technology and/or imports. Structural job losses can best be reduced through retraining and improving labour mobility.
- **Seasonal unemployment.** Agriculture, construction and tourism are especially vulnerable to seasonal variation.
- **Residual unemployment.** This is the hard core of people who

Table 5.4 **Unemployment**

Standardised definition, as % of labour force

	Unemployment rate								Long-term unemployed[a]	
	1960	1970	1980	1990	2000	2005	2008	2008[b]	1998	2008
Australia	1.4	1.4	6.1	6.9	6.3	5.0	4.2	4.2	29.7	14.9
Austria	2.4	1.4	1.9	3.2	3.6	5.2	3.8	3.9	30.3	24.2
Belgium	3.3	1.9	8.1	8.9	7.0	8.4	7.0	7.0	61.7	52.6
Brazil[b]	–	–	2.8[e]	3.7	9.4	9.3	7.9	–	–	–
Canada	7.0	5.7	7.5	8.1	6.8	6.8	6.1	6.2	13.8	7.1
China[b]	–	–	4.9	2.5	3.6	4.2	4.2	4.2	–	–
Finland	1.5	1.9	4.7	3.2	9.8	8.4	6.4	6.4	27.5	18.2
France	1.3	2.2	5.8	8.3	8.6	8.9	7.5	7.9	44.2	37.9
Germany[c]	1.0	0.6	3.2	4.8	7.8	11.2	7.5	7.4	52.6	53.4
Ireland	5.7	5.9	7.4	13.0	4.3	4.3	5.2	6.1	55.3[d]	29.4
Italy	5.7	5.5	7.7	11.5	10.7	7.8	6.8	6.8	59.6	47.5
Japan	1.7	1.1	2.0	2.1	4.7	4.4	4.0	4.0	20.3	33.3
Mexico	–	3.8	3.0	2.7	2.6	3.5	3.5	–	0.8	1.7
Netherlands	0.7	1.0	6.2	7.6	2.7	4.7	2.8	2.8	47.9	36.3
South Korea	–	4.4	5.2	2.4	4.4	3.7	3.2	3.2	1.5	2.7
Spain	1.5	1.5	11.5	16.3	13.9	9.2	11.4	11.3	54.3	23.8
Sweden	1.7	1.5	2.2	1.8	5.9	7.8	6.2	6.2	33.5	12.4
Switzerland	0.0	0.0	0.2	0.5	2.6	4.3	3.3	2.7	34.8	34.3
UK	1.4	2.2	5.7	6.9	5.5	4.7	5.3	5.5	32.7	25.5
US	5.5	4.9	7.1	5.6	4.0	5.1	5.8	5.8	8.0	10.6

a Those unemployed for 12 months or more as % of total unemployed.
b National definition.   c Data up to 1990 refer to Western Germany.   d 1999.   e 1979.
Sources: EIU; Eurostat; OECD; ILO; IMF

are virtually unemployable, perhaps owing to their inability to integrate with the modern world.

The natural rate

Economists argue that there is a natural rate of unemployment (NRU) or non-accelerating inflation rate of unemployment (NAIRU), at which the demand and supply for labour are in balance.

The basic premise is that an increase in demand can be translated

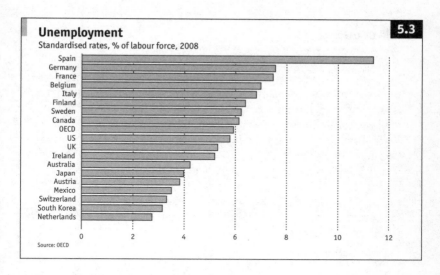

Unemployment 5.3
Standardised rates, % of labour force, 2008

Spain
Germany
France
Belgium
Italy
Finland
Sweden
Canada
OECD
US
UK
Ireland
Australia
Japan
Austria
Mexico
Switzerland
South Korea
Netherlands

0   2   4   6   8   10   12

Source: OECD

into higher employment only up to the NAIRU, at which point employment stops growing and the increase in demand spills over into higher inflation.

Estimates of the NAIRU are subjective and vary from country to country and over time, depending on the level of minimum wages, benefit rates, payroll taxes, unionisation and demographic factors such as the age structure of the labour force.

The cycle

There is a clear cyclical pattern in unemployment. As demand increases, companies take on more workers and unemployment decreases. When there is no more labour available (when the NAIRU is reached), demand bubbles over into inflation or imports. Strong consumer demand is less likely to be inflationary if the unemployment rate is well above the NAIRU rather than close to it. During the mid- and late 1990s, unemployment continued to decline in America and Britain below the unemployment rate previously thought to be the NAIRU, with few signs of inflationary pressure. Economists therefore think that the NAIRU declined in these two countries during the 1990s.

Longer-term trends

Unemployment in the industrial countries started to rise again in the early 1990s. It reached 7.4% of the labour force in 1995, and has since

Hire or fire?

Where employers are most optimistic, and pessimistic

In 27 out of 36 countries surveyed by Manpower, an employment-services firm, more companies said they expected to add jobs in the three months to the end of June than said they reckoned on reducing their workforce. The difference between the proportion of hirers and firers was highest in Brazil and India. Throughout Asia companies have become more optimistic about hiring than they were a year ago, most dramatically in Singapore but only slightly in Japan. Things look less rosy in Europe. In several countries, including Spain and Ireland, more companies expect to see cuts to their workforce than expect it to grow. Of the four countries where the outlook has darkened, three are in Europe.

Employment outlook
Balance of employers expecting an increase or decrease in employment, Q2 2010, percentage points

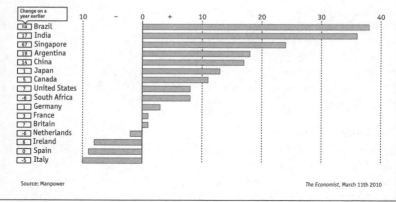

Source: Manpower

The Economist, March 11th 2010

fallen back to 5.9%. The rate is higher in Europe (7.5% in 2008) than in America (7.4%), where flexible labour markets and strong economic growth have pulled unemployment down.

The structure of unemployment helps to identify problem areas. In 2008 long-term unemployment in the euro area (those unemployed for more than 12 months) was 48% of total unemployment. However, it was lower in Japan (33%) and in America (11%).

A job to do

As countries climb out of recession, employers begin to recruit again

Recruitment in both Europe and America rose in October, according to the Monster Employment Index, which measures the strength of companies' hiring intentions by counting online advertisements. In Europe this was the first increase since February. In America there were more openings in health care and public administration in October, but fewer retail jobs on offer. Steep declines in most of the second half of 2008 mean that the American index is still more than 20% lower than a year earlier. The picture is worse in Europe, where recruitment was more than a third lower than 12 months earlier. Recruitment continued to fall in Germany in October, but it rose substantially in Britain.

Job vacancies
% change on a year earlier

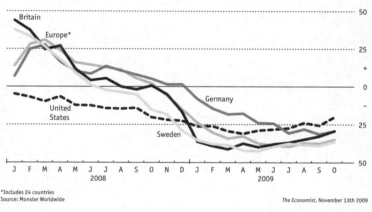

*Includes 24 countries
Source: Monster Worldwide

The Economist, November 13th 2009

Other clues

The monthly change in unemployment is a good guide to economic developments. Compare the last 2–3 months with the average change in the same period of the previous year. Most figures are seasonally adjusted, but watch out for the effects of severe weather or industrial disputes.

Other figures, such as weekly claims for unemployment benefit, job advertisements for help wanted and vacancies, provide a useful back-up to unemployment figures.

Regional unemployment figures provide a guide to structural unemployment since they highlight the relationship between job losses and the location of known twilight industries.

Surveys, such as of employers, also give an indication of the employment outlook.

6 Fiscal indicators

Blessed are the young, for they shall inherit the national debt.

Herbert Hoover

Fiscal indicators are concerned with government revenue and expenditure, which are significant influences on the circular flow of incomes (see pages 42–43). Taxes and duties take money out, while spending is an injection. In any one day or year the American government spends more than any other government, company or other organisation anywhere in the world.

Fiscal activities allow governments to provide services, redistribute incomes and influence the overall level of economic activity. They are one of the government's tools for controlling the economy. Others include monetary policy (see Chapter 12) and direct intervention and controls over wages, prices and industrial activity.

Level of government

Various problems of definition arise because of different treatment of financial transactions by central government, local authorities, publicly owned enterprises, and so on.

In an attempt to standardise, international organisations such as the OECD focus on general government, which covers central and local authorities, separate social security funds where applicable, and province or state authorities in federations such as in North America, Australia, Germany, Spain and Switzerland.

Watch out for fiscal fraud: spending can be shifted to publicly owned enterprises which are generally classified as being outside general government. Net lending to such enterprises is part of government spending, but it is not always included in headline expenditure figures.

Timing

Many governments run their accounts on a calendar-year basis. Britain, Canada and Japan have financial years which cover the 12 months to March 31st; Australia's fiscal year runs to June 30th; and America's ends on September 30th.

Total tax revenue

Tax revenues have risen as a share of GDP across the OECD over the past 30 years. In 2007 Denmark's government collected nearly half its GDP as taxes, making it the most heavily taxed among all the rich countries. The Danes narrowly edged out Sweden, the previous year's most heavily taxed country. France, Norway and Italy also have tax revenues of more than 40% of GDP. At the other end of the spectrum, America and South Korea are relatively lightly taxed, with ratios of under 30%. However they are not as lightly taxed as Mexico, where the government's tax revenues are barely a fifth of GDP. In general Europe is the most heavily taxed region in the OECD and taxes are lowest in the Americas.

As % of GDP, 2007

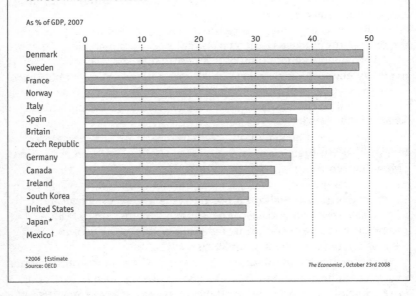

*2006 †Estimate
Source: OECD

The Economist , October 23rd 2008

Public expenditure

Measures:	Spending by the government.
Significance:	Affects aggregate demand, size of the budget deficit.
Presented as:	Monthly and annual totals in current prices.
Focus on:	Total, trends.
Yardstick:	OECD average public expenditure was 40.2% of GDP between 2000 and 2008.
Released:	Monthly, at least one month in arrears.

The cycle and the automatic stabiliser

Government spending provides services including law and order, defence, education and health, roads, and so on. Such spending is an injection into the circular flow of income and has a considerable effect on aggregate demand. It is a stabilising influence to the extent that payments of welfare benefits increase when unemployment rises, which helps to maintain consumer spending.

Classification

Public spending may be classified in several different ways.

- **By level of government:** central and local authorities, state or provincial authorities for federations, social security funds and public corporations.
- **By department:** agriculture, defence, trade, and so on.
- **By function:** such as environmental services, which might be provided by more than one department.
- **By economic category:** current, capital, and so on.

Breaking down the economic effect of public spending into current and capital spending is a useful way to interpret it.

Current spending

Major categories of current spending include the following.

- **Pay of public-sector employees:** this generally seems to rise faster than other current spending.
- **Other current spending:** on goods and services such as stationery, medicines, uniforms, and so on.
- **Subsidies:** on goods and services such as public housing and agricultural support.
- **Social security:** including benefits for sickness, old age, family allowances, and so on; social assistance grants and unfunded employee welfare benefits paid by general government.
- **Interest on the national debt.**

Interest payments reflect the size of the national debt (see page 87) and the level of interest rates. In 2008 net interest payments ranged from 4.9% of GDP in Italy to -3.8% in Norway.

Social security transfers do not directly create output and are not included when measuring GDP. Their size reflects the level of state support, demographics and the economic cycle. Payments are mostly financed by specific employers' and employees' contributions. Where these are passed through a separate social security budget, headline spending figures are lower. National accounting conventions also affect the figures. For example, the British government counts the working families' tax credit, a means of support for low-paid people with children introduced in 1999, as a deduction from tax revenues. The payment it replaced, family credit, was counted as social-security expenditure. The effect of the change is to reduce the headline spending figure.

Subsidies are caught in the market price measure of GDP, but are added back in as part of the adjustment to a factor cost basis. They range from around 0.5% of GDP in America and Japan to nearly 2% in Sweden.

Other current spending on pay and other goods and services makes up the "government consumption" component of GDP on an expenditure basis. This exceeds 25% of GDP in countries such as Sweden and Denmark where many services are supplied by the government rather than the private sector.

Capital spending

Capital spending is mainly fixed investment in infrastructure and dwellings. Note that some spending is arbitrarily classified as current spending even when there is a considerable capital outlay, such as in defence. Also current spending on things such as education, industrial training, and research and development might be regarded as investment although they are never classified as such in economic figures.

This capital spending is part of investment in the expenditure measure of GDP. Public-sector investment ranges from around 2% of GDP in Britain and America to 5% in South Korea.

Patterns and targets

Monthly public spending figures are rarely seasonally adjusted, although there is often a definite pattern of spending during the fiscal year. Eliminate this by comparing the latest 2–3 months with the same period 12 months earlier, or the fiscal year to date with the same part of the previous year, but note that the smoothing effect will be smaller at the start of the year (perhaps covering only two months) than the end (when perhaps 11 months are included).

The year-to-date comparison is useful for judging spending in relation to budget projections. For example, if in the first six months of the fiscal

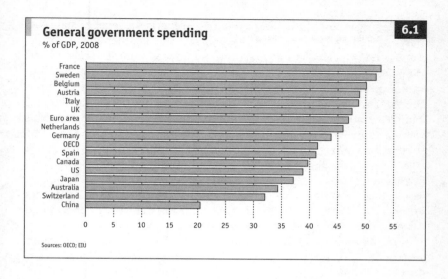

General government spending
% of GDP, 2008

6.1

Sources: OECD; EIU

year spending is 5% up from the previous first half and expenditure is projected to rise by 2% during the year as a whole, it is a fair bet that the government is overspending. However, watch for any erratic items which distort the seasonal pattern.

Spending tends to rise above target if the economy grows more slowly than expected. Always ask whether government economic forecasts are realistic when looking at expenditure projections.

Prices

Monthly government spending figures are always presented in nominal money terms. Judge their influence on the real level of economic activity by deflating them. For example, if government consumption rises by 10% and inflation is 6%, the real level of such consumption is approximately 4% higher.

Choosing an appropriate deflator requires care. Table 13.1 shows that prices in the public and private sectors can increase at different rates. If public servants tolerate larger price rises than private individuals, then prices in the public sector will rise faster than in the private sector. If the public sector is facing a cash squeeze, then prices may rise more slowly in the public sector.

Quarterly and annual spending figures are available in volume terms. The consumption component can be found in GDP data, although

Table 6.1 **General government spending**
      % of GDP, 2006

	Total	Health	Education	Defence
Austria	49.3	7.2	5.9	0.9
Belgium	48.3	6.9	5.8	1.0
Canada	39.2	7.3	7.2	1.0
Finland	48.9	6.8	5.8	1.5
France	52.7	7.2	6.0	1.8
Germany	45.4	6.2	4.0	1.1
India[a]	28.2	1.1	3.6	2.1
Ireland	33.7	7.7	4.1	0.5
Italy	49.9	7.0	4.5	1.4
Japan	36.1	7.1	3.8	0.9
Netherlands	45.6	5.9	5.1	1.5
OECD	43.5	6.5	5.6	1.4
South Korea	30.2	4.1	4.7	2.8
Spain	38.5	5.6	4.3	1.1
Sweden	54.3	6.8	7.1	1.7
UK	44.3	7.1	5.8	2.5
US	36.7	7.7	6.2	4.3

a Financial year 2006–07.
Sources: OECD; national statistics

public investment is not usually distinguished separately from private investment in the main GDP breakdowns.

Government revenues

Measures: Government receipts mainly from taxes and duties.
Significance: Affects aggregate demand; finances (partly) government spending.
Presented as: Monthly and annual totals in current prices.
Focus on: Total; trends.
Yardstick: Compare with spending (see Budget balance, page 83). OECD receipts averaged 38.0% of GDP between 1998 and 2008.
Released: Monthly, at least one month in arrears.

Overview
Government revenues are raised largely through taxes, social security

contributions, fees or charges for services and some miscellaneous sources such as interest on government loans. A few governments also conduct trading activities which generate income.

For the industrial countries as a group in 2007, personal income taxes, payroll taxes (largely social security) and taxes on spending each accounted for 25–30% of the total tax take. The remaining 20% came mainly from taxes on company profits and property.

Asset sales. One other source of income is receipts from the privatisation of activities previously undertaken by the public sector. In some countries, such as Britain, the receipts are classified as "negative expenditure". Either way, they have a one-off effect on public finances which is perhaps akin to selling the family silver and should not be mistaken for an underlying improvement.

The cycle and the automatic stabiliser

In addition to financing government spending, taxes have a major effect on economic activity.

They also have an important automatic stabilising influence. The government tax take increases and helps to moderate consumer demand when more people are earning and spending more at the top of the economic cycle. Similarly, the tax take declines during recession and to some extent helps to offset falling wage incomes.

Progressive or regressive

- **Progressive taxes** take a larger proportion of cash from the rich than from the poor, such as income tax where the marginal percentage rate of tax increases as income rises.
- **Proportional taxes** take the same percentage of everyone's income, wealth or expenditure, but the rich pay a larger amount in total.
- **Regressive taxes** take more from the poor. For example, a flat-rate tax of £200, such as Britain's controversial and short-lived poll tax, takes a greater proportion of the income of a lower-paid worker than of a higher-paid worker.

Direct or indirect

Direct taxes. These are levied directly on people or companies. They include taxes on personal and corporate income, capital gains, capital transfers, inheritances and wealth; and royalties on mineral extraction.

Direct taxes are usually charged at percentage rates; frequently they are progressive. Payroll taxes tend to be regressive if considered separately from the associated social security benefits.

As mentioned in the previous brief, social security payments are mostly financed by specific employers' and employees' contributions. Where these are passed through a separate social security budget, headline revenue figures are lower. But Denmark's social security bill is mainly met from general taxation, which depresses the apparent level of social security revenues.

Indirect taxes. Levied on goods and services, these include the following:

- Value-added tax (VAT) charged on the value added at each stage of production; this amounts to a single tax on the final sale price.
- Sales and turnover taxes which may be levied on every transaction (for example, wheat, flour, bread) and cumulate as a product is made.
- Customs duties on imports.
- Excise duties on home-produced goods, sometimes at penal rates to discourage activities such as smoking.

Indirect taxes tend to be regressive, as poorer people spend a bigger slice of their income. They are charged at either flat or percentage rates. Flat-rate duties do not rise with inflation and have to be "revalorised", usually in the annual budget, if the government is to retain its real tax-take.

GDP at market prices includes indirect taxes, which increase selling prices and have to be subtracted as part of the adjustment to a factor cost basis (see page 38).

Monthly figures

As with spending figures, revenues are usually published monthly in nominal values. Erratic movements can be smoothed out by taking several months together. They can be converted into real terms using the same deflator that is used for public expenditure.

When comparing revenues against budget projections, remember that revenues will tend to be below expectation if the economy grows more slowly than forecast.

Budget balance, deficit, surplus

Measures:	Net total of government spending less revenues in one month/year.
Significance:	Indicator of government's fiscal stance.
Presented as:	Monthly and annual totals in current prices.
Focus on:	Totals; trends.
Yardstick:	The average OECD deficit was 3.2% of GDP during the 1990s and 3.5% in 2008.
Released:	Monthly, at least one month in arrears.

Overview

Balanced budgets (revenues equal spending) sound prudent but may not always be in the best interests of economic management. Perfect balance is hard to achieve anyway, because of the automatic stabilisers in spending and revenue.

Budget deficits (spending exceeds revenues) boost total demand and output through a net injection into the circular flow of incomes. As with personal finances, a deficit on current spending may signal imprudence. However, a deficit to finance capital investment expenditure helps to lay the basis for future output and can be sustained so long as there are private or foreign savings willing to finance it in a non-inflationary way.

Deficits are more common than surpluses. In the 1970s and early 1980s many OECD governments went on a borrowing binge, often with adverse consequences. High levels of government borrowing tend to push up interest rates and so may crowd out private-sector investment. The average budget deficit of OECD countries rose in the early 1990s. However, after peaking at 5.0% of GDP in 1993 it became a 0.2% surplus in 2000 (see Table 6.2 on page 86). In that year, 16 of the 30 countries in the OECD ran a surplus. In the new century, deficits became more common but were not excessive until the financial crisis. Governments stepped in to support the financial system, sending the average budget deficit to an estimated 8.2% in 2009. Norway was the only OECD member expected to show a surplus. At the other end of the scale, Iceland, Greece, Ireland and Britain were estimated to be running deficits of over 11% of GDP.

Budget surpluses (revenues exceed expenditure) may be prudent if a government is building up a large surplus on its social security fund in order to meet an expected increase in its future pensions bill as the population ages. However, a surplus may be undesirable if it takes too much money out of the circular flow.

The world's largest relative budget surpluses (20–40% of GDP) have been run up by Kuwait after the 1970 oil price hikes and Botswana, as a result of income from the sale of oil and diamonds respectively. The receipts come from foreigners rather than the domestic circular flow, so the surpluses manage to stimulate even though they appear deflationary. Other countries' surpluses tend to be smaller, typically up to 5% of GDP.

Tighter or looser. Fiscal policy is said to have tightened if a deficit is reduced or converted into a surplus or if a surplus is increased, after taking into account the effects of the economic cycle. A move in the opposite direction is called a loosening of fiscal policy.

The cycle and the automatic stabiliser

There is an automatic stabiliser built into the budget balance. Surpluses reduce or tip into the red and deficits grow during a recession when tax revenues fall and welfare spending increases. This helps to maintain aggregate demand. The opposite happens during an economic boom.

The cyclically adjusted budget balance is the normal balance with cyclical fluctuations removed. This helps to identify the underlying fiscal stance, but such figures should always be regarded with suspicion because it is difficult to get the adjustments right.

Definitions

There are three main ways of looking at the budget balance. One is the published headline balance which depends on national definitions and accounting practices. The other two are the borrowing requirement and net savings, both of which are usually tricky to identify precisely from published figures.

The borrowing requirement. The net total of government spending less revenues is the gap which has to be financed by borrowing or which allows debt to be repaid. The announced budget balance in Britain used to be exactly this figure: the public-sector borrowing requirement (PSBR), or for surpluses the public-sector debt repayment (PSDR). However, the PSBR (renamed the public-sector net cash requirement) has now been downgraded in favour of the "current balance" (see below).

In most countries the precise definition varies depending on what is included in the "budget". There are two important areas to consider.

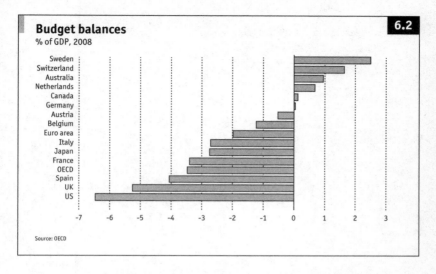

Budget balances
% of GDP, 2008

6.2

Source: OECD

- ◪ **Level of government.** Headline budget figures for the United States are for federal government only and for France cover just central government. At the other extreme, those for Germany cover federal, Länder and local authorities, and Switzerland's include federal, confederations, cantons and local government.
- ◪ **On or off budget.** Many government activities fall outside the normal budget, including lending by government agencies and government farm crop or export insurance, as well as government-guaranteed borrowing by publicly owned enterprises and government-guaranteed lending by private-sector bodies. During the financial crisis that began in 2008, America was one of several countries that were forced to bail out banks and other financial institutions, with the rescue expected to cost around $350 billion.

Net savings. The balance of current spending and receipts indicates the public sector's net savings: the extent to which the public sector is adding to or subtracting from the circular flow of incomes. This differs from the budget balance in that it includes only current, not capital, transactions. Britain's current balance corresponds to the government's net savings.

Table 6.2 **General government budget balances**
Surplus or deficit (-) as % of GDP

	1995	2000	2005	2007	2008	Net financial liabilities, % of GDP, 2008
Australia	-3.7	0.9	1.7	1.8	1.0	-7.3
Austria	-5.9	-1.9	-1.7	-0.7	-0.5	32.7
Belgium	-4.5	-0.1	-2.8	-0.2	-1.2	74.1
Canada	-5.3	2.9	1.5	1.6	0.1	22.4
Finland	-6.2	6.9	2.6	5.2	4.4	-51.1
France	-5.5	-1.5	-3.0	-2.7	-3.4	44.3
Germany	-9.7	1.3	-3.3	0.2	0.0	45.0
Ireland	-2.0	4.8	1.7	0.2	-7.2	11.4
Italy	-7.4	-0.9	-4.4	-1.5	-2.7	89.6
Japan	-4.7	-7.6	-6.7	-2.5	-2.7	84.4
Netherlands	-9.2	2.0	-0.3	0.2	0.7	25.2
South Korea	3.8	5.4	3.4	4.7	3.3	-37.4
Spain	-6.5	-1.0	1.0	1.9	-4.1	22.8
Sweden	-7.3	3.7	2.0	3.8	2.5	-18.2
Switzerland	-2.0	0.1	-0.7	1.6	1.6	9.0
UK	-5.8	3.7	-3.3	-2.7	-5.3	33.1
US	-3.3	1.5	-3.3	-2.8	-6.5	47.2
Euro area	-7.6	-0.1	-2.6	-0.6	-2.0	44.8
OECD	-4.8	0.2	-2.7	-1.3	-3.5	41.9

Source: OECD

Monthly figures and targets

Budget balances are usually published monthly in nominal values. Erratic movements can be smoothed by taking several months together. They can be converted into real terms by deflating spending and revenue separately.

When comparing cumulative budget balances with projections, remember that deficits tend to expand if the economy grows more slowly than forecast.

National debt; government or public debt

Measures: Long-run cumulative total of government spending less revenues.
Significance: Inter-generational transfer, interest payments add to borrowing.
Presented as: Annual totals in current prices.
Focus on: Total, particularly as a percentage of GDP; trends.
Yardstick: Varies widely; see text.
Released: Mainly annually; not easily found.

Overview

The public or national debt is the cumulative total of all government borrowing less repayments. It is financed mainly by citizens and may be seen as a transfer between generations. This contrasts with external debt (see page 152) which has to be financed out of export earnings.

Size of debt

Chart 6.3 shows the relative size of various national debts in 2008. Italy and Japan headed the list with debt that was almost as much as their annual GDP.

The debt is often understated since governments carry various liabilities which do not show on their balance sheets. For example, public-sector pensions are usually unfunded, that is, paid out of current income rather than from a reserve created during the individual's working life as happens with private-sector pensions.

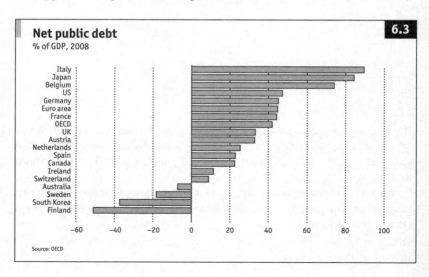

Net public debt
% of GDP, 2008

6.3

Source: OECD

Oceans of red ink
Comparing rich-country budget deficits

Most rich-country governments will struggle with huge budget deficits in 2010. A decade ago small surpluses were common in many rich countries (although not in Japan), but these are long gone. As economies pull out of recession, government spending will have to be cut and, with luck, tax revenues will gradually rise again. But paying off debts will be an enormous and painful task, which could also prolong the pain inflicted by the economic slump. On Monday February 1st Barack Obama made a start for America, unveiling his budget for 2011 which proposes cutting or consolidated 120 programmes, with savings expected to total $20 billion.

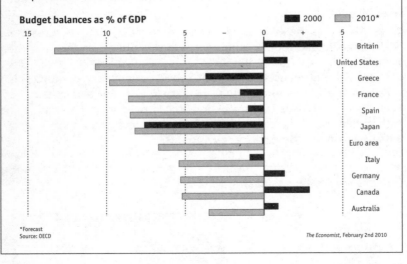

Budget balances as % of GDP ■ 2000 ▢ 2010*

*Forecast
Source: OECD

The Economist, February 2nd 2010

Economic theory provides few clues to the optimum ratio of public debt to GDP. Trends over time are often a better measure of a government's creditworthiness than the absolute level of debt. A country with an ever-rising debt ratio is clearly heading for trouble. In 2010 Greece's sharply rising debt triggered a sovereign-debt crisis that threatened to spread to other weaker euro-zone members. A €110 billion rescue plan for Greece from the European Union and the IMF was not enough to calm market fears, and was followed by a further package of up to $750 billion for the euro area.

7 Consumers

Live within your income, even if you have to borrow money to do so.

Josh Billings

Overview

Consumers are important since personal consumption accounts for between half and two-thirds of GDP.

In general, if consumers' incomes increase (perhaps because of wage rises or tax cuts) they will save some and spend the rest. The part which is spent becomes income for someone else, who in turn spends and saves. The process is repeated and the multiplier effect makes everyone better off, provided that the growth in spending goes into extra production rather than higher prices.

At the same time, the proportion of consumers' income that is saved provides the finance for investment, which is essential for future production, income and consumption.

Consumers, persons and households

For the most part, economic analysis is most effective if focused on a clearly defined group of economic agents, such as households. However, national accounting practices vary and figures are not generally available for such neat units. Terminology can become cloudy.

- **Household.** A group of people living under one roof and sharing cooking facilities.
- **Consumer sector and personal sector.** These terms are generally used interchangeably and are usually defined to include: households and individuals; owners of unincorporated businesses; non-profit-making bodies serving individuals; private trusts; and private pension, life insurance and welfare funds.
- **Private consumption.** The same as personal consumption since, by national accounts definition, companies do not consume. But businesses invest, so private (personal plus business) investment is different from personal investment.
- **Total consumption.** Personal (private) consumption plus government consumption.

Personal income, disposable income

Measures: Personal sector total income and income after tax.
Significance: Basis for consumption and savings.
Presented as: Money totals.
Focus on: Growth rates.
Yardstick: 3% a year in real terms.
Released: Mainly quarterly, monthly in USA; 1–3 months in arrears.

Personal income. Current income received by the personal sector from all sources. The bulk is wages and salaries, but the total also covers rents (including the imputed rental value to owner-occupiers of their homes), interest and dividends (including those received by life insurance and pension funds), and current transfers such as social security benefits paid to persons and business donations to charities.

Personal disposable income (PDI). Personal income after the deduction of personal direct taxes and fees (such as passport fees), and current transfers abroad. The figures in Table 7.1 give an indication of the composition of income and disposable income in the United States.

Real personal income and PDI. Personal incomes and personal disposable income are occasionally quoted in nominal terms, that is, before allowing for inflation. Real personal income and real PDI are incomes adjusted for inflation. Consumer prices can be used if no other deflator is available. Loosely, if incomes rise by 5% and prices increase by 3%, real incomes are 2% higher.

International comparisons

International comparisons are affected by differences in the provision or treatment of private pensions, life insurance, social security, household interest payments, and current and capital transfers.

In general PDI is reasonably consistent internationally, but personal income is less so. For example, British personal income includes employers' social security contributions and excludes employees' contributions. Both sets of contributions are deducted from personal income to arrive at PDI. In America social insurance payments are excluded from both total income and disposable income. Thus British personal income is inflated slightly relative to that in America, but PDI is on the same social security basis in both countries.

Similarly, personal income in Britain includes net interest receipts. In

Table 7.1 **Personal income, outlays and savings in the United States, 2008**
$bn

Wages and salaries	6,545.9
of which:	
Private industries	5,404.6
Government	1,141.3
Proprietors' income	1,106.3
of which:	
Farm	48.7
Non-farm	1,057.5
Rental income	210.4
Interest income	1,308.0
Dividends	686.4
Transfers	1,875.9
Less social-insurance contributions	990.6
Less taxes, etc	1,432.4
Personal disposable income (PDI)	**10,806.4**
Total deductions	10,520.0
of which:	
Personal consumption	10,129.9
Interest payments	237.7
Transfers to government	87.9
Transfers overseas	64.5
Personal savings	**286.4**
Savings ratio (savings as % of PDI)	**2.7**

Source: US Department of Commerce

American income includes interest received on savings but interest paid on loans is treated as part of expenditure. In this case American income and PDI are both inflated relative to Britain's.

Interpretation

Incomes are affected by the economic cycle. In general it is advisable to look for sustainable growth in real incomes – too rapid an increase may be inflationary (see Chapter 13). The main components are as follows.

Income from employment. The major influence on personal income. The total depends mainly on the number of people in employment, hours worked (see Chapter 5) and their pay (see Chapter 13).

Income from self-employment. The next most important component of PDI. Self-employed incomes are linked to the general health of the economy. They will increase when nominal GDP rises.

Interest and dividends. Dividends are sensitive to company profits and the state of the economy, while interest payments obviously move in line with interest rates. When borrowing is high relative to savings, an increase in interest rates can mean a fall in net interest income. Generally an increase in interest rates boosts PDI because in most countries (Britain is the main exception) the personal sector has more assets with adjustable interest rates than liabilities.

Taxes and benefits. Changes in the rates of tax or benefits have a rapid effect on PDI (but not, of course, on personal income). The magnitude will depend on the nature of the change; see Chapter 6.

Consumer and personal expenditure, private consumption

Measures:	Spending by persons.
Significance:	Key component of GDP.
Presented as:	Money totals.
Focus on:	Growth rates.
Yardstick:	The OECD average real growth in consumer expenditure was 3.2% a year during the late 1970s and 1980s and 2.5% during the 1990s and 2000s.
Released:	Quarterly with GDP figures, monthly in USA; frequently revised.

Overview

Consumer expenditure is personal (mainly household) spending on goods and services. Thus it includes imputed rents on owner-occupied dwellings; the outlays which would be required to buy income in kind; and administrative costs of life insurance and pension funds. It excludes interest payments; the purchase of land and buildings; transfers abroad; all business expenditure; and spending on second-hand goods, which reflects a transfer of ownership rather than new production.

Strictly speaking, expenditure takes place when goods are purchased, while consumption may take place over several years. For example, the benefit derived from a car or television is enjoyed (consumed) over several years. In practice it is hard to measure consumption and the term is used loosely to mean expenditure. Thus consumer expenditure, personal expenditure and private consumption are all the same thing.

Significance

Spending by consumers accounts for between half and two-thirds of GDP. Arithmetically a 1% rise in consumer expenditure contributes to around a 0.6% increase in total GDP, all else being equal, which it rarely is of course. In particular some of the extra consumer spending will go into higher imports.

Spending decisions

Personal income is either spent or saved. Decisions about consumption are intertwined with decisions about savings (see next brief).

The best guesses at what determines spending and saving are the broadly similar permanent-income hypothesis and life-cycle hypothesis, which suggest that consumption is linked to income over a lifetime. Young and old households have a high propensity to spend their income, while those in mid-life save for retirement. In addition, households tend to run down savings or borrow to maintain consumption during a recession (spreading spending over their lifetimes).

Major influences on the level of consumption include the following.

- **Incomes.** In general higher personal incomes allow more spending.
- **Price expectations.** Experience shows that consumers tend to save more (and spend less) during periods of high inflation (see next brief). They may bring spending forward, however, if they expect a one-off increase in prices because of inflation or higher indirect (sales) taxes.
- **Interest rates.** Higher interest rates push up the cost of existing loans and discourage borrowing and, perhaps, encourage savings, all of which depress spending. Nevertheless, higher interest rates also redistribute income from young mortgage payers to their elders whose deposits are greater than their borrowings and who may spend their additional interest income.
- **Consumer credit.** Easier consumer credit may encourage borrowing, which translates directly into higher spending.
- **Wealth.** A rise in asset values, such as share or house prices, may make consumers feel wealthier and inclined to spend more.

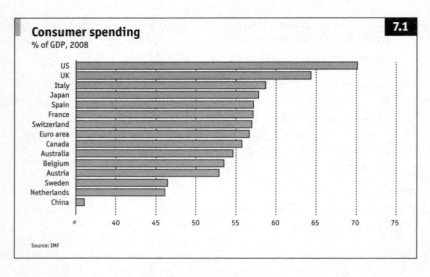

Consumer spending
% of GDP, 2008

7.1

Source: IMF

■ **Stock level and price of durables.** Consumers tend to regard
durables such as cars and electrical appliances as wealth. A sudden
end to a period of restricted supply of durables as in east Germany
in 1990, or a fall in their prices, may encourage a temporary
consumer boom. This may set up replacement cycles, with bouts
of spending on durables every few years.

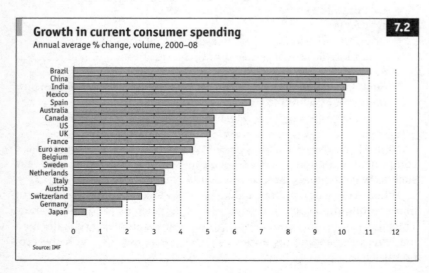

Growth in current consumer spending
Annual average % change, volume, 2000–08

7.2

Source: IMF

Table 7.2 **Consumer spending**

	% of GDP		Real annual average % change				
	2000	2008	1986–95	1996–2005	2006	2007	2008
Australia	59	55	2.7	3.9	3.2	4.4	2.6
Austria	57	53	2.6	1.7	1.9	0.9	0.6
Belgium	53	53	2.0	1.6	1.8	1.6	1.0
Canada	55	56	2.3	3.4	4.1	4.6	3.0
China	46	36	1.6	1.8	4.4	2.4	-0.2
Finland	56	51	1.3	3.4	4.2	3.3	1.5
France	59	57	1.9	2.5	2.6	2.4	1.0
India	64	55	3.0	1.0	1.4	-0.3	0.2
Ireland	49	50	3.3	6.3	6.4	5.6	-0.7
Italy	60	59	2.2	1.6	1.3	1.2	-0.9
Japan	56	58	3.3	1.0	1.5	0.7	0.6
Mexico	55	66	8.3	3.3	4.7	5.1	0.9
Netherlands	67	46	1.8	4.3	5.7	3.9	1.6
South Korea	50	54	2.1	2.6	-0.3	1.7	1.3
Spain	60	57	2.9	3.8	3.8	3.6	-0.6
Sweden	49	46	1.3	2.7	2.5	3.1	-0.4
Switzerland	60	57	1.5	1.6	1.6	2.4	1.7
UK	66	64	3.0	3.7	1.5	2.1	1.2
US	69	70	3.0	3.8	2.9	2.7	-0.2
Euro area	49	57	2.5	2.1	2.1	1.6	0.3

Sources: IMF; OECD

■ **Social factors.** These may encourage saving to allow bequests or retirement spending.

The cycle

There is a cyclical pattern in consumer expenditure. The most volatile component is spending on durables: goods with a life of over one year such as washing machines, furniture and cars.

When economic conditions are tight, spending on durables can be cut more readily than spending on non-durables such as food and heating. Thus there is a stable core of spending on non-durables, and a fluctuating level of spending on durables which moves in line with the economic cycle.

International comparisons

Total spending is affected by the level of services provided by the state. For example, in Belgium and France, where health care is initially paid for by the user, the outlays are included in consumer expenditure. Where health services are more or less free at the point of use, as in Britain and Nordic countries, no entry appears under consumer spending. In developing countries a greater proportion of spending is on essentials such as food.

Interpretation

The focus should be on real percentage change. Some countries, such as America, publish monthly figures in nominal terms, which may be deflated by consumer prices to obtain a feel for the real growth. For example, if nominal personal spending grows by 6% and consumer prices rise by 4%, spending has risen by about 2% in real terms. Changes in spending on durables can be an early signal of developments.

Retail sales (page 129), car sales (page 123) and consumer confidence (page 98) also provide leading indicators of spending patterns.

Personal and household savings; savings ratio

Measures:	Savings by households.
Significance:	Key component of total national savings.
Presented as:	Money totals and as a percentage of disposable income.
Focus on:	Trends.
Yardstick:	The OECD average savings ratio has been about 6.5% during the 2000s.
Released:	Quarterly or annually; frequently revised.

Overview

Personal savings, an important chunk of national savings (see page 109), are personal disposable income less personal consumption. Many governments also produce savings data for households alone. The household savings ratio is household savings as a percentage of household disposable income.

The household or personal sector's financial deficit or surplus (the net balance of deposits and loans) is different from savings. For this reason consumer borrowing – which influences spending and saving – can be considered separately (see page 92).

International comparisons

Household savings ratios are shown with national savings in Table 8.3.

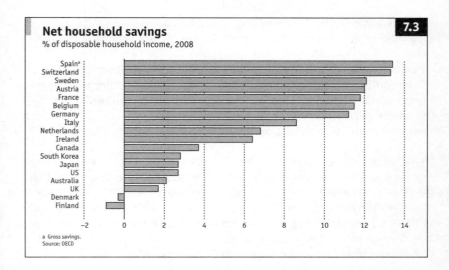

Net household savings   7.3
% of disposable household income, 2008

a Gross savings.
Source: OECD

Household savings ratios vary widely between countries. For example, in 2008 net household savings were 2.7% of household income in the United States and 11.8% in France (see Chart 7.3). There are a number of reasons for this.

As far as definitions are concerned, the calculations depend on the treatment of consumer durables, private pensions and life insurance payments, social security, household interest payments, capital transfers and depreciation. Adjusting for such factors can change savings ratios by several percentage points.

Other factors which account for differences in savings ratios include the age structure of the population and the labour force; the distribution of incomes; the availability of consumer credit; the tax treatment of savings; the social security system; and economic variables such as those discussed below.

Influences on household savings

The experience of the industrial countries in recent decades highlights some factors which affect savings. Note that savings appear to be relatively unaffected by changes in interest rates.

The 1970s. Economists were confounded by the rise in savings which accompanied the high inflation of the 1970s. Theory said that with falling real disposable incomes and negative real interest rates the savings ratio should have fallen. It seems that households save more during high inflation in order to maintain the real value of their savings.

The 1980s. Savings ratios fell in the 1980s for several reasons. There was lower inflation; stockmarkets were rising; in some countries higher house prices boosted personal wealth and so encouraged spending; financial liberalisation made borrowing easier; public pensions improved; and the population was ageing (older people save less).

The 1990s and 2000s. Perhaps the most striking feature of savings trends in the 1990s was the continuing fall in America's already low household savings rates, which was 1.4% in 2005. One reason may be that Americans felt wealthier because of the rise in the stockmarket. Or prolonged economic growth may have made them more optimistic about future earnings. However, since the credit crunch of 2007–08 most OECD countries have seen a significant increase in their savings ratios.

Interpretation
See National savings, page 109, for hints on interpretation. Note that the ageing population (see Population, page 63) is likely to reduce savings rates.

Consumer confidence

Measures:	Consumers' perception of their economic well-being.
Significance:	Determines short-term spending/borrowing/savings plans.
Presented as:	Usually index numbers.
Focus on:	Trends.
Yardstick:	Watch for changes in direction.
Released:	Monthly, one month in arrears.

Overview
Survey evidence of consumer perceptions is valuable as a leading indicator. In general, the more optimistic consumers are, the more likely they are to spend money. This boosts consumer spending and economic output.

Surveys of consumer confidence are conducted by private sector organisations such as the Conference Board in America and GfK in Britain and universities such as the University of Michigan. The results are presented in index form or as percentage balances (of consumers feeling more optimistic minus those feeling less optimistic).

Other indicators

Other popular indicators of consumer confidence include:

- **The misery index I:** The rate of consumer-price inflation plus the unemployment rate.
- **The misery index II:** The rate of consumer-price inflation plus annual interest rates.

In each case the higher the number, the more miserable consumers are assumed to be. However, once inflation falls below zero or close to it, the misery index becomes less meaningful. Falling prices can have damaging economic effects.

8 Investment and savings

Saving is a very fine thing. Especially when your parents have done it for you.

Sir Winston Churchill

Overview

Investment deserves special attention because it is so important for the future health of an economy. It lays the basis for future production.

Investment is spending on physical assets with a life of more than one year. This should be distinguished from financial transactions which are known as investment in everyday language but which are – from an economic viewpoint – savings.

It is conventional to say that businesses invest while individuals consume. If a household buys itself a personal computer, this is recorded in the national accounts as personal consumption. If a business buys the same model, the spending is classed as investment. The rationale is that the household uses a PC for "pleasure" while a business uses it in the production of future output. A company's stocks of raw materials and goods are classed as investment.

The circular flow of incomes

Chapter 4 (page 42) outlined the concept of the circular flow of incomes. Savings and investment are often considered to be the most important leakage and injection. It is easiest to understand their significance through an example.

Imagine a simple system in which firms produce $100m of goods a year. Suppose that households save $20m. Output is $100m, incomes are $100m and consumption is $80m. Since the firms sell only $80m of their output, the remainder is left in stock at the end of the year. The $20m increase in stocks is classed as investment spending. In order to meet their wage bills, the firms have to borrow $20m from the banks where the households saved their $20m. Output is $100m, incomes are $100m, and total spending is $80m consumption plus $20m investment which equals $100m.

The leakage of $20m for saving is matched by an injection of $20m for investment. Investment (in stocks or fixed assets) can take place only when some consumption is deferred. By definition, investment = savings.

Table 8.1 **Investment and savings**
% of GDP

	1995–99	2000–04	2005	2008
World				
Saving	22.4	21.5	22.9	24.2
Investment	22.5	21.7	22.6	24.0
Net lending	–0.1	–0.2	0.3	0.2
Industrial countries				
Saving	22.0	20.2	20.2	19.5
Investment	21.9	20.7	21.1	21.0
Net lending	0.1	–0.5	–0.9	–1.5
US				
Saving	17.8	17.8	15.1	12.6
Investment	19.6	19.5	20.3	18.2
Net lending	–1.8	–1.7	–5.2	–5.6
EU 27				
Saving	20.8	20.1	20.1	20.5
Investment	20.3	20.1	20.1	21.5
Net lending	0.5	0.0	0.0	–0.1
Euro area				
Saving	21.7	21.2	21.2	21.4
Investment	20.7	20.7	20.8	22.2
Net lending	1.0	0.5	0.5	–0.7
Japan				
Saving	29.6	29.6	27.2	26.6
Investment	27.3	23.8	23.6	23.5
Net lending	2.3	5.8	3.6	3.1

Source: IMF

Of course there is no automatic mechanism which ensures that the amount that households wish to save matches the amount that firms wish to invest. Investment and savings are each determined by different factors which are discussed in the following briefs.

Economic effects of imbalance. Loosely, if planned savings exceed planned investment, stocks pile up and companies cut back their production: GDP falls. If planned savings are less than planned investment, companies produce more to meet the extra demand and GDP rises. (See Cyclical indicators, page 55.)

The golden rule. It is difficult to identify the ideal level of saving and investment. Less saving means more consumption today but less investment and so less future consumption. Economists talk about the "golden rule" which maximises the consumption per head of all generations. Significantly, an IMF study suggested that America's national savings in the period 1986–1990 were only half the amount required by the golden rule.

National savings and investment. All sectors of the economy save and invest. Real life is not as simple as business investment and household savings. Table 8.1 shows flows of funds around the world. The following briefs discuss the topics in more detail.

Fixed investment and GDFCF

Measures: Spending on goods with a life of more than one year.
Significance: Contributes directly to GDP, lays basis for future output.
Presented as: Value, volume and index numbers.
Focus on: Volume trend.
Yardstick: OECD average fixed investment grew by 1.6% a year during the period 2000–08.
Released: Quarterly, 1–3 months in arrears; frequently revised.

Overview

Fixed investment is spending on physical assets. Total investment is fixed investment plus investment in stocks of raw materials and goods (see Stocks, page 107).

Physical assets include infrastructure such as roads and docks; buildings such as dwellings, factories and offices; plant and machinery; vehicles; and equipment such as computers. These generally provide the potential for higher output in the future. The economic (as opposed to

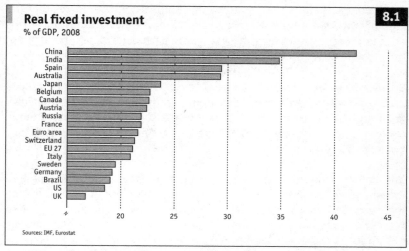

Real fixed investment
% of GDP, 2008

8.1

China
India
Spain
Australia
Japan
Belgium
Canada
Austria
Russia
France
Euro area
Switzerland
EU 27
Italy
Sweden
Germany
Brazil
US
UK

20   25   30   35   40   45

Sources: IMF, Eurostat

the social) benefit of dwellings and some infrastructure is more
arguable, but most infrastructure boosts economic efficiency. For example, new roads help to get delivery teams back for more work rather
than crawling at 10kph through the world's congested cities.

Investment and consumption. By convention, only businesses invest.
All personal spending is consumption for national accounts purposes,
except the purchase of new dwellings. These have such a long life that
they are classed as investment. Most government spending, including
that on defence equipment, is classified as consumption (see page 34).

GDFCF. Economists pompously call new investment in physical assets
"gross domestic fixed capital formation". Gross because it is before depreciation; domestic because it is at home rather than overseas; fixed because
it does not include stocks; and capital formation since it distinguishes
physical from financial investment.

Fixed investment is rarely shown net because of the problem of
accounting for capital retirements and obsolescence.

Interpretation

Fixed investment accounts for an average of around 20% of GDP in
industrial economies. So as a crude rule of thumb, a 1% rise in fixed
investment adds around 0.2% to GDP in the same period, all else being
constant.

Table 8.2 **Real fixed investment**

| | % of GDP, 2007[a] | | | | | Annual % change | |
| | — Construction — | | | | | | |
	Machinery & equipment	Non res'l	Residential	Other	Total	1995–2000	2000–07
Australia	–	–	–	–	28.3	3.8	8.9
Austria	8.4	6.9	4.8	1.8	21.8	2.9	0.9
Belgium	–	–	–	–	21.7	3.7	2.8
Canada	6.1	7.8	7.1	1.5	22.6	6.7	5.6
France	5.6	5.1	4.8	5.1	20.6	4.7	3.0
Germany	8.1	4.1	5.5	1.1	18.8	2.4	0.4
Italy	8.5	5.4	4.4	2.8	21.1	3.6	1.8
Japan	9.6	7.8	3.8	2.1	23.3	-0.6	-0.1
Netherlands	6.5	5.2	6.4	1.8	20.0	6.6	1.1
Spain	7.6	8.6	9.3	5.3	30.7	7.2	5.4
Sweden	7.9	4.7	3.3	3.0	19.0	5.5	4.2
Switzerland	–	–	–	–	21.5	2.5	1.8
UK	6.0	8.1	4.9	1.5	17.8	6.2	4.1
US	5.6	4.8	5.6	3.1	19.1	8.6	1.5
Euro area	–	–	–	–	21.8	4.3	2.3

a 2006 France, Italy, Japan and USA.
Source: OECD

The potential for future output will also be boosted (see Productivity, pages 52–54), especially by investment in plant and machinery. Table 8.2 shows that this is typically 6–8% of GDP.

The direct relationship between investment and output is complex. Investment is shown gross and the increase in productive capacity will be less after allowing for depreciation, and so on, but in developing countries at least, a given change in investment this year can be used as the basis for a moderately reliable forecast of the change in GDP next year.

The cycle. Investment is highly cyclical. Firms are more likely to invest if they are operating at a high level of capacity, if they expect demand to remain high and if interest rates are low. (See Business conditions and Capacity use, pages 115 and 118.) When these conditions are reversed, businesses are likely to cut back on fixed investment. However, invest-

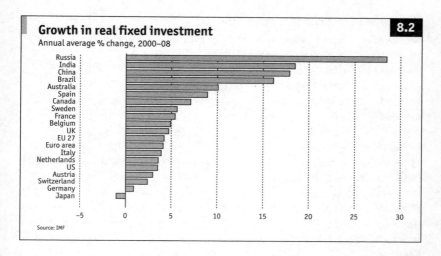

Growth in real fixed investment 8.2

Annual average % change, 2000–08

Source: IMF

ment projects have long lead times and a cut in new investment does not automatically imply a fall in total investment spending.

A 1% increase in demand may be translated into a greater than 1% increase in output if firms respond by increasing investment spending. (See "accelerator principle" in Cyclical indicators, page 55.)

Government intervention. Government incentives for investment should be treated with caution as they can be counter-productive in the long run. Tax subsidies make poor investment projects viable.

Changes in government investment spending should also be scrutinised. In more mature economies government expenditure can crowd out private-sector investment with detrimental effects, but in developing countries public and private investment are often complementary.

Other indicators. GDP investment figures are released with a lag. Other indicators should be used for advance signals, especially investment intentions, construction spending, housing starts, auto sales, manufacturing production and imports of capital goods.

Sectoral. Investment is classified by ownership rather than end-use. Sectoral investment figures should not be taken at face value. Investment by service companies may reflect spending on goods which are subsequently leased to industrial firms.

Investment intentions

Measures:	Plans for capital spending, sometimes just in manufacturing.
Significance:	Investment adds to current and future GDP.
Presented as:	Value, volume totals or changes.
Focus on:	Trend: planned volume increases.
Yardstick:	Look for planned increases of several percentage points.
Released:	Monthly, one month in arrears.

Overview

Governments and trade associations such as the US Institute for Supply Management and the Confederation of British Industry (CBI) publish the results of surveys of investment intentions. These may be wholly subjective ("Do you expect more or fewer capital authorisations over the next 12 months?") or misleadingly quantitative ("How many dollars' worth of capital spending will you undertake in the calendar year?"). See also Business conditions, page 115.

Value and volume

Where surveys are in value terms, the first step should be to consider how closely the figures relate to volumes. Respondents tend to indicate the value of investment after allowing for any expected price increases, so the totals should be deflated to arrive at the planned volume increase. As a crude deflator use producer prices. If these are rising by 5% and companies expect the value of their investment to increase by 7%, the volume of investment will be about 2% greater. If inflation is accelerating or decelerating, use the consensus view (at the time of the survey) of expected inflation for the period ahead.

Outcomes

Intentions are rarely turned into spending on a one-for-one basis. Investment intentions surveys tell you something about future trends in the economy, but at the same time you should interpret the survey results in the light of developments in the economy. For example, a rise in interest rates after a survey may lead to a lower than announced level of investment.

Stocks (inventories)

Measures: Stocks held by producers and distributors.
Significance: Indicator of demand pressures; potential sales.
Presented as: Value and volume totals and changes.
Focus on: Totals in relation to sales, changes.
Yardstick: See text.
Released: Quarterly, sometimes monthly, 1–3 months in arrears; frequently
                 revised.

Overview

Stocks or inventories are materials and fuel, work-in-progress and finished goods held by companies.

The book value of stocks changes for two reasons.

- **Stock appreciation** is an increase in the money value of stocks owing to inflation. It adds to nominal income (the inventories can be sold at a profit) but there is no addition to real output.
- **Stockbuilding** (or destocking) is a change in the physical volume of inventories. It reflects the production of goods and affects nominal and real output.

Data are generally collected in value terms and deflated into volume terms using assumptions about accounting practices, stockholding patterns and price changes. The breakdown between the physical change and stock appreciation can be unreliable, especially during periods of rapid inflation.

Cycles

In general the level of stocks rises as national income increases, but there are wide fluctuations which reflect the economic cycle.

Stocks are a buffer between production and consumption. When demand increases unexpectedly, the first sign is a decrease in inventories before manufacturers can respond by increasing output. Alternatively, if an increase in demand is expected, stocks may be built up in advance ready to meet the extra demand. Either way, production can increase faster than demand for short periods during restocking or stockbuilding.

Stocks accumulate when demand turns down unexpectedly; production might fall faster than sales as excess stocks are consumed.

Inflation. Stocks of raw materials react violently to expected changes in world commodity prices (see also page 205).

Interpretation

The stocks:sales ratios at each stage of activity (manufacturing, wholesaling, retailing) are important leading indicators.

If the ratios are higher than normal (look at a long run of figures), this implies that production and imports will be cut unless demand increases. If the ratios are lower than normal the implication is that production and imports will rise unless demand falls (but note that stock ratios fell sharply in the industrial countries during the 1980s because of better stock control techniques such as just-in-time). If the ratios are low and there are capacity constraints (high capacity utilisation and/or low unemployment), the excess demand might go into higher inflation or imports.

High or low stocks:sales ratios all the way through the economy give fairly clear signals. Different ratios at different stages imply bottlenecks or structural problems. For example, a low ratio in retailing and a high ratio in manufacturing may indicate that an increase in consumer demand has not yet fed through to manufacturers, or it might suggest that domestic producers cannot provide the required goods and the excess consumer demand is going into imports.

Surveys (see Business conditions, page 115) provide useful evidence about companies' perceptions of their stocks. If, say, manufacturers think that their stocks are too high, they will cut production over the next few months unless demand increases.

GDP

It is not the total level of stocks but the change in the rate of stockbuilding which affects the GDP expenditure measure. An increase in stocks reflects extra output that has not been consumed. Note, however, that a fall in the level of stocks can lead to an increase in GDP if the rate of destocking slows.

The effects of changes in stocks are limited when measured over several years, but stockbuilding is highly volatile quarter-by-quarter. Accordingly, changes in the rate of stockbuilding can be a major influence on demand and GDP. The snag is that stockbuilding is the trickiest component of GDP to forecast.

National savings, savings ratio

Measures:	Total savings in an economy.
Significance:	Major influence on investment and interest rates.
Presented as:	Totals; percentage of GDP.
Focus on:	Trends.
Yardstick:	The OECD average was around 20% during the 1990s and 2000s.
Released:	Quarterly with GDP figures. Total savings = investment.

Overview

Savings (deferred consumption) affect investment (the basis for future output and consumption). For the economy as a whole it is the national savings rate which is important: the sum of savings by the private sector and the government.

Gross savings are the savings required to finance gross investment. Net savings are those required to finance investment net of capital consumption. The national savings ratio is savings as a percentage of GDP.

Private savings

Private savings are the sum of savings by persons and companies. (See also Personal savings, page 96.) Company savings are cyclical since businesses hold liquid reserves to cushion themselves against the economic cycle and to provide funds for expansion.

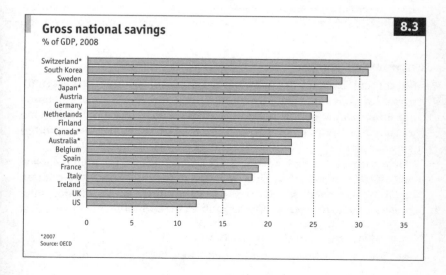

Gross national savings   8.3
% of GDP, 2008

*2007
Source: OECD

Table 8.3 **Savings ratios**

	Households[a]				National[c]			
	1995	2000	2005	2008	1995	2000	2005	2008
Australia	6.4	1.8	-0.8	2.1	18.7	19.7	21.6	22.5[d]
Austria	11.8	9.2	9.7	12.0	22.2	23.6	24.7	26.4
Belgium	16.4	12.3	10.0	11.5	25.4	26.0	23.7	22.4
Canada	9.2	4.7	2.1	3.7	18.3	23.6	23.8	23.7[d]
Finland	4.1	-1.7	0.3	-0.9	21.9	28.7	25.4	24.6
France	12.8	11.9	11.7	11.8	19.1	21.6	18.5	18.9
Germany	11.0	9.2	10.5	11.2	21.0	20.2	22.1	25.8
Ireland	–	–	5.6	6.4	20.4	23.9	23.6	16.9
Italy	17.0	8.4	9.9	8.6	22.0	20.6	19.5	18.2
Japan	12.6	8.6	3.9	2.7	29.3	27.5	26.8	27.0[d]
Netherlands	14.0	6.7	6.3	6.8	27.2	28.4	26.5	24.7
South Korea	16.0	9.3	7.2	2.8	35.5	32.9	32.0	30.9
Spain[b]	17.5	11.1	11.3	13.4	21.7	22.3	22.0	20.0
Sweden	9.5	4.8	6.8	12.1	20.9	22.8	23.4	28.0
Switzerland	12.7	11.7	10.1	13.3	29.6	34.7	36.0	31.2[d]
UK[b]	10.3	4.7	3.9	1.7	15.9	15.0	14.6	15.1
US	5.2	2.9	1.4	2.7	16.0	17.8	14.6	12.1

a Net household savings as % of disposable personal income.
b Gross household savings as % of disposable personal income.
c Gross national savings as % of GDP.
d 2007
Source: OECD

Government savings

Government savings are general government revenue less current expenditure. Government capital spending is classed as investment. Thus although the budget balance is often taken as a proxy for government savings, there can be a large difference between the two (amounting to, for example, 5.0% of GDP for Italy during the early 1990s).

Government savings or, frequently, dissavings reflect political decisions and are largely cyclical. Budget cuts in the industrial countries led to higher government savings or lower government dissavings as a percentage of GDP in several OECD countries in the 1990s.

National savings and the investment gap

A net inflow of foreign capital implies that domestic savings are less than domestic investment: foreigners' excess savings fill the gap. A net outflow of capital implies that domestic savings are bigger than domestic investment. Net foreign savings are conveniently defined as the balance on the current account of the balance of payments with the sign reversed (see Current-account balance, page 146).

Current-account deficits indicate the extent to which domestic investment is financed by foreign savings. For example, the American current-account deficit (averaging 5.5% of GDP in 2005–08) represented a net inflow of foreign savings of the same proportion.

Interpretation

Trends in domestic savings are an important indicator to watch. The comments in this chapter suggest that an increase in domestic savings rates would be no bad thing.

9 Industry and commerce

If economists were any good at business, they would be rich men instead of
advisers to rich men.

Kirk Kerkorian

Partly for historical reasons, there is an abundance of economic indicators relating to industry and commerce in general and
manufacturing in particular. These provide useful, timely signals of
activity, but it should be borne in mind that their coverage is relatively
narrow.

Interpretation

Industrial and commercial indicators provide a guide to both the output
and expenditure measures of GDP. These should be used in conjunction
with cyclical indicators (page 55) to assess overall economic activity.

Output. The main clues to output include manufacturing and industrial
production, car production and sales, construction spending, housing
starts, and wholesale and retail sales.

Table 9.1 shows the relative importance of the main sectors. Note that
services account for 66-77% of output in the major industrialised countries, according to the OECD, but they are relatively neglected among the
commonly followed indicators of output. Employment (page 66), consumer spending (page 92) and government consumption (page 34) also
provide clues to services.

It is value added that matters: the value of output less the cost of raw
materials and other inputs. This is what manufacturing and industrial
production figures measure, but the other indicators are before the
deduction of input costs.

Expenditure. The main indicators of industrial and commercial expenditure are fixed investment and investment in stocks (see Chapter 8).

Fixed investment figures are available only after a lag. This chapter
will show that business conditions, construction spending and housing
starts provide a useful advance guide; so do manufacturers' production
of capital goods and net imports of capital goods. Manufacturing,

Table 9.1 **Output by sector, 2007 or latest**

	% of GDP				Average annual % change, 2000–07 or latest		
	Agriculture	Industry	of which manufacturing	Services	Agriculture	Industry	Services
Australia	2	36	10	63	0.1	2.5	3.7
Austria	2	31	20	67	-0.4	3.2	2.2
Belgium	1	24	17	75	-0.5	1.7	2.3
Brazil	6	28	17	66	1.6	1.1	-0.5
Canada	2	32	16	66	0.4	2.2	3.0
China	11	49	34	40	-4.7	0.7	0.9
Finland	3	32	24	65	3.0	5.6	2.3
France	2	21	12	77	-0.7	1.6	2.2
Germany	1	30	23	70	-0.2	1.5	1.8
India	18	30	16	52	-3.9	2.0	0.7
Ireland	2	35	23	63	-2.3	6.3	6.5
Italy	2	27	18	71	-0.8	1.1	1.7
Japan	1	30	21	68	-0.2	1.5	1.5
Mexico	4	36	19	60	2.5	2.1	3.9
Netherlands	2	24	13	74	0.9	1.5	2.5
Russia	5	38	19	57	5.4	6.4	7.2
South Korea	3	37	27	60	1.3	6.6	4.4
Spain	3	30	16	67	0.2	2.8	4.0
Sweden	2	29	–	70	3.7	4.1	2.7
Switzerland	1	28	–	71	0.1	2.1	2.1
UK	1	23	14	76	0.3	0.5	3.4
US	1	22	14	77	2.8	1.1	3.3
Euro area	2	27	18	71	-0.5	2	2.4

Sources: OECD; World Bank

wholesale and retail inventories provide clues to changes in total stocks.

Investment figures should be used with consumer spending, government consumption and exports and imports to assess total GDP on an expenditure basis. This chapter's briefs on retail and vehicle sales provide clues to consumer spending and imports. Manufacturers' orders from abroad are indicative of export demand.

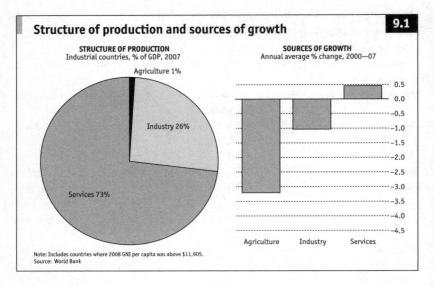

Structure of production and sources of growth `9.1`

STRUCTURE OF PRODUCTION
Industrial countries, % of GDP, 2007

Agriculture 1%

Industry 26%

Services 73%

SOURCES OF GROWTH
Annual average % change, 2000—07

Agriculture   Industry   Services

Note: Includes countries where 2008 GNI per capita was above $11,905.
Source: World Bank

Coverage

Many figures such as orders and productivity can be related to the whole economy, but for convenience are often produced for manufacturing alone. It is important to be clear about the coverage of any figures you use. Where they relate to manufacturing alone, consider whether other sectors of the economy might be moving differently.

Key indicators

The following briefs are arranged broadly from top to bottom: from the whole economy through to individual sectors, and from manufacturing through wholesaling to retailing.

Business conditions; indices and surveys

Measures: Anecdotal evidence of business climate.
Significance: Valuable early warning of changes in economic cycle.
Presented as: Index number or percentage balance of companies optimistic or pessimistic.
Focus on: Trends.
Yardstick: Watch for indicators of rising or falling confidence. The US ISM index has a breakpoint of 50 (see text).
Released: Monthly or quarterly, one month in arrears; rarely revised.

Overview

Surveys provide valuable evidence of perceptions and expectations relating to business conditions, usually in manufacturing. Responses are subjective but they give early signals of changes in economic trends. (See briefs on Orders, Inventories, Prices, Retail sales, and so on, for comments on individual parts of the surveys.)

Private-sector bodies conduct surveys in some countries (for example, confederations of industry in Australia, Britain, Finland; IFO in Germany), but some government agencies do the work (for example, Statistics Canada, the Bank of Japan). Many surveys are quarterly, although where they are monthly some questions are asked only 3–4 times a year (for example, capacity use in France and Germany).

America

The US Institute for Supply Management (previously National Association of Purchasing Managers) publishes monthly indices covering factors such as the state of order books, inventories, production and prices, and a composite index of industrial conditions (the PMI).

A composite index reading above 50 indicates an expanding manufacturing sector, a figure below that indicates a contracting manufacturing sector. A reading below 44 is taken as a sign of a declining economy overall.

Also useful are the US Federal Reserve's report on regional trends (known as the Tan or Beige Book) and the Conference Board's surveys of business conditions.

The UK

The Confederation of British Industry (CBI) conducts several surveys. About 450 manufacturers take part in its monthly surveys, providing a guide to their expectations, mostly for the three months ahead. Its monthly distributive trades surveys, covering 20,000 outlets of firms

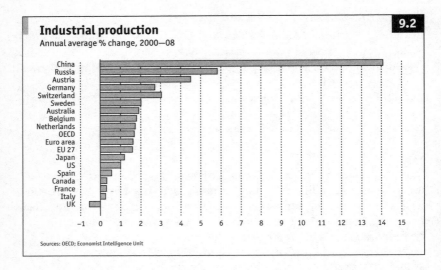

9.2

Industrial production
Annual average % change, 2000—08

Sources: OECD; Economist Intelligence Unit

responsible for 40% of employment in retailing, provide information about current and expected conditions in retailing and wholesaling outlets.

The CBI surveys are presented in the percentage balance of companies' reporting orders, exports, etc up minus those reporting them down. The OECD uses a similar style. Interpretation is not as clear-cut as with

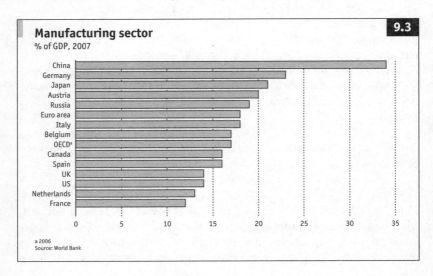

9.3

Manufacturing sector
% of GDP, 2007

a 2006
Source: World Bank

the American surveys, but trends provide a good indication of perceived conditions. The CBI confidence measure is reckoned to provide a guide to corporate earnings nine months in advance.

British economists also watch the monthly indices published by the Chartered Institute of Purchasing and Supply (CIPS) and Markit Economics. They produce separate surveys of manufacturing, service and construction companies. As with the PMI in America, a CIPS index above 50 indicates expanding output; below 50 implies contraction.

Japan

The Tankan survey of business sentiment, issued quarterly by the Bank of Japan, covers about 9,000 firms. It is regarded as an influential guide to the health of the Japanese economy and of business confidence.

Industrial and manufacturing production

Measures:	Value-added output of mines, manufacturing companies, utilities and, in some cases, construction.
Significance:	Indicator of industrial activity.
Presented as:	Index numbers in volume terms.
Focus on:	Trends in volume terms.
Yardstick:	OECD average industrial production grew by 1.7% a year during 2000–08. Manufacturing production in the euro area grew by 0.6% during the same period.
Released:	Monthly, at least one month in arrears; revised.

Coverage

There are two main series, which are usually released together.

- **Manufacturing production.** This is the value-added output of manufacturing companies.
- **Industrial production.** This is manufacturing production plus the supply of energy and water, and the output of mines, oil wells and quarries, and, sometimes, construction. It generally excludes agriculture, trade, transport, finance and all other services.

National coverage varies widely eg, Germany covers construction, Eurostat data excludes it. Russia includes estimates of hidden production by registered enterprises and the production of entrepreneurs operating without a corporate legal entity (obtained from tax records).

In total, for industry the index in Japan covers about 60%, Spain around 70%, Germany and Italy 80%, and the Netherlands, Sweden and Britain up to 100%. France conducts a monthly survey covering 65% and a fuller quarterly survey covering 85% of industry. Australia and Switzerland have quarterly indices only.

The importance of manufacturing and industry

Manufacturing. Broadly speaking, in advanced economies, manufacturing ranges from about 12% of GDP in France to 23% in Germany and 34% in China (see Table 9.1). Manufacturing is tiny in some African states, but it rises to 30–35% of GDP in emerging markets such as Malaysia and Thailand. Chart 9.3 shows the importance of manufacturing across 13 countries, the euro area and OECD.

Industry. The difference between manufacturing and industrial production accounts for about 10% of GDP on average. This takes total industrial production to about 22% of American GDP and about 30% of Japan's (see Table 9.1).

The gap is more significant where the energy-producing sector is large; OPEC members' industrial production often exceeds half of GDP.

Interpretation

Industrial production as a whole is broadly indicative of the state of the economic cycle. The output of industries producing capital goods and consumer durables tends to be squeezed most during a downturn. Some countries produce separate figures for various sectors (see Motor vehicles, page 123). Steel production is a useful lead indicator since it is an input to many other industries.

Capacity use and utilisation

Measures:	Extent to which plant and machinery is in use.
Significance:	Indicator of output and inflationary pressures.
Presented as:	Percentage of total capacity.
Focus on:	Absolute level and trends.
Yardstick:	80–90%; more may be inflationary, less indicates room for growth.
Released:	Monthly, 1–3 months in arrears; revised.

Overview

Total capacity. Capacity is a vague, hard-to-measure concept which varies over time and according to economic conditions. The term is generally used to refer to the sustainable maximum output that could be produced by existing (installed) manufacturing plant and machinery, although sometimes other factors such as labour are taken into account. Either way "normal capacity" will vary if working practices are changed, even if only by increasing the working week by one hour. (See Productivity, page 53.)

Capacity use. Capacity use is usually defined as output divided by sustainable maximum capacity. Sustainable maximum output is lower than temporarily attainable peak production, so use of (sustainable) capacity can and occasionally does exceed 100% in some industries.

Overall capacity use does not go as high as 100% because different companies reach their peaks at different stages of the economic cycle. Also bottlenecks in one industry restrict supplies and therefore output in another: in major cyclical peaks, a shortage of metals can limit output of consumer durables and business machinery, and restrain capacity utilisation in those industries.

Capital investment. Figures for capital investment are sometimes taken as indicators of changes in capacity, but investment is usually measured gross, with no allowance for scrapping. Even where allowance is made, the net capital stock may not be representative of output potential. Moreover, the increase in capacity derived from a unit of new capital is affected by factors such as new technology, an increasingly shorter life for capital equipment, a longer work week for capital, restructuring of industry and the closure of plants.

Interpretation
Strong economic growth with high capacity use usually suggests inflationary pressures. However, if demand is expected to remain buoyant and if interest rates are low, producers may invest in new plant and machinery.

If the economy is expanding, but there is low capacity use and no evidence of recent new investment, it may be that the economy is recovering from recession.

American capacity utilisation
The US Federal Reserve is one of the few national official bodies to produce estimates of capacity use and its figures are undoubtedly the most detailed and consistent available, but not even the Fed conducts surveys of capacity or capacity utilisation. Instead it uses data from the Census

Bureau and various trade organisations to estimate capacity in various industries. Overall capacity utilisation is industrial production divided by the capacity index.

The Fed defines capacity as the realistically sustainable maximum capacity, rather than unsustainable short-term peak capacity.

American capacity use exceeded 90% during the Korean and Vietnam wars, but it has been below 90% since 1967; in 2009 it dipped below 70%. A figure of 88% overall would indicate severe strains (but 88% would be normal in certain individual industries which operate a high level of capacity use, such as paper and pulp).

Surveys

In most other countries measures of capacity use are derived from survey evidence (see Business conditions, page 115).

Defining terms such as "capacity", "satisfactory" or "normal" is left to respondents. Accordingly, survey results are better for examining short-term rather than long-term changes in capacity use.

Manufacturing orders

Measures: New orders received by manufacturing companies.
Significance: Indicator of output in the near term.
Presented as: Money, index or percentage balance form.
Focus on: Trends.
Yardstick: Total orders can change by 10–20%. Generally the higher the better, but watch for bottlenecks and inflation.
Released: Monthly, 1–2 months in arrears; revised.

Overview

- **The US Census Bureau** publishes new orders received by manufacturing companies and their unfilled orders in current dollars, with an advance report on orders for durable and a more detailed report including non-durable goods about a week later.
- **The German Federal Statistical Office** publishes volume index numbers for manufacturing orders, distinguishing between domestic and foreign orders.
- **The Confederation of British Industry** publishes survey results indicating the percentage of respondent companies which think that order books are above normal less the percentage of companies reporting below normal order books. This subjective assessment is broken down into domestic and export orders.

Manufacturing orders ripple through the economy. An order for a washing machine may prompt an order for a metal pressing which in turn will provoke an order for sheet steel. Each order will reflect the output price, while manufacturing output and GDP will rise by the value-added component only. Orders are therefore much more volatile than manufacturing production.

Total orders

Buoyant order books indicate upward pressure on employment and output over the next few months. This is basically good, but it may suggest: a rise in inflation if unemployment is low; capacity use is high; there is an order backlog (orders are high in relation to shipments or sales); and/or inventories are low. Strong orders will also tend to increase imports of materials and intermediate goods, but this may be offset by exports (see below).

Orders provide an early signal of changes in the economic cycle. A rise in orders may indicate the end of a recession; a fall may indicate that the cycle is peaking.

Where orders are presented in value terms they should be adjusted for inflation. Producer prices can be used. If orders rise by 6% in value and producer prices increase by 4%, the volume of orders is about 2% higher. It is important to ascertain that this adjustment does not reflect, say, a movement in refined oil prices, which are erratic and can falsely suggest changes in the volume of new orders. There may also be other blips. In the American series the transport component jumps by perhaps a third in a month when new aircraft are ordered. Try to use a series which excludes misleading influences.

Domestic orders

Domestic orders by sector are indicative of the structure of home demand. Bigger orders for capital goods suggest more investment activity and more output in the future. Machine tool orders sometimes receive special attention: an increase is encouraging because they are used to manufacture yet more machines which in turn make more goods.

Defence orders tend to reflect political decision-making. If they are identified separately, as they are in America, subtract them from capital or durable orders to get a better feel for underlying demand.

Orders for durable and capital goods react to changes in the economic cycle ahead of other orders. Orders for consumer goods are obviously indicative of trends in the consumer sector.

Manufacturing activity

Surveys of purchasing managers indicate that manufacturing industries in most of the world's big economies are growing. In big emerging
economies such as Brazil, China and India, the indices compiled by
Markit, a provider of financial information, were well above 50 in
January, indicating robust growth. In each of those countries manufacturing was still shrinking in January 2009. There has also been a
pronounced turnaround in America, where the Institute for Supply
Management's index for January was 58.4, in contrast to 35.5 in
January 2009. Manufacturing is also expanding in Germany, France
and Britain. But it is still shrinking in Greece and Spain, though much
less markedly than a year earlier.

Manufacturing activity

Purchasing Managers' Index*, January:

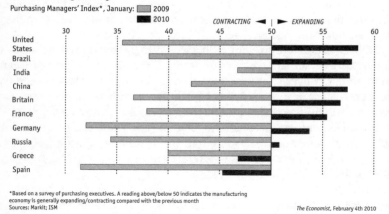

*Based on a survey of purchasing executives. A reading above/below 50 indicates the manufacturing
economy is generally expanding/contracting compared with the previous month
Sources: Markit; ISM

The Economist, February 4th 2010

Export orders

Orders from overseas reflect export competitiveness (see page 168) and
the economic cycle in overseas markets. A rise is good, but see comments above about inflation. If orders are booked despite a stronger currency, profits may be squeezed and repeat business may not be
sustained.

Motor vehicles

Measures: Activity involving cars and trucks.
Significance: Indicator of manufacturing production as well as consumer demand.
Presented as: Number of units.
Focus on: Trends.
Yardstick: Volatile, but a 12-month change of more than a few percentage points is worrying.
Released: Monthly; more frequently in the United States.

Overview

There are three main series relating to motor vehicles:

- manufacturers' production;
- sales; and
- registrations of new vehicles with national licensing authorities.

Registrations and sales are broadly similar; the difference mainly reflects the method of data collection.

The figures usually relate to the number of units, that is, volume rather than value. They may not reveal very much about the pattern of demand for cheap or expensive vehicles or about changes in quality. However, they are a useful indicator of manufacturing production; demand for a durable good which is vulnerable to the economic cycle; competitive pressures, especially between domestic and overseas producers; and import and export trends.

Interpretation

Vehicle sales are a reasonable leading indicator of economic activity. A vehicle purchased by an individual is classed as consumption expenditure. The same vehicle purchased by a business is investment spending. Generally, then, figures for cars are suggestive of consumption; light vans and trucks are indicative of investment.

Production and sales may not tally due to changes in stocks (see Wholesale sales and stocks and Retail sales and stocks, pages 128 and 129) and net exports.

Seasonality. There is a marked seasonal pattern in car sales, with turnover bunched into January and, if different, the start of a new model year or registration-plate year identifier. Discounting price wars can also shift demand into a different month from normal. Short-term figures

Table 9.2 **Motor vehicle markets, 2007**

	Stock of cars (per '000 persons)	New registrations ('000)	Production ('000)
Australia	545	–	–
Austria	512	42	200
Belgium	471	82	790
Brazil	108	1,707	2,388
Canada	561	858	1,342
China	22	6,225	6,381
Finland	474	22	24
France	509	520	2,551
Germany	569	334	5,709
India	13	1,606	1,708
Ireland	430	46	–
Italy	604	281	911
Japan	542	4,579	9,945
Mexico	152	762	1,209
Netherlands	442	97	62
Russia	191	374	1,289
South Korea	525	1,037	3,724
Spain	487	325	2,196
Sweden	467	54	317
Switzerland	528	31	–
UK	516	396	1,535
US	453	7,835	3,924
Euro area	518	2,295	13,324
EU 27	478	2,987	17,321

Source: Euromonitor

should be interpreted with care. Take 2–3 months together and compare with similar periods of earlier years.

Construction orders and output

Measures: Activity in the construction sector.
Significance: Indicator of new investment and future output.
Presented as: Value of orders, volume of construction.
Focus on: Trends in volume terms.
Yardstick: In OECD countries, the growth rate of real capital formation in non-residential construction averaged 2.8% a year between 2000 and 2008.
Released: Monthly, at least one month in arrears.

Overview

There are several main series, including the following.

- Orders (volume in Britain; value in Japan and America).
- Permits issued (number in Belgium and France; value in Australia, Germany, the Netherlands).
- The value of work put in place (Germany, America).
- Value added in money and real terms (with GDP figures for expenditure on investment for many countries).

Construction normally covers buildings and infrastructure (such as roads and ports). Orders are sometimes based on contracting work. This may include projects such as oil rigs which really belong in manufacturing production under steel fabrication. The figures may exclude residential dwellings, so this should be checked.

Significance

Construction work is fixed investment. This boosts current-period GDP and lays the basis for future economic growth. Its share of GDP in different countries is shown in Table 8.2.

New factories and offices provide a direct foundation for higher economic output. New infrastructure improves social welfare and generally boosts productivity. The only real exception to the "future output" rule is investment in new dwellings, but this still brings benefits (see Housing, page 127).

Interpretation

Seasons and cycles. Construction work is highly seasonal and cyclical. Data are frequently (but not always) seasonally adjusted, but it is wise to take 2–3 months together and compare them with the same periods in earlier years. It is important to look out for the adverse effects of a wet or freezing month.

Construction activity is sensitive to expectations of future demand, to interest rates and to the availability of finance. Low interest rates increase the return from investment and encourage capital spending, especially when they are coupled with strong demand and high usage of existing capacity. (See also Investment, page 100.)

Orders. Construction orders signal demand for building materials and labour over the coming months (and years – depending on the size of the individual projects). Knock-on effects include implications for service industries such as architects and surveyors, manufacturers of industrial plant to go into new factories, and providers of office fittings and furnishings.

Orders are often given on a value basis. These should be adjusted for inflation to arrive at the volume change. For example, if the value of orders rises by 10% and inflation is 8%, real growth is about 2%. Producer prices might be used for deflation if there is no obviously better indicator to hand. Figures sometimes cover construction permits; these provide no guide to the size of the projects, and they might not be translated into construction activity if economic conditions change.

Output. Construction output in volume terms helps you to judge the effect on total output. Construction accounts for about 5% of GDP, so a 10% rise in construction value-added contributes around 0.5% to GDP.

A large construction project spread over several months or years adds a little bit to output in each of several periods. (See above for knock-on effects.)

Housing starts, completions and sales

Measures: Number of new houses begun and finished; sales of new and existing homes.

Significance: Indicator of construction activity; industrial and consumer demand.

Presented as: Number of units per month.

Focus on: Trends.

Yardstick: Volatile; number of starts can change by 30% a year. In OECD countries, the growth rate of gross capital formation in residential construction averaged −0.1% a year between 2000 and 2008.

Released: Monthly, at least one month in arrears.

Overview

There are three main series indicating:

- the number of residential dwellings started;
- the number of residential dwellings completed; and
- the number of residential dwellings sold.

Each series applies to a given period, usually one month. They are often seasonally adjusted, but it is wise to take 2–3 months together and compare with the same periods in earlier years since house building is highly sensitive to the weather.

Figures usually distinguish between public and private dwellings. Activity in the private sector is a good guide to underlying activity, but there are also knock-on effects from public-sector building.

Starts

A housing start is counted on the date that foundations are begun (not when the site is cleared). It implies a given level of demand for construction materials and labour over the next few months and a housing completion at the end of that period.

If the existing housing stock is old, there may be an element of replacement building. Generally, however, housing starts (and completions) are closely linked to population growth rates, earnings and employment, and interest rates.

Completions

A housing completion implies a house sale, a new mortgage advance and increased consumer demand for carpets, furnishings and other durables – possibly accompanied by extra consumer credit.

Sales

Housing sales are linked to the level of completions, but turnover of existing homes is more important. House prices are highly relevant. People are more inclined to move home and buy rather than rent when house prices are rising and are expected to provide capital gains. Housing turnover is also stimulated by incomes rising relative to house prices and by lower mortgage rates which encourage borrowing.

Effect on GDP

The construction of new houses is classed as fixed investment in residential dwellings. This accounts for only a few percentage points of GDP (see Table 8.2), so arithmetically a 10% rise in house building may add less than 0.5% to total output.

The sale of existing houses is a transfer of production scored in earlier periods and does not itself add to output, but real estate, legal and financial fees and commissions do, as does demand for new furnishing and other durables.

Wholesale sales or turnover, orders and stocks

Measures: Most common indicator measures sales by wholesalers.
Significance: Indicator of demand.
Presented as: Monthly index numbers.
Focus on: Rates of change in volume of sales.
Yardstick: More volatile than retail sales; look for gains of 3–4% a year.
Released: Monthly, 1–2 months in arrears; revised.

Overview

Wholesale sales (called wholesale turnover in Germany) are an important link in the supply chain. Wholesalers channel imports and domestically produced or processed goods through to final users. Where stocks and orders are available, these provide a useful check on trends. A fall in wholesale sales or a rise in wholesale inventories suggests or confirms slack in business and retail demand.

There are relatively few figures on the services sector, but wholesale sales provide extremely loose indicators of demand from, for example, hotels and catering establishments. They are also indicative of demand for business goods including, in some countries, building materials. Wholesale sales are a reasonable signal of consumer demand (but retail sales are better – see below).

Value and volume

It is important to watch the volume of sales, particularly for durable goods (an early indicator of demand pressures). Where figures are in value terms they can be converted to volume using wholesale or producer prices. For example, if producer prices increase by 3% and sales value rises by 5%, volume is up by about 2%.

Effect on GDP

Wholesale sales are included in the distributive trades sector of GDP. Their direct contribution is wholesalers' value added (income from sales less the cost of purchases and other inputs).

Retail sales or turnover, orders and stocks

Measures:	Most commonly sales by retailers.
Significance:	Indicator of consumer demand.
Presented as:	Monthly index numbers.
Focus on:	Rates of change in volume of sales.
Yardstick:	3% a year is reasonable; any lower and the economy might slow down. More than 4–5% suggests overheating.
Released:	Monthly, at least one month in arrears.

Coverage

Retail sales figures provide an important and timely indicator of spending at retail outlets. Most series include VAT or sales taxes and many are in volume terms (that is, after adjustment for inflation) as well as value terms. Retail e-commerce, or business-to-consumer (B2C), estimates are published by some official statistics offices eg, Britain's National Statistics started to issue monthly retail internet sales at the beginning of 2009.

The International Council of Shopping Centers-Goldman Sachs index tracks weekly US retail chain store sales; the John Lewis Partnership in Britain publishes weekly data for its stores.

Basis. Information is presented by type of business, rather than by commodity. For example, food sales appear under at least two subheadings: food retailers and mixed businesses. Where an establishment sells items outside its main classification, such as sales of food by a petrol filling station, these are usually excluded from the statistics. Credit sales are treated as a sale, valued at the date of the transaction at the total credit price including charges levied by the retailer.

Interpretation

Retail sales cover up to half of total consumer spending although there is not a direct correlation between the two since some items sold by retailers are bought by businesses. Nevertheless, retail sales are a key indicator of consumer confidence and demand.

It is important to focus on volume increases. Where figures are in value terms they can be converted to volume using consumer prices. Arithmetically, a 1% rise in retail sales adds roughly 0.3% to GDP, all else being constant.

Seasonality. Retail sales data are usually seasonally adjusted, but they should be interpreted with care. Promotional sales price discounting, warm weather or an expectation of increases in sales taxes can encourage consumers to bring forward their spending. An upward blip may not be sustained.

Cyclical variations. In times of financial stress consumers cut back on non-essential spending, which results in a decline or less rapid growth in retail sales. Spending on durables (items with a life of over one year, such as washing machines) goes first. For example, in Britain during the 1991–92 recession, the volume of food sales rose by 3% while new car registrations fell by 20%.

Although retail sales are very nearly coincident with GDP, retail sales figures are published with a much shorter lag. They therefore provide an early indication of economic trends.

A downturn in retail sales could lead to lower wholesale sales, slacker factory orders, an accumulation of stocks and, eventually, a cut in production.

Stocks and orders. Where figures for retail stocks and orders are also available they provide useful advance warning. For example, excess retail demand might show up first in a fall in the ratio of retailers' inventories to sales. This spells trouble if wholesalers' and manufacturers' stocks are also low and there are constraints on manufacturers' ability to increase output (high capacity use and low unemployment). Look out for price inflation and a surge in imports.

10 The balance of payments

No nation was ever ruined by trade.

Benjamin Franklin

The balance of payments is a continual source of misunderstanding and misconception. Yet it is no more than a simple accounting record of international flows. Moreover, trade between two countries is exactly the same as trade between two individuals. Once seen in this light, interpreting external flows is no different from interpreting any other economic transactions.

Accounting conventions

Balance of payments accounts record financial flows in a specific period such as one year. Financial inflows (such as receipts for exports or when a foreigner invests in the stockmarket) are treated as credits or positive entries. Outflows (such as payments for imports or the purchase of shares on a foreign stockmarket) are debits or negative entries. When a foreigner invests in (acquires a claim on) the country, there is a capital inflow which is a credit entry. Conversely, the acquisition of a claim on another country is a negative or debit entry.

Debits = credits. The accounts are double entry, that is, every transaction is entered twice. For example, the export of goods involves the receipt of cash (the credit) which represents a claim on another country (the debit). By definition the balance of payments must balance. Debits must equal credits.

Current = capital. One side of each transaction is treated as a current flow (such as a receipt of payment for an export). The other is a capital flow (such as the acquisition of a claim on another country). Arithmetically current flows must exactly equal capital flows.

Balances

The accounts build up in layers. Balances may be struck at each stage. What follows reflects the IMF's methodology in the fifth edition of the

Balance of Payments Manual. By the late 1990s most countries had moved to the new international standards.

Net exports of goods (exports of goods less imports of goods)
= the visible trade or merchandise trade balance
+ net exports of services (such as shipping and insurance)
= the balance of trade in goods and services
+ net income (compensation of employees and investment income)
+ net current transfers (such as payments of international aid and workers' remittances)
= the current-account balance (all the following entries form the capital and financial account)
+ net direct investment (such as building a factory overseas)
+ other net investment (such as portfolio investments in foreign equity markets)
+ net financial derivatives
+ other investment (including trade credit, loans, currency and deposits)
+ reserve assets (changes in official reserves), sometimes known as the **bottom line**
= overall balance
+ net errors and omissions
= zero

Thus the current account covers trade in goods and services, income and transfers. Non-merchandise items are known as invisibles. All other flows are recorded in the capital and financial account. The capital part of the account includes capital transfers, such as debt forgiveness, and the acquisition and/or disposal of non-produced, non-financial assets such as patents. The financial part includes direct, portfolio and other investment.

Balancing items

In practice it is impossible to identify all flows: invisibles are hard to track, some speculative flows go unmeasured and some transactions are concealed by tax evasion or organised crime. Even visible trade is sometimes overlooked. In the late 1980s British customs officials stumbled upon £1.5 billion of aircraft imports which had previously gone unnoticed. In addition, the balance of payments accounts relate to specific periods such as calendar years. Lags mean that one-half of a transaction may not be recorded in the same period as the other half.

To cover timing differences and unidentified items, government statisticians make the accounts balance with a residual or balancing item or statistical discrepancy shown as net errors and omissions.

Interpretation. Every country has discrepancies and Britain's have been among the worst. In 2008 the accounts showed a current-account deficit of £25.1 billion with a capital and financial-account surplus of £21.5 billion, leaving a £3.6 billion figure for net errors and omissions.

Aggregating international current-account figures show that world credits in 2007 exceeded world debits by over $300 billion, a very large amount but only 1.4% of total credits. The implication is that many countries have small current-account deficits rather than surpluses.

Deficits and surpluses

The balance of payments must balance. When commentators talk about a balance of payments deficit or surplus, they mean a deficit or surplus on one part of the accounts.

Attention is usually focused on the current-account balance, but capital flows have become increasingly important as many industrial countries relaxed exchange controls and other barriers to world capital flows during the 1980s. The stock of foreign direct investment (FDI) more than tripled between 1999 and 2008. FDI is long-term investment in companies in a foreign country, implying a certain degree of control of those companies.

The balance to watch. The bottom line gives an indication of imbalances in the economy. Acute imbalances will trigger changes in the exchange rate. Large negative errors and omissions can be indicative of capital flight or unrecorded outflows to avoid exchange controls. Large positive discrepancies could be proceeds from illegal activities. Adjustments are made to Britain's import figures to allow for VAT Missing Trader Inter-Community fraud. Carousel fraud relates to goods being imported VAT-free from an EU member state, sold through a series of companies and then re-exported to another EU member state.

Balance of payments accounting quirks

Balance of payments figures must be interpreted with care. As a brief illustration, consider a company which borrows $500 in foreign currency from a domestic bank (which itself borrows the cash from overseas) and invests the money in an overseas operation which earns profits of $1,750, only $750 of which are repatriated.

If the balance of payments accounts are drawn up in accordance with IMF recommendations and if all transactions are identified, the entries will be as follows.

	$
Current account	
Income: profits earned abroad	1,750
Financial account	
Private investment overseas	−1,500
of which:	
Financed by borrowing	−500
Unremitted profits	−1,000
Banks' overseas borrowing	+500
Change in reserves (− = additions)	−750

At first glance the accounts suggest that there was an investment outflow of $1,500. Yet the net currency movement is the inflow of $750 profits.

Analysis of balance of payments accounts requires careful review of all entries and a good measure of imagination. Do not be misled by changes in reserves, where negative entries indicate an increase in official holdings of foreign currencies.

Published figures

National accounting practices vary, but in general governments produce two sets of figures relating to external flows.

- ◪ Overseas trade statistics (OTS), which measure imports and exports of goods.
- ◪ Balance of payments (BOP) accounts, which record all cross-border currency flows including movements of capital, with emphasis on transactions rather than physical movement.

Apart from the fact that BOP accounts have a wider coverage, the main difference between the two is that BOP accounts exclude goods passing across borders where there is no change of ownership, but include changes of ownership which take place abroad (such as ships built and delivered abroad).

In addition, overseas trade statistics usually record the value of trade at the point of customs clearance, measuring exports FOB (free on board) and imports CIF (including cost, insurance and freight). For BOP purposes insurance and freight are separated out and imports of goods are shown FOB. Transport and insurance are shown as imports of services if the payments are made to overseas companies; otherwise they are domestic transactions which are excluded from the accounts.

Using OTS figures. Figures on an OTS basis are usually the first available and they are preferable for examining the effect of imports on domestic economic activity. They sometimes show imports CIF which is the cost at the point of arrival and is directly comparable with the cost of goods produced at home, but most OTS figures for developed countries are now shown FOB/FOB.

Using BOP figures. BOP figures should be used for analysis of external trade in relation to GDP, usually as a percentage. Exports and imports of goods and services on a BOP basis match the figures in GDP. The total income plus net current transfers is shown as "net income from abroad" in national accounts statistics (the difference between GDP and GNP). The BOP position can be vulnerable if the current account is being financed by portfolio investment, financial derivatives and external borrowings rather than by long-term funds for direct investment, as an abrupt withdrawal of funds is easier.

Other figures. The briefs in this section should be read in conjunction with the exchange-rate briefs (Chapter 11).

Export and import unit values (prices) are included with other price indicators in Chapter 13.

Exports of goods and services

Measures: Sales in other countries.
Significance: Exports generate foreign currency and economic growth.
Presented as: Value and volume figures in money and index numbers.
Focus on: Growth; total in relation to imports (see trade balance) and as a percentage of GDP.
Yardstick: OECD average growth in the volume of exports of goods and services was 4.5% during the period 2000–08.
Released: Monthly, at least one month in arrears.

Overview
Exports generate foreign currency earnings. Export growth boosts GDP

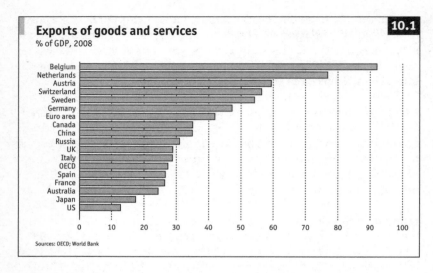

Exports of goods and services 10.1
% of GDP, 2008

Sources: OECD; World Bank

which in turn implies more imports, so exports should never be considered in isolation.

Goods and services. Merchandise or visible exports relate to physical goods. Exports of services are payments from foreigners for invisibles such as shipping, travel and tourism; financial services including insurance, banking, commodity trading and brokerage; and other items such as advertising, education, health, commissions and royalties.

In practice, many countries give prominence to visible trade figures because they are among the most reliable and rapidly available figures on external flows. Even so, they are available only after a lag, are frequently revised as more information comes to hand and are subject to various errors and omissions. Figures for invisibles are harder to collect, less reliable and are published only quarterly by some countries.

Value and volume. Demand for exports depends on economic conditions in foreign countries, prices (relative inflation and the exchange rate) and perceptions of quality, reliability, and so on. Real exchange rates (see page 168) help to identify inflation and currency effects. Export volume indicates "real changes", and value gives the overall balance of payments position.

Export composition and destinations. Dependence on a few commodities increases vulnerability to shifts in demand, while dependence

Table 10.1 **Exports of goods and services**

	% of GDP	Annual average % change				
	2008	1990–94	1995–99	2000–04	2005–08	2008
Australia	24.3	3.8	8.5	7.1	2.2	3.6
Austria	59.4	0.8	3.2	7.6	6.9	6.2
Belgium	92.1	2.2	3.8	5.0	3.9	3.1
Brazil	14.3	-0.6	6.5	3.7	11.2	5.1
Canada	34.1	-4.7	7.4	8.4	1.9	-0.3
China	35.0	7.9	13.6	9.8	24.8	18.6
Finland	47.0	7.3	6.4	9.7	5.6	8.5
France	26.4	-0.2	5.0	7.5	3.7	2.6
Germany	47.3	2.9	4.7	7.6	7.3	7.7
India	24.0	7.5[a]	10.4	13.0	15.6	13.6[a]
Ireland	83.5	-1.0	10.6	17.7	8.2	4.4
Italy	28.8	-3.7	5.9	4.1	2.8	2.0
Japan	17.4	1.8	3.6	4.0	7.0	6.7
Mexico	28.4	1.4	8.1	16.5	5.4	6.1
Netherlands	76.8	2.7	5.6	8.0	5.0	5.6
Russia	31.0	5.7	–	5.5	5.2	6.4
South Korea	52.9	5.7	11.2	17.0	12.1	9.3
Spain	26.6	-1.0	8.9	10.0	4.8	3.7
Sweden	54.2	1.9	4.7	8.9	5.6	5.8
Switzerland	56.4	2.9	1.7	5.2	3.9	7.6
UK	28.9	0.1	4.5	6.6	3.9	3.6
US	12.7	5.4	6.9	7.3	2.2	7.4
Euro area	41.9	1.2	–	–	5.3	5.1
OECD	28.9	2.2	–	6.7	3.9	5.9

a 2007
Sources: OECD; World Bank

on a few countries increases vulnerability to their economic cycle.

The greater the proportion of exports in relation to GDP, the bigger the boost to domestic output when overseas demand rises. For example, the Netherlands' exports account for over 70% of GDP and it trades heavily with Germany. Consequently, if German imports rise by 10%,

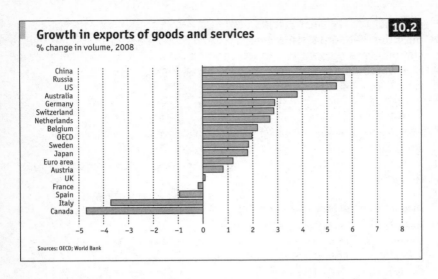

Growth in exports of goods and services `10.2`
% change in volume, 2008

Sources: OECD; World Bank

Dutch GDP jumps by 1.5%. A high exports:GDP ratio also implies a larger slump when foreign demand falls.

Other special factors

Smoothing. Various special factors can cause swings in trade figures even when there is no change in underlying trends. It is always wise to take at least 2–3 months together to smooth out blips.

Many commentators compare the calendar year so far with the same period of the previous year. This has a certain neatness, but economic figures do not respect accounting periods and comparisons of, say, the two months to February are more susceptible to erratic influences than the 11 months to November. Another option is to look at 12-month rolling totals, as can be found for trade balances in the Indicators pages of *The Economist*.

Oil and erratics. The movement of high-value items such as ships, aircraft and precious stones can have a significant effect on trade figures. Oil accounts for a large proportion of imports for many countries (typically up to 20%) and the price can fluctuate widely. For these reasons many countries publish figures for imports and exports excluding oil and erratics, which helps to identify underlying trends.

Seasonal adjustment. Most trade figures are adjusted for obvious seasonal factors such as climatic variation and the effect of holidays on industrial output. However, seasonal adjustment cannot cope with shipping and dock strikes, unusually bad weather or the movement of high-value items. Sensible adjustments should be made for any such factors of which you are aware.

Compatibility

Exports are always measured FOB (free on board) or FAS (free alongside ship) at the point of export, so they present fewer compatibility problems than imports which may be FOB or may include insurance and freight (CIF).

Imports of goods and services

Measures: Purchases from abroad.
Significance Imports add to well-being but may displace domestic production and drain financial resources.
Presented as: Value and volume figures in money and index form.
Focus on: Growth; total in relation to exports (see trade balance) and as a percentage of GDP.
Yardstick: OECD average growth in the volume of imports of goods and services was 4.3% a year during the period 2000–08.
Released: Monthly, at least one month in arrears.

Overview

A country imports goods and services because it cannot produce them itself or because there is some comparative advantage in buying them from abroad. Some commentators worry that all imports are a drain on national resources, which is a bit like saying you should not buy from a domestic neighbour who produces something better or cheaper than you do. Of course, you can only buy to the extent that you can finance the purchase from income, savings or borrowing against future production.

This brief should be read in conjunction with the previous brief on exports. Note especially the comments on goods and services (page 136) and special factors (pages 138–9).

Value and volume. Changes in import values reflect changes in foreign prices, exchange rates and quantity (volume). Real exchange rates (see page 168) are useful for identifying price and currency effects. Import volume indicates "real changes", and value gives the overall balance of payments position.

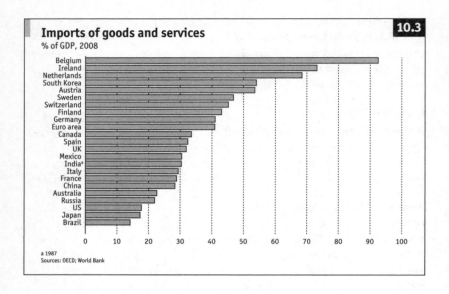

Imports of goods and services
% of GDP, 2008

10.3

Belgium
Ireland
Netherlands
South Korea
Austria
Sweden
Switzerland
Finland
Germany
Euro area
Canada
Spain
UK
Mexico
India[a]
Italy
France
China
Australia
Russia
US
Japan
Brazil

0 10 20 30 40 50 60 70 80 90 100

a 1987
Sources: OECD; World Bank

Cyclical variation. Import volumes tend to move cyclically. In general they increase when home demand is buoyant. For this reason imports might be seen as a safety valve which offsets the inflationary pressures that arise when domestic firms are operating at close to full capacity.

Link to exports. Imports are also linked to exports. An increase in exports boosts GDP because the goods sold overseas are part of domestic production.

When GDP increases, demand for domestic and imported goods rises as well.

Import penetration. Imports of goods and services as a percentage of GDP (or of total final demand) indicates the degree of dependence on imports; the higher the figure the more imports displace domestic output and the more vulnerable is the economy to changes in import prices. A sudden rise in import penetration may signal that domestic companies are operating at full capacity and cannot meet increases in demand.

Import composition and sources

Commodity breakdown. A high volume of imports of intermediate and capital goods is generally good where these are used to manufac-

Table 10.2 **Imports of goods and services**

	% of GDP	Annual average % change				
	2008	1990–94	1995–99	2000–04	2005–08	2008
Australia	22.1	5.3	8.2	7.6	7.9	11.1
Austria	53.6	3.9	5.6	6.0	3.6	-0.7
Belgium	92.6	3.7	4.8	3.7	2.9	3.3
Brazil	14.2	14.1	6.1	2.0	16.4	18.5
Canada	33.5	4.9	7.5	3.3	3.7	0.8
China	28.4	14.9	8.8	21.9	10.7	3.5
Finland	43.1	-0.2	7.5	6.7	6.5	7.0
France	28.9	3.0	7.1	5.3	3.5	0.8
Germany	41.0	5.4	7.2	4.4	5.5	4.3
India	30.3[a]	12.9	12.8	9.9	25.0[a]	7.7[a]
Ireland	73.2	7.6	17.0	7.3	3.6	-2.1
Italy	29.3	2.7	6.4	3.4	1.4	-4.5
Japan	17.3	2.4	4.5	4.5	2.5	0.9
Mexico	30.5	15.3	11.2	6.2	6.4	4.3
Netherlands	68.4	4.5	9.1	4.4	4.6	3.7
Russia	21.9	–	-3.3	21.1	21.2	19.4
South Korea	54.1	12.8	7.8	10.2	6.7	3.7
Spain	32.4	6.4	12.3	7.0	4.0	-4.9
Sweden	46.8	1.5	7.8	3.7	5.5	3.0
Switzerland	45.2	1.2	5.5	3.9	3.9	0.4
UK	32.0	2.3	8.4	5.5	2.8	-0.6
US	17.7	6.1	10.7	5.7	2.1	-3.2
Euro area	40.9	–	–	4.8	4.0	1.1
OECD	29.0	–	7.8	5.7	5.1	2.2

a 2007
Sources: OECD; World Bank

ture other items or to generate invisible earnings. This adds value to GDP and perhaps contributes to future export growth. For example, a country buying aircraft from abroad records these as imports. In later years the aircraft will be used to move passengers and generate profits which are invisible export earnings.

Note though that manufacturing output declines in the short term when imports displace locally processed or manufactured items. Devel-

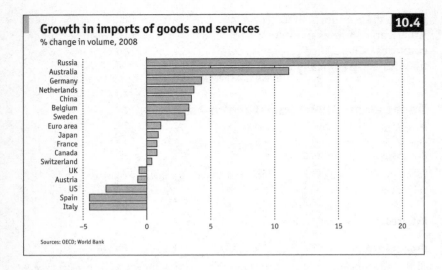

Growth in imports of goods and services `10.4`
% change in volume, 2008

Sources: OECD; World Bank

oping countries increasingly export semi-manufactures (such as cloth and refined petroleum products) and finished goods rather than raw materials (such as cotton and crude oil) and the industrial countries import more semi-manufactures and finished goods and fewer raw materials.

Increases in the volume of imports of consumer goods are a direct signal of consumer demand. They imply that domestic producers cannot meet the required price, quality or quantity.

Compressibility. When examining a developing country it is important to check the compressibility of imports, that is, the extent to which there are non-essential goods which need not be imported in times of stress on the balance of payments. If all imports are essentials such as foods and fuels it may not be possible to reduce the import bill.

Sources. A country which imports from just one or two main trading partners is vulnerable to economic shocks from its suppliers, especially if they cease to export those particular goods, if prices rise sharply or if there is some political disturbance.

International comparisons

The distinction between OTS and BOP figures is discussed on pages 134–5. For international comparisons, aim for consistency and watch the FOB/CIF basis. As a crude rule of thumb, imports CIF are around 10%

greater than imports FOB. The figure varies from 20% for some Latin American countries to under 4% for North America and some European countries where local cross-border trade keeps shipping costs lower than for geographically remote countries.

Trade balance, merchandise trade balance

Measures: The net balance between exports and imports of goods.
Significance: Shows a country's fundamental trading position.
Presented as: Money values.
Focus on: Total balance; balance in relation to the current account.
Yardstick: A deficit is potentially more of a problem than a surplus. See Current-account yardstick (page 146).
Released: Monthly, at least one month in arrears.

Overview

The trade balance is the difference between exports and imports (see above). It may measure visible (merchandise) trade only, or trade in both goods and services.

Invisibles are difficult to measure, so the balance of trade in goods and services is less reliable and more likely to be revised than the visible balance.

This brief should be read in conjunction with the previous briefs on exports and imports. Note especially the comments on goods and services (page 136) and special factors (pages 138–9).

Arithmetic. Small variations in imports or exports can have a significant effect on the trade balance. For example, if exports are $10 billion and imports are $11 billion, a 10% rise in imports to $12 billion will double the trade deficit from $1 billion to $2 billion.

Income elasticity. The relationship of exports and imports to economic growth (their income elasticity) is important. For example, Japan's imports tend to increase by a relatively small amount when its GDP grows by 1%. At the same time its exports rise rapidly when its trading partners' economies expand. Thus if Japan's economy grows at the same pace as the rest of the world, its trade surplus will tend to widen.

Supply constraints. A large trade deficit may signal supply constraints, especially if it is accompanied by high inflation and/or the deficit has

Table 10.3 **Trade and current-account balances**

	Trade balance 2008, $bn	Current-account balance, $bn	1990	1995	2000	2005	2008
			Current-account balance, % of GDP				
Australia	-3.8	-45.6	-5.2	-5.3	-3.6	-6.1	-4.6
Austria	-0.8	13.4	0.7	-2.3	-0.7	2.2	3.2
Belgium	-15.3	-12.8	1.8	5.0	4.9	2.6	-2.5
Brazil	24.8	-28.2	-0.8	-2.4	-3.8	1.6	-1.8
Canada	-45.4	7.6	-3.4	-0.7	2.7	1.9	0.5
China	360.7	426.1	3.4	0.2	1.7	7.2	9.8
Finland	8.6	8.1	-5.0	4.0	8.6	3.6	2.8
France	-86.4	-64.4	-0.8	0.7	1.7	-0.4	-2.3
Germany	265.4	241.6	2.8	-1.1	-1.7	5.1	6.6
India	-128.4	-37.2	-2.2	-1.6	-1.0	-1.2	-2.5
Ireland	36.3	-14.2	-0.8	2.6	-0.4	-3.5	-5.4
Italy	-1.1	-78.4	-1.5	2.2	-0.5	-1.7	-3.4
Japan	37.6	158.4	1.5	2.1	2.6	3.6	3.2
Mexico	-17.3	-15.8	-2.8	-0.5	-3.2	-0.5	-1.5
Netherlands	56.7	41.7	2.7	6.2	1.8	7.4	7.6
Russia	179.8	102.4	-	1.8	18.0	11.1	6.0
South Korea	6.0	-6.4	-0.8	-1.7	2.3	1.8	-0.6
Spain	-128.2	-152.7	-3.5	-0.3	-4.0	-7.4	-9.6
Sweden	18.6	29.8	-2.6	1.9	2.7	6.8	6.2
Switzerland	13.9	12.0	2.6	6.6	13.1	14.0	2.3
UK	-171.1	-43.3	-3.9	-1.2	-2.7	-2.6	-1.6
US	-840.6	-706.1	-1.4	-1.5	-4.3	-5.9	-4.9
Euro area	-16.6	-209.5	0.1	0.6	-1.5	0.5	-0.8
OECD	-868.6	-718.7	-0.6	1.0	-1.2	-1.4	-1.6

Sources: OECD; World Bank

emerged recently owing to a rise in imports. This suggests that companies are unable to boost output to match higher domestic demand. The deficit may act as a safety valve and divert potentially inflationary pressures. Alternatively, an increasing trade deficit may signal a loss of competitiveness by domestic companies.

Net savings and the resource gap. The balance of trade in goods and services measures the relationship between national savings and investment. A deficit indicates that investment exceeds savings and that absorption of real resources exceeds output.

For developing countries, the difference between exports and imports of goods and services is more usually called the resource gap; that is, the extent to which the country is dependent on the outside world. Many developing countries have resource gaps equivalent to 25–50% of GDP. In 2007 Liberia's was over 150% of GDP.

Current flows. For the industrial countries a trade imbalance is not necessarily a problem; it reflects choice as much as necessity.

For most of the past 200 years Britain has run a deficit on visible trade which has been more than offset by one of the world's largest surpluses on invisibles. Countries with large manufacturing sectors, such as Japan and Germany, have tended to run visible-trade surpluses and invisibles deficits. The current account is a better indicator of overall current flows (see pages 146–8).

Eliminating a trade deficit

There are two main ways in which an external trade deficit might move back into balance.

- **A change in the volume of trade.** If demand in the deficit country contracts or grows more slowly than that in the surplus country, the volume of exports will increase relative to the volume of imports.
- **A change in relative prices through a change in the exchange rate or a change in domestic prices.** Imports become dearer and exports cheaper if the deficit country's currency falls in value or if inflation is lower in the deficit country than in the surplus country. This will tend to depress the demand for imports and boost exports.

Attempts to regain balance through government export subsidies or import barriers such as quotas or tariffs are essentially imposed volume or price changes (which also cause market distortions). For example, a ban on imports will generate extra, possibly inflationary, demand for domestic goods.

Similarly, trade surpluses may be eroded by faster economic growth, a stronger currency or higher inflation in the surplus country.

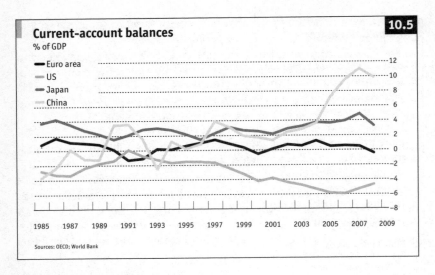

Current-account balances
% of GDP

- Euro area
- US
- Japan
- China

Sources: OECD; World Bank

Current-account balance

Measures:	Net current payments, the difference between national savings and investment.
Significance:	Identifies international payments which arithmetically must be matched by capital flows and changes in official reserves.
Presented as:	Money total.
Focus on:	Trends; size in relation to GDP.
Yardstick:	The OECD average current-account balance was -0.4% of GDP during the late 1980s, -0.2% during the 1990s and -1.2% in 2000–2008.
Released:	Usually monthly, quarterly by some countries; at least one month in arrears.

Overview

The current-account balance is the balance of trade in goods and services (see above) plus income and current transfer payments.

Countries which produce monthly current-account figures base their initial estimates on simple projections of previous income and transfers, which themselves may be revised. Consequently this component of the current account is even less reliable than the goods and services balance and is subject to heavy revision.

Income. This mainly reflects past capital flows. Countries with current-account surpluses acquire foreign assets which generate further current-account income in future periods. Also referred to as RIPD (rents,

146

Global imbalances

In its latest *World Economic Outlook*, the IMF forecasts that this year the current-account balances of the main trading regions will fall below 2% of world GDP for the first time since 2004. America's deficit is expected to shrink by almost half as a share of global GDP from its level last year. The oil exporters' current-account surplus is set to drop by more than two-thirds. But China and South-East Asia's surplus is forecast to be broadly unchanged. International deficits and surpluses should offset each other, but the data are subject to measurement error. The figures since 2005 suggest the world is running a surplus with itself. The discrepancy is thought to arise from delays in the recording of imports.

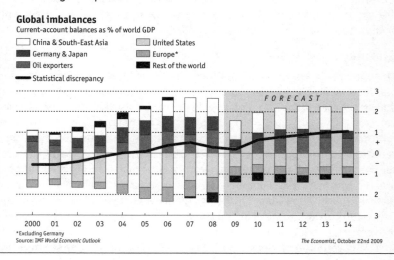

Global imbalances
Current-account balances as % of world GDP

- ☐ China & South-East Asia
- ☐ United States
- ☐ Germany & Japan
- ☐ Europe*
- ☐ Oil exporters
- ☐ Rest of the world
- ▬ Statistical discrepancy

*Excluding Germany
Source: IMF *World Economic Outlook*

The Economist, October 22nd 2009

interest, profits and dividends). Compensation to non-resident employees is also included here.

Transfer payments. These include foreign workers' remittances to their home countries, pension payments to retired workers now living abroad, government subscriptions to international organisations and payments of foreign aid.

Host countries with large populations of foreign workers (including Germany) experience transfer outflows. However, for many developing countries workers' inward remittances save the current account from becoming an unmanageable deficit. Remittances are a particularly important source of foreign currency for poor countries with workers in the rich oil-exporting Gulf states.

Current-account deficits

A visible-trade deficit can be covered by exports of services or net inflows of income and transfers, but the overall current account cannot remain in deficit indefinitely. It has to be financed by any or all of inward investment, loans from overseas, sales of overseas assets and depletion of official currency reserves.

Direct inward investment in businesses may create new employment, output and exports which should help to eliminate future current-account deficits. Nevertheless capital inflows might be withdrawn at inconvenient times, and they create potential RIPD current-account outflows.

Savings

The current account is sometimes taken as a measure of the gap between domestic savings and investment, although strictly speaking this is measured by the balance of trade in goods and services (see above).

Since government budget deficits represent government dissaving, some commentators argue that if a budget deficit is cut any current-account deficit will fall automatically. This line of reasoning became popular when America developed large current-account and budget deficits in the mid-1980s. The fallacy of the argument was demonstrated when the American current-account deficit subsequently fell without a corresponding reduction in the budget deficit.

The correlation between the budget deficit and the current-account deficit holds good only if private-sector savings and investments remain unchanged, which they generally do not.

Acquisition of net foreign assets

Although the current account does not quite measure net savings, it does measure the net acquisition of foreign assets. In other words, external debt grows by the size of a current-account deficit (see above).

Foreign direct investment

The flow of foreign direct investment (FDI) fell by 39% in 2009 to just over $1 trillion, from a shade under $1.7 trillion in 2008, according to the UN Conference on Trade and Development. All kinds of investment – equity capital, reinvested earnings, and intra-company loans – were affected by the downturn. Rich countries saw FDI inflows plunge by 41%, and foreign investment into developing countries fell by more than a third. Not every country was badly hit. FDI into China, where economic growth remained robust, declined by only 2.6%. Foreigners actually invested more in Germany and Italy last year than in 2008. Despite FDI plunging by 57% last year, America remained the world's top investment destination.

Foreign direct investment
FDI inflows, 2009 estimate, $bn

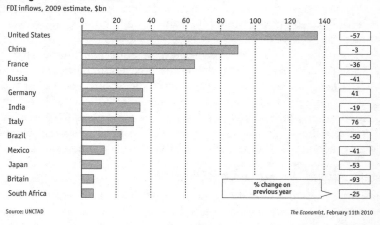

Source: UNCTAD

The Economist, February 11th 2010

Capital- and financial-account flows

Measures:	International capital flows.
Significance:	Major contributor to exchange-rate fluctuations. Outflows represent the acquisition of assets overseas.
Presented as:	Money totals.
Focus on:	Direct and portfolio investment.
Yardstick:	Use current-account balance as indicator.
Released:	Quarterly, at least one month after the quarter end. Revised often.

Overview

The capital and financial account records international capital and financial flows. These are frequently neglected by commentators but they are important because they are directly related to the current-account balance and to exchange rates. The increase in direct investment flows particularly reflect the increased globalisation of the world economy.

Foreign direct investment (FDI) refers to an investment made to acquire lasting interest in enterprises operating outside of the economy of the investor. Further, in cases of FDI, the investor's purpose is to gain an effective voice in the management of the enterprise. The foreign entity or group of associated entities that makes the investment is termed the "direct investor". The unincorporated or incorporated enterprise – a branch or subsidiary, respectively, in which direct investment is made – is referred to as a "direct investment enterprise". Some degree of equity ownership is almost always considered to be associated with an effective voice in the management of an enterprise; the IMF suggests a threshold of 10 per cent of equity ownership to qualify an investor as a foreign direct investor.

An outflow of capital today implies current-account income in the future. Indeed, with global deregulation, it is easier for companies to raise their market share by setting up production facilities overseas. The initial direct investment shows as a capital-account outflow. Subsequently remitted profits add to current-account inflows and boost GNP relative to GDP. The value of goods sold, however, does not show up in external trade or increase GDP in the way that exports from home would.

International investment position (IIP)

Measures: Balance sheet levels of external assets and liabilities.
Significance: Indicates cumulative cross-border activity.
Presented as: Value at end-quarter or end-year.
Focus on: Changes in totals and main components and holders.
Yardstick: US-owned assets abroad were $19.9 trillion at the end of 2008; foreign-owned assets in the United States were $23.4 trillion.
Released: Normally annually, about six months after year-end.

Overview

This is a stock indicator rather than a flow. The IIP measures the level of inward and outward investment with the rest of the world.

Official reserves

Measures:	Gold and foreign currencies held by the government.
Significance:	Indicates a country's ultimate ability to pay for imports; signals pressures on the balance of payments.
Presented as:	Nominal value at end-month, often in dollars; watch for unrealistic value or revaluation of gold and currencies.
Focus on:	Totals and changes.
Yardstick:	A crude rule of thumb is that reserves should be sufficient to cover three months' imports. A sudden large change of tens or hundreds of millions of dollars in one month may indicate exchange-rate pressures.
Released:	Monthly; in some countries immediately after the month-end.

Overview

Central banks hold stocks (reserves) of gold and currencies which have widespread acceptability and convertibility, such as the dollar. These reserves are used to settle international obligations and to plug temporary imbalances between supply and demand for currencies.

Intervention

Central banks frequently intervene in the markets to influence their currency's exchange rate. This affects their reserves.

For example, if the Federal Reserve (the American central bank) decides that the dollar is too strong against the yen it may sell (anonymously) dollars in exchange for yen on the open market. The extra supply of dollars creates new demand for yen and tends to depress the exchange rate of the dollar relative to the yen. The Fed increases its foreign currency reserves by the value of the yen purchased.

Conversely, if the Fed thinks that the dollar is too low, it might use its currency reserves to buy dollars and prop up the dollar exchange rate. Intervention in this direction can continue only so long as the central bank has reserves that it can sell.

Central banks might sensibly intervene to smooth erratic fluctuations in currencies, but it is a fool's game to use intervention alone to try to hold a currency at, or move it to, some previously determined level if that is not the level at which market supply and demand are in equilibrium. Such an exchange-rate objective can only be met in the longer term through domestic economic policies (see Exchange rates, page 154).

Sterilisation. When a central bank sells reserves and buys its own currency, the domestic money supply is reduced in size by the amount of

151

domestic currency swallowed up by the bank. Purchases of foreign currencies boost the money supply. Such intervention is said to be sterilised if the central bank neutralises the effect on the money supply with some other action, such as the purchase or sale of government bonds.

Interpretation

Changes in the level of official reserves suggest foreign-exchange intervention and, therefore, pressures on the currency:

- a fall in the reserves suggests that there was intervention to offset currency weakness;
- a rise suggests intervention to hold the currency down.

However, reserves change for reasons other than intervention, including government borrowing or payments overseas, and fluctuations in the rates used to convert holdings of gold and currencies into a common unit of account. The total value of reserves can also be misleading if gold is valued at some anachronistic rate, as it frequently is.

Strictly speaking, the level of reserves alone is not a guide to a coun-

Table 10.4 **External debt, 2007**

	Total, $bn	% of GDP	As % of goods and services	Debt service ratio[a]
Largest in $				
China	373.6	11.6	23.0	2.2
Russia	370.2	29.4	83.9	9.1
Turkey	251.5	38.8	165.7	32.1
Brazil	237.5	18.7	119.4	27.8
India	221.0	18.9	75.7[b]	7.7[b]
Poland	195.4	25.6	104.1	25.6
Largest relative to GDP				
Liberia	2.5	442	440.3	111.6
Samoa	1.1	223	714.5	26.9
Guinea-Bissau	0.7	214	684.9[c]	40.2[c]

a Debt service (principal repayments plus interest paid) as % of exports of goods and services.
b 2006   c 2004
Source: World Bank

try's ability to pay its way. That is determined in the short term at least by the government's ability to borrow overseas. If the reserves are running low it is a good idea to look at the country's IMF position (see SDR, page 160), its current level of external debt and its ability to borrow overseas.

External debt, net foreign assets

Measures: Net borrowing by the public and private sectors.
Significance: Liability which can be repaid only from export earnings.
Presented as: Money totals.
Focus on: Total and debt service in relation to exports.
Yardstick: See Table 10.4.
Released: Annually without fanfare.

Overview

Countries which persistently run current-account deficits accumulate external debt. This can become a major problem since essentially the debt repayments and interest can be financed only from export earnings. Table 10.4 indicates the problems for some of the world's largest debtors.

Net foreign assets. Rather than being debtors, many countries, including some industrial countries and oil exporters, have accumulated stocks of assets in other countries. The figures tend to understate the true position because of under-declaration and book values that are way out of line with market values.

The stock, however, may not be of any help for offsetting any current-account deficits. Residents may have no wish to repatriate their assets, especially if the current-account deficit is a signal of fundamental economic problems.

11 Exchange rates

Devaluation ... would be a lunatic self-destroying operation.
Harold Wilson in 1963; in 1967 he devalued the pound.

Exchange rates are nothing more than the price of one currency in terms of another. They are determined mainly by supply and demand, which reflect trade and other international payments, and, much more important, volatile capital flows which are constantly shifting around the world in search of the best expected investment returns.

The prime indicator of market pressures on a currency is the figure for total currency flows in the balance of payments account (see Chapter 10). Other important influences are relative interest rates and yields (Chapter 12) and inflation (Chapter 13).

A history of exchange rates

The easiest way to understand exchange rates and their influence on the balance of payments is to review previous experiences.

The gold standard. Before 1914 exchange rates were fixed in terms of gold, trade was mainly in physical goods and capital flows were limited. A country which developed a deficit on its current account would first consume its reserves of foreign currencies. Then it would have to pay for the imports by shipping gold. The transfer of gold would reduce the money supply in the deficit country and boost it elsewhere, since currencies were then backed by convertibility into gold.

In the deficit country the contracting money supply would tend to depress output and prices. Elsewhere the expanding money supply would boost output and inflation. The deficit country could then only afford to import a lower quantity of dearer foreign goods. The surplus countries could import a higher quantity of the deficit country's cheaper goods. Thus the current account would automatically return to equilibrium.

That was the theory. It seemed to work in practice until the system got out of balance in the 1920s. The gold standard was temporarily suspended during the first world war. Countries experienced rapid and varying rates of inflation and exports were grossly underpriced or overpriced when the gold standard was reintroduced at pre-war rates. Large current-account surpluses and deficits developed. The gold standard fell from favour and was abandoned almost universally by the early 1930s.

The 1930s. There were widespread experiments with fixed and floating exchange rates during the 1930s. Almost every country tried to alleviate the unemployment of the Depression by limiting imports and boosting exports with measures such as import duties, quotas and exchange-rate devaluation or depreciation. It may seem obvious, but world exports cannot rise if world imports fall. The international payments system fell further into disrepute.

Adjustable pegs. An international conference was convened in America at Bretton Woods, New Hampshire, in June 1944. Participants agreed to form the IMF and World Bank to promote international monetary cooperation and the major currencies were fixed in relation to the dollar. Fluctuations were limited to 1% in either direction, although larger revaluations and devaluations were allowed with IMF permission. In addition, the American government agreed to buy gold on demand at $35 an ounce, which left only the dollar on a gold standard.

Floating rates. The Bretton Woods system broke down in the 1970s. Persistent American deficits had led to an international excess of dollars and American gold reserves came under pressure. In August 1971 the Americans suspended the convertibility of the dollar, imposed a 10% surcharge on imports and took other measures aimed at eliminating its balance of payments deficit. The major currencies were allowed to float, some within constraints imposed by exchange controls (dirty floats).

Fixed rates with some flexibility were reintroduced in December 1971 following a meeting of the IMF Group of Ten at the Smithsonian Institution in Washington (the "Smithsonian agreement"). However, sterling was floated "temporarily" in June 1972 and by the following year all major currencies were floating or subject to managed floats. Despite bouts of extreme turbulence, most major currencies have remained floating ever since. The exceptions are EU currencies. Several of these spent the 1980s and most of the 1990s linked to one another in the exchange-rate mechanism of the European monetary system. At the start of 1999, 11 countries fixed their exchange rates irrevocably and joined a single European currency, the euro. Greece joined on January 1st 2001. Slovenia, Cyprus, Malta and Slovakia followed in 2007–09. The euro floats freely against other currencies.

Nominal exchange rates

Measures:	Price of one currency in terms of another.
Significance:	Influences external trade, capital flows, and so on.
Presented as:	Units of one currency for one unit of another.
Focus on:	Trends.
Yardstick:	Annual movements of more than a few per cent in either direction can be destabilising.
Released:	Minute-by-minute.

Jargon

An exchange rate indicates how many units of one currency can be purchased with a single unit of another. For example, a rate of ¥100 against the dollar indicates that one dollar buys 100 yen: $1 = ¥100.

Stronger and weaker. If the rate changes from $1 = ¥100 to $1 = ¥200 the dollar has risen or strengthened by 100% against the yen (it will buy 100% more yen). The yen has fallen or weakened against the dollar, but not by 100% or it would be worthless. It has moved from ¥100 = $1 to ¥100 = $0.50, a fall of 50%.

When currencies get stronger or weaker, they are said to have appreciated or depreciated if they are floating-rate currencies or to have been revalued or devalued if their rates are fixed by the central bank.

Spot rates. Rates for immediate settlement are spot rates.

Forward rates and futures. Exchange rates fixed today for settlement on a given future date reflect nothing more than spot exchange rates and interest rate differentials.

For example, if a bank agrees to buy dollars in exchange for yen in one month, essentially it borrows the dollars today, converts them into yen, and places the yen in the money markets to earn interest for one month. At the end of the month the bank hands over the yen, takes the dollars and uses them to repay the dollar loan. Nobody takes an exchange-rate risk.

Moreover, arbitrage ensures that forward rates, futures and options move in line.

Forward exchange rates and futures should not therefore be regarded as explicit indicators of expected exchange rates.

Exchanging blows
Our Big Mac index shows the Chinese yuan is still undervalued

Recent renewed American calls for China to revalue its currency have so far fallen on deaf ears. China has rejected accusations that America's huge trade deficit with it is caused largely by an artificially weak yuan, which has been pegged to the dollar since July 2008. Economists point out that an appreciation of the yen did little to help reduce America's trade deficit with Japan in the 1980s. But the yuan is unquestionably undervalued. Our Big Mac index, based on the theory of purchasing-power parity, in which exchange rates should equalise the price of a basket of goods across countries, suggests that the yuan is 49% below its fair-value benchmark with the dollar.

Big Mac index
Local currency under (-)/ over (+) valuation against the dollar, %

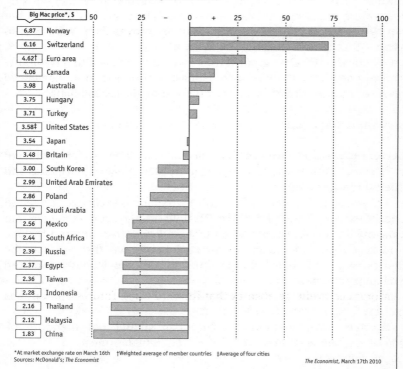

Big Mac price*, $		
6.87	Norway	
6.16	Switzerland	
4.62†	Euro area	
4.06	Canada	
3.98	Australia	
3.75	Hungary	
3.71	Turkey	
3.58‡	United States	
3.54	Japan	
3.48	Britain	
3.00	South Korea	
2.99	United Arab Emirates	
2.86	Poland	
2.67	Saudi Arabia	
2.56	Mexico	
2.44	South Africa	
2.39	Russia	
2.37	Egypt	
2.36	Taiwan	
2.28	Indonesia	
2.16	Thailand	
2.12	Malaysia	
1.83	China	

*At market exchange rate on March 16th   †Weighted average of member countries   ‡Average of four cities
Sources: McDonald's; *The Economist*

The Economist, March 17th 2010

What determines exchange rates

There is no neat explanation for what determines exchange rates. The two main theories are based on purchasing power and asset markets (investment portfolios).

Purchasing power parity (PPP). The traditional approach to exchange rates says that they move to keep international purchasing power in line (parity). If American inflation is 6% and Canadian inflation is 4%, the American dollar will fall by 2% to maintain PPP. With floating exchange rates this would happen automatically. If exchange rates are fixed, demand pressures will instead equalise inflation in the two countries.

Another version of this, favoured by some economists, is to define purchasing power parity as the exchange rate which equates the prices of a basket of goods and services in two countries. In the long term, it is argued, currencies should move towards their PPP. *The Economist* has a simpler approach with its Big Mac index.

Portfolio balance. The portfolio approach suggests that exchange rates move to balance total returns (interest plus expected exchange-rate movements). If yen deposits pay 6% and dollar deposits pay 8%, investors will buy dollars for the higher return until the exchange rate has been pushed up so far that the dollar is expected to depreciate by 2%. The expected return from the dollar will then exactly match the expected return from the yen.

Overshooting. The best guess is that exchange rates are determined by PPP in the long run, but that this is overridden in the short term by portfolio pressures. These tend to cause currencies to overshoot PPP equilibrium.

Who determines exchange rates

Clearly there is a complex interaction between exchange rates and various economic and financial variables, many of which are outside domestic control (they are determined exogenously). Central banks can either try to control these variables in order to fix their exchange rate, or leave the exchange rate to the markets.

In fact, of the 150 or so IMF members' currencies in 1990, less than one-sixth were freely floating, including those of Australia, Canada, Japan, New Zealand and America. Of the remaining currencies, 32 had managed floats or limited flexibility, while around 25 were pegged to the dollar, 14 to the French franc, five to other single currencies and 50 to the

SDR (see page 160) or other baskets of currencies. By 2008, however, 40 of the world's 180-odd IMF members had independently floating currencies and a further 44 had managed floats.

Monetary policy. All economic policies affect exchange rates, although changes in interest rates have probably the most direct and visible influence. The exchange rate is thus the broadest indicator of monetary policy.

Table 11.1 **Exchange rates**
Currency units per $, period average

Country	Currency	1990	1995	2000	2005	2008
Australia	dollar	1.28	1.35	1.72	1.31	1.19
Austria	schilling/euro	11.37	10.08	1.09	0.80	0.68
Belgium	franc/euro	33.42	29.49	1.09	0.80	0.68
Brazil	real	0.02	0.92	1.83	2.43	1.83
Canada	dollar	1.17	1.37	1.49	1.21	1.07
China	yuan	4.78	8.35	8.28	8.19	6.95
Finland	markka/euro	3.82	4.37	1.09	0.80	0.68
France	franc/euro	5.45	4.99	1.09	0.80	0.68
Germany	D-mark/euro	1.62	1.43	1.09	0.80	0.68
India	rupee	17.50	32.43	44.94	44.10	43.51
Ireland	pound/euro	0.60	0.62	1.09	0.80	0.68
Italy	lira/euro	1,198	1,629	1.09	0.8	0.68
Japan	yen	144.80	94.10	107.80	110.20	103.40
Mexico	peso	2.81	6.42	9.46	10.90	11.13
Netherlands	guilder/euro	1.82	1.61	1.09	0.80	0.68
Russia	rouble	-	4.56	28.13	28.28	24.85
South Korea	won	707.76	771.27	1,130.00	1,024.1	1,102.1
Spain	peseta/euro	101.90	124.70	1.09	0.80	0.68
Sweden	krona	5.92	7.13	9.16	7.47	6.59
Switzerland	franc	1.39	1.18	1.69	1.25	1.08
UK	pound	0.56	0.63	0.66	0.55	0.54
US	dollar	1.00	1.00	1.00	1.00	1.00
Euro area	euro	0.79	0.77	1.09	0.80	0.68
SDR		0.74	0.66	0.76	0.68	0.63

Source: IMF

Intervention. Central banks frequently intervene in the currency markets. They buy or sell their currency in order to alter the balance of supply and demand and move the exchange rate. This is essentially a short-term smoothing activity since they can buy one currency only if they have another to sell. (See Reserves, page 151.)

Effects of exchange-rate movements

The most immediate effect of a weaker currency is higher domestic inflation owing to dearer imports. At the same time, exports priced in foreign currencies and inflows of rents, interest, profits and dividends generate more income in domestic-currency terms. Thus the trade and current-account balances deteriorate.

Later, after perhaps as much as 12–18 months, relative price movements cause a shift from imports to domestic production and exports. This boosts GDP and the trade and current accounts improve. (Their deterioration followed by improvement is known as the J-curve effect.) However, higher inflation caused by a weaker currency can wipe out any current account improvement within a number of years.

Capital account. With regard to the capital account of the balance of payments, a weaker currency makes inward investment look more attractive. In foreign-currency terms outlays are lower and returns are higher, but this may not be enough to attract investors if the currency weakened because of unfavourable domestic economic conditions.

Special drawing rights (SDRs)

Measures:	The value of a basket of four major currencies, see Table 11.2.
Significance:	Stable international currency and reserves asset.
Presented as:	Absolute value per unit of currency.
Focus on:	Market rate against any currency.
Yardstick:	Average: SDR1 = $1.18 in the 1980s, $1.40 in the 1990s and $1.43 in 2000–2008.
Released:	Several times daily.

Overview

The SDR (special drawing right) has some of the characteristics of a world currency. It was introduced by the IMF in 1970 to boost world liquidity after the ratio of world reserves to imports had fallen by half since the 1950s. Through book-keeping entries, the Fund allocated SDRs to member countries in proportion to their quotas (see below). Countries

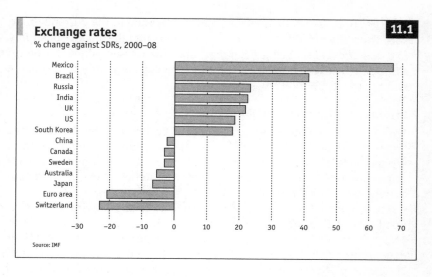

Exchange rates `11.1`
% change against SDRs, 2000–08

Mexico
Brazil
Russia
India
UK
US
South Korea
China
Canada
Sweden
Australia
Japan
Euro area
Switzerland

−30   −20   −10   0   10   20   30   40   50   60   70

Source: IMF

in need of foreign currency may obtain them from other central banks in exchange for SDRs.

Advantages. The SDR is stable. It is used for accounting purposes by the IMF and even some multinational corporations. Commercial banks accept deposits and make loans in SDRs, and it is used to price some international transactions.

Disadvantages. Since the SDR is an average of four currencies it is less

Table 11.2 **Currencies in the SDR**
%

Country	Currency	1986–90	1991–95	1996–98	1999–2000	2001–05	2006–10
US	dollar	42	40	39	39	45	44
Germany	D-mark	19	21	21	–	–	
Japan	yen	15	17	18	18	15	11
France	franc	12	11	11	–	–	
UK	pound	12	11	11	11	11	11
Euro area	euro	–	–	–	32	29	34

Source: IMF

Table 11.3 **SDR exchange rates**
Currency units per SDR, end of period

Country	Currency	1990	1995	2000	2005	2008
Australia	dollar	1.84	2.00	2.35	1.95	2.22
Austria	schilling/euro	15.19	15.00	1.40	1.21	1.11
Belgium	franc/euro	44.08	43.73	1.40	1.21	1.11
Brazil	real	0.09	1.45	2.55	3.34	3.60
Canada	dollar	1.65	2.03	1.95	1.66	1.89
China	yuan	7.43	12.36	10.78	11.53	10.53
Finland	markka/euro	5.17	6.48	1.40	1.21	1.11
France	franc/euro	7.30	7.28	1.40	1.21	1.11
Germany	D-mark/euro	2.13	2.13	1.40	1.21	1.11
India	rupee	25.71	52.30	60.91	64.41	74.63
Ireland	pound/euro	0.80	0.93	1.40	1.21	1.11
Italy	lira/euro	1,607.80	2,355.70	1.40	1.21	1.11
Japan	yen	191.21	152.86	149.70	168.61	139.78
Mexico	peso	4.19	11.36	12.47	15.40	20.85
Netherlands	guilder/euro	2.40	2.38	1.40	1.21	1.11
Russia	rouble	–	6.90	36.69	41.14	45.25
South Korea	won	1,019.20	1,151.60	1,647.50	1,445.80	1,940.00
Spain	peseta/euro	137.87	180.49	1.40	1.21	1.11
Sweden	krona	8.11	9.90	12.42	11.37	12.03
Switzerland	franc	1.84	1.71	2.13	1.88	1.64
UK	pound	0.74	0.96	0.87	0.83	1.06
US	dollar	1.42	1.49	1.30	1.48	1.54
Euro area	euro	–	–	1.40	1.21	1.11

Source: IMF

valuable than the strongest and is among the first to go when reserves are sold off. Developing countries argue that it would help their liquidity if they had more SDRs, but the quota system ensures that the rich industrial countries have most of them.

Value

SDRs were first allocated in 1970 equal to $^{1}/_{35}$ of an ounce of gold, or exactly $1 ($1.0857 after the dollar was devalued in 1971). When the dollar came off the gold standard the SDR was fixed from 1974 in terms of a basket of 16 currencies. This proved too unwieldy and in 1981 the basket was slimmed to five major currencies with weights broadly reflecting their importance in international trade. With the creation of the euro in 1999, the number of currencies was reduced to four (see Table 11.2). The next review is due in 2010.

Since 1981 the IMF has paid the full market rate of interest on the SDR, based on a weighted average of rates paid by the individual constituents.

Quotas

The IMF allocates to each member country a quota which reflects the country's importance in world trade and payments. The size of the quota determines voting powers, subscriptions in gold and currencies, borrowing powers and SDR allocations.

Any member with balance of payments difficulties may swap its SDRs for reserve currencies at IMF-designated central banks. It can also use its own currency to buy (draw) foreign currency from the Fund's pool. The first chunk of currencies (the reserve tranche), amounting to 25% of the member's quota, may be taken unconditionally. Four additional credit tranches each worth another 25% of the quota may be taken under progressively tougher terms and conditions. When these options are used up there are other borrowing facilities available. The IMF also arranges standby credits in times of severe strain on a currency.

EMU, ecu, ERM and euro

Measures:	The euro became the single currency of 11 EU countries on January 1st 1999. By January 1st 2009 there were 16 members.
Significance:	Reserve asset, international currency and basis of the European exchange-rate mechanism. Now in circulation in the form of notes and coins.
Presented as:	Dollars per euro; yen per euro; (British) pence per euro.
Focus on:	Rate against other currencies, especially the dollar.
Yardstick:	The euro began life at around $1.17 to the euro. By late 2000 it was trading at just over $0.82 but at the end of 2004 it was $1.36. In 2010 it stood at around $1.20.
Released:	Continuously.

Overview

A timetable and criteria for the creation of a single currency as part of economic and monetary union (EMU) was agreed by the EU at Maastricht in 1991. The programme built on the exchange rate mechanism

Table 11.4 **Permanent conversion rates against euro area currencies**

Country	Currency	€1 =
December 31st 1998		
Austria	Sch	13.7603
Belgium/Luxembourg	BFr/LFr	40.3399
Finland	FM	5.94573
France	FFr	6.55957
Germany	DM	1.95583
Ireland	I£	0.787564
Italy	L	1,936.27
Netherlands	Fl	2.20371
Portugal	Es	200.482
Spain	Pta	166.386
December 31st 2000		
Greece	Dr	340.750
December 31st 2006		
Slovenia	SIT	239.640
December 31st 2007		
Cyprus	CYP	0.585274
Malta	MTL	0.429300
December 31st 2008		
Slovakia	SKK	30.1260

Euro value against leading currencies	Dec 31st 1998	Dec 31st 2009
US	1.1668	1.4406
Japan	134.88	132.62
UK	0.7055	0.8895
Switzerland	1.6061	1.4845

Source: IMF

(ERM) and the European currency unit (ecu), which was replaced by the euro.

The ecu

Introduced on March 13th 1979, the ecu superseded the European unit of account (EUA). While the EUA was no more than a common unit for book-keeping purposes, the ecu was a reserve asset and a currency in its own right used for commercial transactions and bond issues.

The ecu was based on a basket of EC currencies weighted according to the relative size of GDP and trade volume.

The ERM

Before the creation of the euro, the ERM linked most of the EU's national currencies, including all those who adopted the single currency. Britain and Italy withdrew in September 1992. The Italians later rejoined.

Each ERM currency had a fixed central rate against the ecu. From these rates a "parity grid" of cross-rates between each pair of currencies was calculated. In most countries, central banks were required to keep their own currencies within 2.25% of all other cross-parities. For some countries, however, the limit was 6%, and was raised to 15% after the near-collapse of the ERM in mid-1993.

When the euro was created on January 1st 1999, the ERM was superseded by a new arrangement, ERM2. Countries that wanted to join the euro were expected to be members of ERM2 before acceding. Two of the four EU countries that were not members of the euro, Denmark and Greece, were members of ERM2. The British pound and Swedish krona float freely against other currencies.

In ERM2, central rates are defined against the euro, rather than the ecu, and the maximum divergence permitted from the cross-parities is 15%. However, the Danes negotiated a narrower band of 2.25%.

The euro

The December 1995 EU summit in Madrid confirmed the intention to introduce a single European currency, to be known as the euro, on January 1st 1999.

The summit adopted changeover recommendations presented in a 1995 European Commission Green Paper and a report by the European Monetary Institute (the forerunner of the European Central Bank). On the basis of economic and financial indicators of "convergence" (including budget deficits, ratios of debt to GDP, interest rates and inflation rates), initial participants were selected in early 1998. Eleven countries that wanted to join were deemed to have qualified. Britain and Denmark decided to opt out. Greece and Sweden were deemed not to have qualified. Greece was admitted from January 1st 2001. Slovenia, Cyprus, Malta and Slovakia joined subsequently (see Table 11.4).

On January 1st 1999 the exchange rates of the 11 countries were irrevocably fixed. The euro replaced the ecu at a rate of one to one. On January 1st 2002 euro notes and coins were introduced. National currency notes and coins were withdrawn from circulation two months later.

Official interest rates in the 16 euro area countries are now set by the European Central Bank. The governors of the national central banks and six members of the Executive Board sit on the ECB's rate-setting governing council.

Effective exchange rates

Measures: Average exchange rate against a basket of currencies.
Significance: Shows overall exchange-rate movements.
Presented as: Index numbers.
Focus on: Trends.
Yardstick: An increase indicates a strengthening currency. Movements of more than a few percentage points a year can be destabilising.
Released: Daily or monthly.

Overview

An effective exchange rate (EER) measures the overall value of one currency against a basket of other currencies. Changes indicate the average change in one currency relative to all the others.

Effective exchange rates are weighted averages of many currency movements with weights chosen to reflect the relative importance of each currency in the home country's trade. For example, if the dollar appreciates by 10% against the Japanese yen but is unchanged against all other currencies, and if the yen accounts for 25% of American trade, the dollar's effective exchange rate has risen by 2.5%.

For obvious reasons EERs are sometimes known as trade-weighted exchange rates. There are many ways of selecting the weights, based on imports of manufactured goods, total trade, and so on.

MERMs. Most indices use weights from the IMF's multilateral exchange-rate model (MERM). This tries to measure the effect of exchange-rate changes on prices of exports and imports, and the response of trade flows to such price changes.

Main sources. The IMF, the major central banks and some other organisations calculate effective rates for all the major currencies. The Bank of England indices published on *The Economist*'s website and some daily newspapers for non-euro area countries are based on the IMF's model. The IMF publishes monthly indices for most countries including euro area members.

Table 11.5 **Effective exchange rates**
Annual averages, 2005 = 100

Country	2000	2002	2004	2006	2008
Australia	84.9	81.9	97.6	98.8	103.8
Austria	95.0	95.5	100.2	100.2	102.5
Belgium	91.5	93.6	99.8	100.3	104.7
Brazil	146.0	96.8	83.2	110.4	122.9
Canada	83.4	79.7	93.5	106.8	111.9
China	106.1	111.5	99.9	102.7	111.2
Finland	89.9	92.6	100.5	100.0	104.9
France	91.7	93.5	99.9	100.2	105.1
Germany	89.8	92.5	100.5	100.3	104.9
India	103.1	100.7	97.1	96.8	97.5
Ireland	87.2	89.9	99.8	100.3	109.0
Italy	89.4	93.3	100.6	100.1	104.4
Japan	109.8	96.4	103.3	93.0	99.3
Mexico	117.9	116.8	97.0	99.5	95.9
Netherlands	91.2	93.3	100.1	100.1	105.2
Russia	104.1	103.7	99.7	103.1	103.4
South Korea	96.4	91.5	90.1	107.0	85.3
Spain	93.9	95.3	99.9	100.2	103.9
Sweden	100.8	94.2	102.5	100.6	101.2
Switzerland	91.1	98.9	100.6	98.7	102.3
UK	101.1	100.0	101.0	1007.0	90.2
US	109.7	115.4	102.7	98.5	90.8
Euro area	79.9	85.6	101.2	100.2	109.4

Sources: IMF; Eurostat

Interpretation

If, for example, the effective exchange rate for the dollar rises by 1%, this indicates that the various exchange-rate changes that have taken place are the same as a flat 1% rise in the dollar against every individual currency. In other words, the observed movements will have the same effect on the American trade balance as a 1% overall rise in the dollar.

Effective exchange rates do not take account of inflation so they do not reveal anything about changes in a country's competitiveness (see Real exchange rates below).

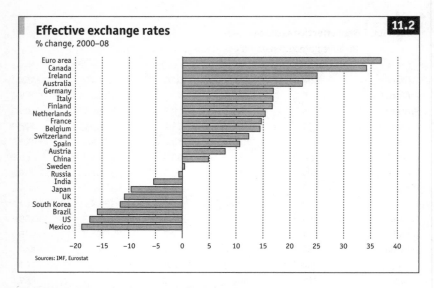

Effective exchange rates
% change, 2000–08

Euro area
Canada
Ireland
Australia
Germany
Italy
Finland
Netherlands
France
Belgium
Switzerland
Spain
Austria
China
Sweden
Russia
India
Japan
UK
South Korea
Brazil
US
Mexico

−20 −15 −10 −5 0 5 10 15 20 25 30 35 40

Sources: IMF, Eurostat

Real exchange rates; competitiveness

Measures: International competitiveness.

Significance: Indicative of a country's ability to sell abroad and of net price (inflation and exchange rate) pressures on the balance of payments.

Presented as: Index numbers.

Focus on: Trends.

Yardstick: The lower the index, the more competitive the country.

Released: Monthly, one month in arrears.

Overview

The international competitiveness of goods and services produced in a country depends on relative movements in costs or prices after adjusting for exchange-rate movements. For example, if prices increase by 4% in Germany and 6% in America, American competitiveness appears to have fallen by 2%. However, if over the same period the dollar fell by 3%, overall American competitiveness has actually improved by 1%. Such measures of overall competitiveness are known as "relative costs or prices expressed in a common currency" or, more simply, real exchange rates.

Indicators of prices and costs

There is no ideal measure of competitiveness. Those in common use are

Table 11.6 **Real effective exchange rates**
Relative normalised unit labour costs, period averages, 2005 = 100

Country	2000	2002	2004	2006	2008
Australia	80.1	80.6	97.1	100.0	105.6
Austria	94.5	95.4	99.8	99.8	101.9
Belgium	91.3	93.3	99.1	100.0	105.0
Brazil	109.4	96.8	83.2	110.4	122.9
Canada	83.5	80.4	94.2	105.9	108.8
China	108.1	110.1	100.2	102.1	116.2
Finland	95.3	97.3	102.0	99.3	104.2
France	92.6	93.7	100.4	99.7	103.1
Germany	93.9	94.8	101.2	99.7	103.1
India	97.2	96.8	97.6	96.6	95.7
Ireland	80.9	88.4	99.6	102.0	114.0
Italy	90.1	93.6	101.0	99.9	103.5
Japan	128.5	103.1	101.3	93.4	99.8
Mexico	104.9	111.1	96.3	100.1	98.6
Netherlands	88.6	94.1	100.5	99.3	102.5
Russia	67.0	82.8	92.0	109.6	123.3
South Korea	90.5	88.6	89.6	107.0	85.1
Spain	88.5	92.1	98.5	101.7	106.9
Sweden	111.7	100.7	104.7	96.8	93.9
Switzerland	87.7	97.6	99.5	99.3	103.8
UK	102.1	101.2	100.3	102.5	90.2
US	119.9	126.9	103.8	99.5	90.0
Euro area	82.3	87.1	101.7	99.7	107.0

Sources: IMF, Eurostat

listed in Table 11.6 above. They are described in terms of America, but the calculations are the same for any country.

Relative export prices. American export prices divided by a weighted average of competitors' export prices, all expressed in a common currency. This might seem to be a logical basis for assessing price competitiveness but there are several drawbacks. Such an exchange rate covers only goods that are traded; it does not take account of competition

Real effective exchange rates
% change, 2000–08

11.3

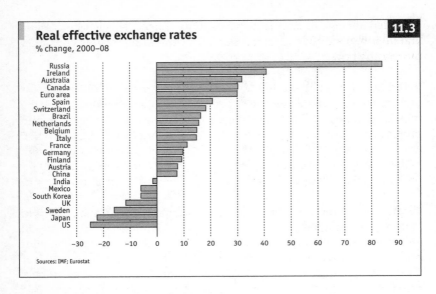

Sources: IMF; Eurostat

between imports and domestic production in home or overseas markets; it measures orders but ignores unsuccessful quotations; and it fails to take account of profitability (exporters in general are price-takers; they may be forced to absorb exchange-rate movements in profits).

Relative export profitability. American export prices divided by American producer prices. This is not a measure of international competitiveness, but it is a useful supplement to relative export prices. It indicates the extent to which changes in export prices reflect changes in the profit margins on exports against home sales. If export prices rise less rapidly than domestic prices, export profitability has declined.

Import price competitiveness. American producer prices divided by American import prices. This provides a guide to import competitiveness, but again it ignores relative profitability.

Relative producer prices. American producer prices divided by a weighted average of competitors' producer prices. This compares home prices with prices that they will be competing against overseas. It tends to overemphasise domestic markets.

Relative consumer prices. American consumer prices divided by a weighted average of competitors' consumer prices. This ignores capital and intermediate goods, but it is good for comparing relative consumer purchasing power.

Relative GDP value-added deflators. The American GDP deflator divided by a weighted average of competitors' GDP deflators. This is the most comprehensive basis for comparison, covering unit labour costs and profits per unit of output. One drawback is that some of the items in GDP are not traded, although it might be argued that inflation pressures are ultimately transmitted uniformly through all goods and services. Another problem is that the deflators are available only after a sizeable lag.

Relative unit labour costs. An alternative to price competitiveness is to look at cost competitiveness. This has the advantage of covering all industries: exporters, potential exporters and those competing with imports. However, because of a lack of data the only sensible indicator is relative unit labour costs (or ULCs – say, American ULCs divided by a weighted average of competitors' ULCs, all in a common currency). This excludes profits and prices of materials.

Normalised relative unit labour costs. These are relative unit labour costs adjusted to allow for short-term deviations in productivity from long-term trends. This smooths out differences in the cyclical position of the countries being compared, but because of the difficulties of adjusting productivity for the cycle it should be treated with care.

Interpretation
Common practice. Relative unit labour costs in manufacturing and relative export prices are the most popular measures, partly because they are available quickly and easily. However, rather than relying on just one indicator it is a good idea to look at several to get a feel for "average" changes.

The indicators are expressed in index form. The index rises if domestic costs or prices increase faster than foreign costs or prices. Thus a larger index number (stronger real exchange rate) indicates that the home country is less competitive. The broad implication is that to restore competitiveness, the currency must weaken or domestic prices/costs will have to increase less than foreign prices/costs.

Current international practice uses 2005 as a base for index numbers.

The indices do not take account of non-price factors (product differentiation) such as quality, reliability and design.

Terms of trade

Measures: The ratio of export prices to import prices.

Significance: Measures the volume of imports that can be bought with one unit of exports.

Presented as: Index numbers.

Focus on: Changes in the index.

Yardstick: An improvement indicates that export earnings will buy more imports – but the trade balance may worsen.

Released: Monthly.

Overview

The terms of trade indicate the purchasing power of a country's exports in terms of the imports that they will buy.

Favourable or unfavourable. The terms of trade are said to improve if export prices rise more rapidly or fall more slowly than import prices. For example, if export prices rise by 5% and import prices rise by 2%, a given volume of exports buys roughly 3% more imports; the terms of trade have improved by 3%.

Common terminology suggests that movements in the terms of trade are "favourable" or "unfavourable". However, after an "unfavourable" movement in the terms of trade, the trade balance will tend to improve (the smaller rise in export prices than import prices means that exports are more competitive), while a "favourable" movement in the terms of trade may price exporters out of the market and result in a weaker trade balance (see Trade balance and Exchange rates, pages 143 and 154).

Which way is up? Governments usually define the terms of trade as export prices divided by import prices expressed in index form. A rise in the index indicates an improvement in the terms of trade: one unit of exports will buy more imports. Academics sometimes do it the other way around, as import prices divided by export prices. The lower the number, the fewer exports needed to obtain one unit of imports. The message is the same in both cases, but you need to check the basis for the calculation before you can interpret the numbers.

Unit value or average values. Terms of trade indices constructed using import and export unit value indices (see Export and Import prices, page 210) are not affected by changes in the commodity breakdown of imports or exports. Terms of trade indices based on average value indices reflect changes in composition as well as changes in prices.

In general unit values are most commonly used and are a satisfactory basis for the terms of trade, but where there has been a structural shift in the composition of trade, average value indicators are better. For example, if a country imported a larger proportion of oil in 1990 than in 2000 and if oil prices rise, a unit value terms of trade indicator based on 1990 weights will overstate the deterioration in the terms of trade. An average value indicator will show a smaller, more realistic, deterioration.

Devaluation or depreciation. Typically, an exchange-rate devaluation or depreciation increases import prices relative to export prices and causes the terms of trade to deteriorate.

12 Money and financial markets

There have been three great inventions since the beginning of time: fire, the wheel and central banking.

Will Rogers

Money

The cornerstone of the modern economy is money, which is a measure of value, a medium of exchange and a store of wealth. It is also the bridge between real and nominal magnitudes, so understanding it is vital for understanding and controlling inflation.

Markets

Financial markets bring together the supply of savings and the demand for money to finance businesses and consumer spending. The markets also allow people to complete commercial transactions and spread risks. Note that there are two sides to every transaction: for every lender there is a borrower; for every seller, a buyer.

Interest rates

Interest rates are the price of money. They link large stocks of physical and financial assets with smaller flows of savings and investment; they connect the present and the future; and they are sensitive to inflation expectations. As a result they are very volatile and hard to predict. With all these factors at work, it is hardly surprising that there is no simple theory which explains why interest rates behave as they do.

Liberalisation and globalisation

Financial systems changed dramatically in the 1970s, 1980s, 1990s and 2000s. There were three main influences.

- **Liberalisation and deregulation.** Exchange, credit and interest rate controls were abolished or relaxed in the major industrialised countries.
- **Innovation.** Many new financial instruments and derivatives were introduced, including financial futures and options.

◪ **Technological change.** Computers and modern telecommunications have allowed transactions to be completed quickly and cheaply.

As a result the world's major financial markets have become much more integrated. A change in American, Japanese or euro area interest rates is felt immediately throughout the world, which means that domestic monetary policies are influenced by uncontrollable outside influences. Monetary variables are harder to control and the demand for money is less sensitive to domestic interest rates.

Key figures

The following briefs examine money and bank lending, interest rates, bond yields and share prices. They are all interlinked. Nevertheless, the exchange rate (see page 154) is also an important indicator of monetary conditions.

Money supply, money stock, M0 ... M5, liquidity

Measures:	Notes, coins and various bank deposits.
Significance:	Indicator of level of transactions and, perhaps, inflation or output.
Presented as:	Money totals at a point in time, usually end-month; except averages of Wednesdays for Canada and daily averages for Japan and America.
Focus on:	Changes over time.
Yardstick:	OECD average narrow money growth was 7.4% a year during the period 2000–2008.
Released:	Monthly; one month in arrears.

Overview

Money is anything which is accepted as a medium of exchange; essentially currency in circulation plus bank deposits. Notes and coin, issued by the monetary authorities (mainly central banks), account for only a tiny proportion of the money supply. The rest is bank deposits, which are initially created within the banking sector.

The total amount of money in circulation, the money stock or money supply depending how you look at it, is often called M. The number of times it changes hands each year is its velocity of circulation, V.

Multiply the two together ($M \times V$) and you have the amount of money that is spent, which by definition must equal real output Y multiplied by the price index P; that is, $M \times V = Y \times P$.

This equation is the basis for understanding money. Assume for the moment that velocity is fixed or predictable (it is not particularly). In this case, argue the monetarists, controlling the money supply controls money GDP (that is, Y × P); and if the trend in real output Y can be predicted inflation can be controlled. Their opponents argue that cause and effect run in the other direction, that money GDP fixes the demand for money and there is nothing that can be done about it.

Whoever is right, if you are prepared to accept that velocity is fixed in the short term, then as a dangerously crude rule of thumb, subtract the inflation rate from the rate of growth of money to estimate the growth of real output.

Money defined

Narrow money, M1. In most countries the measure of narrow money is called M1. This is fairly uniformly defined as currency in circulation plus sight deposits (accounts where cash is available on demand).

There are some national variations. Britain's narrow money measure is called M0. This consists almost entirely of cash in circulation, but also includes banks' operational deposits at the Bank of England. Britain has no M1 measure. America's M1 measure includes travellers' cheques. Japan's definition includes the government's sight deposits.

The number of national variations was reduced in the run-up to the creation of the euro, with the harmonisation of the definition of monetary aggregates across the euro area. The European Central Bank publishes monetary statistics for the whole euro area from figures compiled by national central banks.

Broad money, M2. The main wider definitions of money are called M2 and M3. In essence, M2 consists of M1 plus savings deposits and time deposits (accounts where cash is available after a notice period). The definition of M3 is wider still.

- In America M2 consists of M1 plus savings deposits, time deposits and retail money-market mutual funds.
- In the euro area M2 is defined as M1 plus deposits with agreed maturity of up to two years plus deposits redeemable at up to three months' notice.
- In America M3 consists of M2 plus institutional money funds, large time deposits, repurchase agreements and Eurodollars.
- In the euro area M3 equals M2 plus repurchase agreements,

money-market funds and paper, and debt securities of up to two years' maturity.

◪ In Japan, the measure of broad money is M2 plus certificates of deposit. M2 consists of currency in circulation plus public- and private-sector deposits.

In Britain, there is no M3. The broad money measure is called M4. It consists of M0 plus sterling deposits held at British banks by the non-bank private sector.

Velocity of circulation

Velocity of circulation, that is, the number of times money changes hands in a year, may be measured by nominal GDP divided by any monetary aggregate such as M2 averaged over the year.

Deposit creation and monetary growth

Commercial banks create money. They can lend out a large proportion of deposits placed with them, since it is unlikely that all customers will ask for their money back at once.

Suppose a bank receives a new $100 deposit and lends $80 of it. By the stroke of a pen the bank creates a loan (debit balance $80) and a new deposit (credit balance $80). Even if the customer withdraws the entire $80 to pay for some consumer goods, the retailer is likely to redeposit the $80, probably in a different bank. The second bank has a new deposit of which it might lend $60. This credit creation will gradually peter out, but not until one new deposit has created loans (= deposits = money) of several times its own size.

Reserve assets

For prudence and monetary control central banks limit the proportion of new deposits which banks can on-lend by requiring them to hold a fixed proportion of their assets in the following.

◪ **High-powered reserves.** Cash (till money) and balances at the central banks (operational deposits) which are used to meet day-to-day requirements for customer withdrawals and interbank settlements.

◪ **Secondary reserves.** "Safe" liquid assets such as Treasury bills which can be used to meet temporary increases in withdrawals.

Monetary control

Monetary authorities attempt to control the size and growth of money in several ways.

- **Changing reserve-asset ratios.** This affects the multiple which banks can lend and is usually done only once every few years.
- **Open-market operations.** Buying or selling government bonds in the open market, which increases or reduces the amount of money in bank reserves and private deposits.
- **Influencing interest rates.** For example, by means of open-market operations (which affects the supply and demand for money), changing the discount rate (see page 182), or imposing fixed rates for certain deposits or loans.
- **Credit controls.** For example, limits on total bank lending, total personal credit, or the margins that borrowers have to put up for any credit purchase.
- **Moral suasion.** For example, central banks hold heart-to-heart talks with commercial bankers, perhaps to persuade them to restrict lending.

Note that direct control over reserve-asset ratios and the monetary base affects the supply of money while the other measures affect demand for it.

Alternative indicators of monetary growth

Monetary growth can be tracked by watching the deposits which are included in the various monetary aggregates. Alternative approaches are to track the following.

- **The banking sector's balance sheet.** Movements on the liabilities side (deposits) must be matched by movements in assets (mainly loans) and liabilities not included in monetary aggregates.
- **Sectoral counterparts.** These are measured by money the public sector takes out of circulation (roughly, the budget surplus plus government bond sales to non-banks) plus net additions by the banking sector (mainly bank lending) plus net additions from overseas (net balance of payments inflows to the private sector).

Monetary targets

Monetary authorities adopt many approaches to monetary control. During the 1980s and for much of the 1990s, many central banks (in Britain, the Treasury) had explicit targets for chosen monetary aggregates.

This has largely fallen out of favour. Several central banks, including the Federal Reserve, the European Central Bank, the Bank of England and the Reserve Bank of New Zealand, now have targets or desired target ranges for inflation instead. Monetary growth is one of several indicators of economic activity that central bankers watch.

Although the European Central Bank targets inflation rather than monetary growth, it has a "reference value", reiterated in December 2002, of 4.5% for the annual rate of growth of M3. It thinks that this is the rate consistent with its inflation target (that consumer prices should rise by less than 2% per year), a trend rate of GDP growth of 2–2.5% and an annual decline of 0.5–1% in the velocity of circulation of M3.

Interpretation

An important reason for the decline in the importance of monetary targets is Goodhart's law, named after an economist who sat on the Bank of England's monetary policy committee, which sets British interest rates. The law says that any monetary variable loses its usefulness within six months of being adopted as a target of monetary policy.

The problem is that if relative interest rates or other influences change, investors quickly move their balances from deposits with one institution (which might be included in a particular definition of money) to another (which might not). This can cause the Ms to jump up and down at different rates and make interpretation tricky. Other complications include international capital flows and changes in the velocity of circulation.

Watch for cash lurking in the sidelines and changes in domestic and international relative interest rates and yields, and for factors which might distort some or all monetary aggregates.

Even though monetary targets no longer enjoy the primacy they once did, central bankers and economists still watch monetary aggregates closely. In interpreting them, the difficulties mentioned in the previous paragraph should be borne in mind. Remember also that although many monetary measures are seasonally adjusted, it is advisable to be on the lookout for erratic influences. It is also wise to take several months together and compare with the same period a year earlier.

Table 12.1 **Money supply**
% change

	Narrow money				Broad money			
	2005	2006	2007	2008	2005	2006	2007	2008
Australia	6.7	10.0	13.9	6.4	8.4	10.8	16.9	19.7
Brazil	13.9	15.0	22.6	13.6	17.4	18.9	17.7	17.3
Canada	6.9	8.2	8.9	8.9	9.7	7.4	10.9	12.0
China	11.8	14.3	20.8	14.1	16.0	16.8	17.5	16.5
India	16.9	21.2	15.5	17.2	14.7	18.6	21.5	21.2
Japan	4.7	3.0	-0.1	-0.5	2.9	3.0	3.2	0.9
Mexico	10.9	15.7	9.7	7.9	14.7	15.2	11.3	12.4
Russia	29.9	34.4	37.4	23.1	33.9	37.0	44.7	30.2
South Korea	8.8	0.2	-5.7	-1.5	7.0	8.0	10.3	11.6
Sweden	9.9	11.8	11.1	6.2	8.7	15.7	16.1	13.4
Switzerland	-1.9	-0.2	-4.9	0.5	4.0	2.6	2.1	2.2
UK	12.1	10.8	11.1	14.3	9.9	12.4	13.8	15.3
US	2.0	0.2	-0.1	4.1	4.2	5.0	5.8	6.9
Euro area	13.5	11.3	6.8	2.5	7.5	8.6	11.1	10.4

Source: OECD

In general, if a monetary aggregate is growing too rapidly (faster than its target rate, or faster than is consistent with the central bank's inflation target), this may be an argument for the central bank to raise interest rates. Slow monetary growth is a sign of weakening economic activity, and may be an argument for lower rates. However, other signals of inflationary pressures will also be taken into account.

Bank lending, advances, credit, consumer credit

Measures: Loans to persons, companies and the public sector.
Significance: Indicator of monetary conditions.
Presented as: Monthly totals.
Focus on: Trends.
Yardstick: Roughly, growth should equal target for monetary aggregates.
Released: Monthly; one month in arrears.

Overview
Changes in overall bank lending figures indicate the effectiveness of

monetary policy. Changes in lending to various sectors may indicate trends in various parts of the economy.

Personal and consumer credit

Net new borrowing by households finances the purchase of homes and consumer goods and services. Such borrowing tends to be sensitive to interest rates and consumer confidence. It is translated directly into higher spending (see also Retail sales, House sales, Motor vehicle sales, Consumer expenditure), output and imports.

Growth in household credit is generally good when demand is slack, but it can be inflationary when demand is already buoyant. Excessive borrowing to finance the acquisition of other financial assets such as shares is also worrying: it may help to drive up their prices, making consumers feel wealthier and ready for a bout of inflationary spending.

Borrowing by companies

Companies borrow to finance their operations, investment and takeovers. Corporate borrowing generally slackens when the economy is booming and funds are generated by buoyant sales. On the other hand, there will be more investment activity when companies are most optimistic (see Business conditions, page 115).

A breakdown by industry will reveal trends in various industrial sectors. High borrowing may reflect either optimism and investment or recession and debts. Output, orders and capacity utilisation figures will indicate which.

Central bank policy rates

Measures:	Interest rates at which central banks lend to banking systems.
Significance:	Indicator of central banks' monetary policy; influences banks reserves, monetary growth and market interest rates.
Presented as:	Annual percentage rate.
Focus on:	Rate, trends.
Yardstick:	See Table 12.2.
Released:	Changed daily, fixed weekly, or moved only at irregular intervals.

Overview

Within the constraints of market pressures, central banks manage their banking systems to keep liquidity and short-term interest rates at or near to officially desired levels. Central banks:

◪ intervene in the interbank money market to manage the daily balance of supply and demand;

◪ often publish formal discount rates at which they provide money to commercial banks to help smooth longer (say, weekly) financing needs; and

◪ occasionally impose penal rates for emergency lending to banks.

Central banks aim to influence monetary conditions by setting the interest rates on which they are willing to lend money to commercial banks. These rates in turn influence the rates at which banks deal with each other and their customers, and hence affect economic activity as a whole. In America, the Federal Reserve aims to control the Federal funds rate. The Bank of Japan works on the overnight call money rate.

For European central banks, such as the European Central Bank, the Bank of England and the Swedish Riksbank, the principal instrument of monetary policy is called the repo rate (or, at the ECB, the refinancing or "refi" rate). A repo is a sale and repurchase agreement where one financial dealer sells securities to another with an agreement to buy them back at a given price on a certain date. In effect, in setting its repo rate the central bank is announcing the terms on which it will provide a short-term loan (say a week) to banks, in return for which the banks pledge securities as collateral. The repo rate is the interest rate on this loan, expressed in annual terms.

Policy rates are usually set at regular meetings of central banks. America's Federal Open Market Committee meets eight times a year. The Bank of England's monetary policy committee and the European Central Bank's governing council meet monthly. Some central banks, including the Fed, Bank of England and the Riksbank, publish the minutes of their meetings a few weeks after they take place. These are watched keenly by economists, as they contain clues to central bankers' thinking – such as, for example, the economic indicators they consider most important. In addition, central banks publish regular economic assessments. In Britain, the Bank of England issues an *Inflation Report* in February, May, August and November, which summarises developments over the previous three months and contains projections of inflation and GDP growth for up to two years ahead.

Interest rates; short-term and money-market rates

Measures: Interest charged on financial paper with maturity up to 12 months.
Significance: Indicator of monetary conditions, expectations, creditworthiness.
Presented as: Annual percentage rates (see also discount rates above).
Focus on: 3-month interbank (or CD/Treasury bill rate if no interbank rate).
Yardstick: See Tables 12.2 and 12.4.
Released: Almost continuously round the clock.

Overview

Money markets are the markets in which banks and other intermediaries trade in short-term financial instruments.

The hub is usually the interbank market (called the Federal funds market in America), which is where banks deal with each other to meet their reserve requirements (see Money supply, page 175) and, longer-term, to finance loans and investments.

Very short-term interbank interest rates are largely determined by central bank intervention (see page 181), although market pressures are also influential. For other maturities and other financial instruments, relative maturities and credit risks are also important.

Maturity. Loans in the short-term market range from call (repayable on demand) and overnight to 12-month money. Interest rates on 12-month paper are higher than on shorter maturities if market participants expect interest rates to rise, or lower if rates are expected to fall. Supply and demand imbalances can cause temporary interest rate bulges at various maturities. It is not unknown for overnight money rates to top 100% on rare occasions. Use three-month rates as the benchmark.

Credit risk. Treasury bills (loans to the government) are regarded as completely safe in the major industrial countries and command the finest (lowest) interest rates, usually below interbank rates. Interest rates are higher on certificates of deposit (CDs – bank deposits which can be sold) and, usually, higher still on corporate or commercial paper (loans to companies).

LIBOR and variants

Interbank rates are quoted bid (to borrow) and offer (to lend). The London interbank offered rate (LIBOR) is a benchmark. The interest rates on many credit agreements worldwide are set in relation to it; for

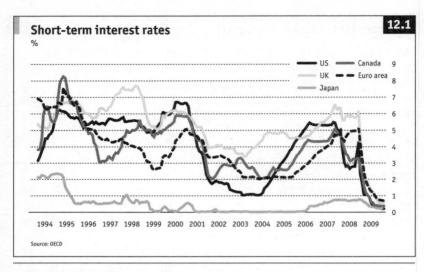

Short-term interest rates
%

Source: OECD

Table 12.2 **Comparative interest rates**
%, 2008 average

	Money market	Deposit	Prime lending	Treasury bills	Gov't bonds
Australia	6.67	5.17	8.91	–	5.73
Belgium	–	–	–	3.63	4.42
Brazil	12.36	11.66	–	13.68	–
Canada	2.96	1.5	4.73	2.39	4.04
Denmark	4.88	–	–	–	4.28
France	–	3.67	–	3.62	4.23
Germany	3.82	–	–	–	3.99
Ireland	2	–	–	–	4.53
Italy	4.67	–	6.84	3.76	4.68
Japan	0.46	0.59	1.91	0.36	1.45
Mexico	8.27	3.04	8.71	7.68	–
Netherlands	–	4.37	4.6	–	4.23
Russia	5.48	5.76	12.23	–	7.53
Spain	3.85	–	–	3.71	4.37
Sweden	–	–	–	3.91	3.89
Switzerland	0.01	0.16	3.34	1.33	2.15
UK	4.65	–	4.63	4.3	4.58
US	–	2.97	5.09	1.46	3.67

Source: IMF

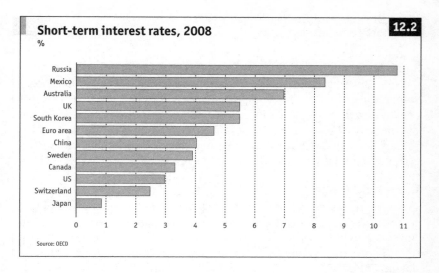

Short-term interest rates, 2008

%

Chart 12.2

Source: OECD

example, as LIBOR plus 0.5%. With the creation of the euro, EURIBOR, a euro-equivalent, has come into being.

There is no direct equivalent in America. Its interbank market is the Federal funds market, while the base for loan contracts is the prime rate (the rate charged to borrowers with prime or excellent creditworthiness). However, whereas LIBOR changes constantly under the direct influence of supply and demand, the prime rate is set by the banks (with reference to market rates) and is changed less regularly.

Two technical points

Interest and discount. Note the difference between interest rates (investment yields) and discount rates. Treasury bills and commercial paper are issued at a discount to their maturity value. A 12-month bill with a face value of $100 might be sold for $92.50, when the discount is $7.50:

- the discount rate is 7.5% (7.50 divided by 100 as a percentage);
- the interest rate is 8.1% (7.50 divided by 92.50 as a percentage).

Basis points. Dealers sometimes talk about basis points, where 100 basis points = 1% (percentage point) or 1 basis point = 0.01%.

Interest rates and the economic cycle

Whether by government action or by constraints of supply and demand, interest rates tend to rise when economic activity is buoyant and fall when it is slack. .

Lower interest rates encourage borrowing, which leads to more consumer spending and investment, increased imports, a higher level of economic activity and possibly faster inflation. Higher interest rates do the opposite. The problem for finance ministers and central bankers is getting the timing right. It can take perhaps 12–18 months for the full effect of a change in interest rates to feed through.

Interest rates and currencies

Changes in interest rates affect the relative attractiveness of holding a currency (see Exchange rates, page 154). For example, an increase in American interest rates will encourage a shift into the dollar, pushing it up and making American imports cheaper and European imports dearer. Other countries which want to maintain exchange-rate relationships or prevent money-market outflows are forced to raise their interest rates as well.

Bond yields

Measures: Interest return on fixed-interest securities.
Significance: Indicator of interest and inflation expectations, creditworthiness.
Presented as: Annual percentage rates.
Focus on: Long-dated government bonds.
Yardstick: See Table 12.3.
Released: Almost continuously round the clock.

Overview

Bonds are loans with fixed regular coupons (interest payments) and usually a fixed redemption value on a given date. Some bonds are perpetual or undated loans which are never repaid or are repaid only at the borrower's option.

The yield (effective rate of interest) on bonds is determined by market conditions. Investors in bonds want to be compensated for loss of interest on other instruments, the time and credit risk of holding bonds and expected inflation. Risks are minimised with government bonds (loans to the government) and unlike shares the maturity value is fixed, so the yield on long-dated government bonds may be taken as an indicator of expected trends in interest rates and inflation.

Table 12.3 **Benchmark yields**
January 8th, 2010

	Coupon %	Redemption date	Price local currency	Yield %
Australia	4.50	Apr 2020	90.37	5.76
Austria	3.90	Jul 2020	100.40	3.85
Belgium	4.00	Mar 2019	102.28	3.70
Canada	3.75	Jun 2019	101.27	3.59
Finland	4.38	Jul 2019	106.44	3.56
France	3.75	Oct 2019	101.40	3.58
Germany	3.25	Jan 2020	98.94	3.38
Ireland	5.90	Oct 2019	108.63	4.77
Italy	4.25	Mar 2020	101.79	4.07
Japan	1.30	Dec 2019	99.40	1.37
Netherlands	4.00	Jul 2019	103.76	3.53
Spain	4.30	Oct 2019	102.77	3.95
Sweden	5.00	Dec 2020	113.96	3.44
Switzerland	2.25	Jul 2020	101.15	2.13
UK	4.50	Mar 2019	103.30	4.06
US	3.38	Nov 2019	96.50	3.80

Sources: *Financial Times*; Thomson Financial

British government bonds are known as gilts, or gilt-edged securities, after the paper on which they were once printed.

Yield calculations

Bonds are traded in secondary markets at prices which in a mechanical sense reflect their redemption value, coupon, credit rating and other interest rates.

For example, a closely watched American Treasury (government) bond with a 5.13% coupon repayable at $100 in 2016 was trading at just under $100 in mid-2006. In return for the $99.83 outlay, a buyer would receive $5.13 a year in coupons and $100 on maturity, making the effective investment yield, or rate of interest, 5.15% a year.

Corporate bonds with the same maturity and redemption details trade at a lower price (higher yield) reflecting the greater risk of default.

Benchmark bonds that professional investors watch are shown in Table 12.3. These change over time as bonds mature and new ones are issued.

Yields and prices. Note the negative relationship between bond yields and bond prices. If prices fall, interest yields increase. If prices rise, interest yields decline.

Yields and the economic cycle

Since interest rates tend to rise when economic activity is buoyant and fall when it is slack, bond prices tend to fall on the upward leg of the economic cycle and rise on the downward leg.

Index-linked issues

The British and some other governments have issued index-linked bonds, where the coupons and redemption value are linked to consumer prices. The yield on such bonds is the real interest rate.

For example, in mid-2006 the real yield on index-linked gilts was roughly 1.7% (depending on inflation assumptions) while the yield on long-dated conventional gilts was 4.5%, implying expected inflation of 2.8% a year.

However, such calculations should be regarded with suspicion, because the volume of index-linked bonds is so small that individual trades can move the market.

Yield curves, gaps and ratios

Measures: Difference between interest yields on different instruments.
Significance: Indicator of interest and inflation expectations.
Presented as: Annual percentage rates.
Focus on: Long-dated government bonds and other interest rates.
Yardstick: See Table 12.4.
Released: Almost continuously round the clock.

Overview

Various yield differentials signal market perceptions of risks, interest rates, inflation and perhaps exchange-rate movements. You can focus on the difference between any two yields. Four common measures are described below.

Yield curve

Strictly speaking, the yield curve is a line on a graph linking interest rates for a whole range of maturities. However, it can be represented numerically by the difference between two maturities, such as the yield on long-term government bonds less three-month Treasury bills (Table 12.4).

Long rates are usually higher than short rates to allow for the time

Table 12.4 **Yields**
      % per year

	Treasury bills		Gov't bonds	
	2005	2008	2005	2008
Australia	–	–	5.32	5.73
Belgium	2.02	3.63	3.41	4.42
Canada	2.73	2.39	4.39	4.04
Finland	–	–	3.35	4.29
France	–	3.62	3.46	4.32
Germany	2.03	–	3.18	3.99
Ireland	–	–	2.90	4.53
Italy	2.17	3.76	3.56	4.68
Japan	–	–	1.36	1.45
Mexico	7.68		9.42	–
Netherlands	–	–	3.37	4.23
Russia	–	–	7.84	7.53
Spain	2.19	3.71	3.05	4.37
Sweden	1.72	–	3.38	3.89
Switzerland	0.71	1.33	1.96	2.15
UK	4.55	4.30	4.39	4.58
US	3.17	1.46	4.29	3.67
Euro area	–	–	3.44	4.36

Source: IMF

and inflation risks of holding bonds. However, the curve flattens or inverts when monetary conditions tighten, mainly because of the increase in short rates. The curve may therefore be used as a signal of monetary conditions and a leading indicator of economic activity.

Bond spread

The bond spread is the gap between bond yields in two countries. For example, it might be defined as American less British long-term government bond yields, in which case a narrowing of the differential indicates a reduction in the relative attractiveness of the dollar. (See Exchange rates and Interest rates, pages 154 and 183.) Or, more frequently, the premium yield required by those investing in many of the emerging economies over American Treasuries.

Widespread worries

Spreads widen alarmingly on government bonds in troubled euro-area economies

Greece's debt was downgraded by Standard & Poor's to "junk" status on Tuesday April 27th, driven in part by fears about delays in aid for Greece from the European Union and the IMF. The agency also cut Portugal's debt rating by two notches. The moves provided another jolt to euro-area bond markets and added to worries that a bail-out for Greece, even if it came soon, would only delay a default. Contagion has already hit other troubled European economies. Yields on two-year Greek notes rose above 25% on Wednesday, from 4.6% a month ago. Spreads between ten-year Greek bonds and benchmark German bunds the day before spiked to nearly seven percentage points. Spreads also rose substantially for bonds issued by Portugal and Ireland, but only slightly for Italian and Spanish government debt.

Ten-year government-bond spreads over German bunds
Percentage points

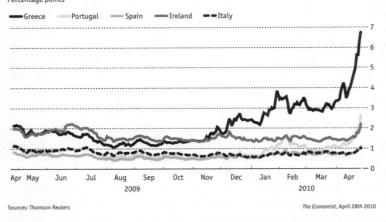

Sources: Thomson Reuters

The Economist, April 28th 2010

Yield gap or reverse yield gap

The yield gap is the yield on long-term government bonds less the average dividend yield on shares. Decades ago, before the markets were worried about inflation, the yield on shares was higher than that on bonds (that is, the gap was negative), reflecting the greater risk of holding equities. The gap is now generally positive (sometimes called a reverse yield gap) because investors demand a higher return from

Table 12.5 **Real yields**
% per year; interest rates and yields less consumer price inflation

	——— Treasury bills ———		——— Gov't bonds ———	
	2005	2008	2005	2008
Australia	–	–	2.65	1.38
Belgium	-0.76	-0.86	0.63	-0.07
Canada	0.5	0.02	2.18	1.67
Finland	–	–	2.49	0.23
France	–	0.81	1.65	1.51
Germany	0.08	–	1.62	1.36
Ireland	–	–	0.47	0.48
Italy	0.18	0.41	1.57	1.33
Japan	–	–	1.63	0.07
Mexico	–	–	5.43	–
Netherlands	–	–	1.67	1.76
Russia	–	–	-4.84	-6.58
Spain	-1.18	-0.36	-0.32	0.30
Sweden	1.27	–	2.93	0.45
Switzerland	-0.46	-1.09	0.79	-0.27
UK	1.72	0.31	1.56	0.59
US	-0.22	-2.38	0.90	-0.17
Euro area	–	–	1.25	1.08

Source: IMF

bonds to compensate for the inflation risk of holding instruments with fixed redemption values. The gap therefore says something about expected inflation.

In the late 1990s and early 2000s, however, worries about inflation were slight in comparison with the early 1990s and the 1980s. Dividend yields in America (and to a lesser extent in other countries, including Britain) were driven lower as the stockmarket boomed. This widened the reverse yield gap. The gap therefore says something about investors' optimism about equities as well as about expected inflation.

Yield ratio

The yield ratio is the yield on long-term government bonds divided by the average dividend yield on shares. The yield ratio was between 1 and 1.6%

in the major markets in mid-2010. Loosely, a high ratio relative to historical experience in the country in question implies that equities are overvalued relative to bonds.

Real interest rates and yields

Measures:	Any interest rate or yield less the rate of inflation.
Significance:	Determinant of investment behaviour.
Presented as:	Per cent per year.
Focus on:	Three-month money, long-dated government bonds.
Yardstick:	See Table 12.5.
Released:	Almost continuously round the clock.

Overview

Real interest rates are nominal interest rates deflated by the rate of inflation. For simplicity, this may be approximated by subtraction. For example, over the period 2005–08 American three-month interest rates averaged 3.4% and consumer prices rose by 3.3% a year, so the real interest rate was about $3.4 - 3.3 = 0.1\%$.

Implicitly at least, investment decisions are based on real interest rates. Since inflation over the period ahead is unknown, it is the expected real interest rate that influences behaviour. This cannot be measured easily, so the latest rate of consumer-price inflation is usually used as a proxy when calculating real interest rates.

Interpretation is tricky. Logic suggests that high real rates will discourage physical investment, but recent studies suggest that cause and effect run in the opposite direction; it is the demand for investment funds that makes real rates high in the first place.

Share prices

Measures:	Prices of company share capital.
Significance:	Reflect economic expectations; useful as a leading indicator.
Presented as:	Individual prices in money and indices of average prices.
Focus on:	Broad market indices.
Yardstick:	See Table 12.6.
Released:	Almost continuously round the clock.

Overview

Share prices reflect the discounted value of future dividend payments, with a premium thrown in to reflect the risks. Future dividends depend on company profits, which in turn reflect the quality of management

Staging a recovery
Shares recovered in 2009 but are still well below their peaks

In 2008 large financial firms suffered the biggest declines in share prices of any industry, falling by 56% overall. In 2009 they rose by 28%, but were still 52% below their peak of May 2007. The Morgan Stanley Capital International (MSCI) world index tracks the equity returns of the world's 1,500 largest companies. Though the index gained 27% last year, it is still 31% below the peak it hit in October 2007. IT and telecoms firms never recovered from the dotcom bust in 2000, though IT companies posted strong gains in 2009.

Share prices by industry
December 31st, % change on a year earlier

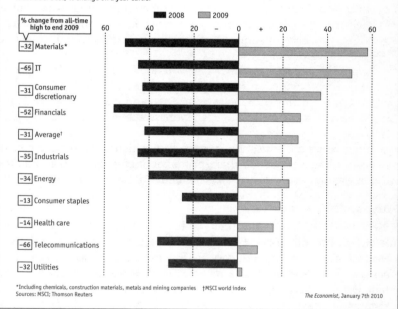

*Including chemicals, construction materials, metals and mining companies †MSCI world index
Sources: MSCI; Thomson Reuters

The Economist, January 7th 2010

and the state of the economy. For the stockmarket as a whole, variations in management quality average out, leaving perceptions about the state of the economy as a key factor in determining overall share prices.

When investors expect recession, they are less keen to buy equities and their prices fall (a bear market). As soon as there is a glimmer of

Table 12.6 **Share prices**
End years, average % change

	Nominal				Real			
	1990–94	*1995–99*	*2000–04*	*2005–09*	*1990–94*	*1995–99*	*2000–04*	*2005–09*
Australia	3.0	10.4	5.4	3.8	-0.9	7.9	1.6	1.4
Austria	-1.9	2.6	15.2	0.5	-5.2	1.0	12.8	-0.9
Belgium	-1.5	19.2	-2.6	-3.1	-4.0	17.4	-4.5	-4.5
Canada	1.2	14.8	1.9	4.9	-1.3	13.0	-0.5	3.8
Denmark	3.4	22.4	3.2	4.1	1.5	19.7	1.2	2.5
France	-1.2	25.9	-8.5	0.6	-3.5	24.4	-10.2	-0.6
Germany	0.9	27.1	-9.4	7.0	-2.8	25.5	-10.8	5.6
Italy	1.9	24.6	-6.2	-5.6	-3.1	21.2	-8.5	-7.0
Japan	-12.7	-0.8	-9.5	-1.7	-14.3	-1.1	-9.1	-1.6
Netherlands	6.6	29.0	-12.3	-0.7	3.7	26.4	-14.4	-2.0
Spain	-0.8	28.8	-1.0	5.3	-5.8	25.3	-4.2	3.4
Sweden	3.1	30.1	-6.9	5.1	-2.1	29.2	-8.3	3.7
Switzerland	8.1	23.6	-5.5	2.8	4.6	22.4	-6.4	2.1
UK	4.8	17.7	-7.0	2.4	0.4	15.5	-8.2	0.1
US	6.8	24.6	-1.3	-0.7	3.2	21.7	-3.7	-2.5

Source: Thomson Datastream

economic recovery, investors switch into equities, pushing up their prices (a bull market). Thus share prices are highly cyclical, and act as valuable leading indicators of expectations.

Broad indices and sectors

For economic fortune-telling, focus on broad market indices which average out erratic influences. For example, use the American Standard & Poor's 500 stock index rather than the Dow Jones Industrial Average of 30 stocks; and the British FTSE (*Financial Times* Stock Exchange) all-share index of nearly 800 shares rather than the narrower FTSE 100 index.

Sector averages, such as indices for consumer goods or building materials companies, may be used to assess market expectations for various parts of the economy.

13 Prices and wages

Inflation means that your money won't buy as much today as it did when you didn't have any.

Anon

Overview

Price indicators tell you about inflation. An increase in the general level of prices is nothing new: records from the days of the Roman empire show rapid inflation. Since 1946 Britain's consumer prices have risen every year, but in fact inflation – in the sense of continuously rising prices – is historically the exception not the rule. Linking together various price series (of admittedly varying quality) suggests that in 1914, on the eve of the first world war, British consumer prices were no higher than during the 1660s. During those 250 years periods of rising prices were interspersed with periods of falling prices.

Inflation has three main adverse effects. First, it blurs relative price signals; that is, it is hard to distinguish between changes in relative prices and changes in the general price level. This distorts the behaviour of individuals and firms, and so reduces economic efficiency. Second, because inflation is never perfectly predictable, it creates uncertainty, which discourages investment. Third, inflation redistributes income: from creditors to borrowers, and from those on fixed incomes to wage-earners.

It has become economic orthodoxy that price stability should be the goal of central banks. Many central banks now say that this is their aim, and several now have explicit inflation targets as the lodestar of monetary policy. In practice, this does not mean zero inflation, because consumer price indices tend to exaggerate annual inflation rates by 1 or 2 percentage points. So the Bank of England, for example, is expected to achieve an inflation rate of 2% (excluding mortgage-interest payments). The European Central Bank's target is a rate of below, but close to, 2%. The Reserve Bank of New Zealand, a pioneer in inflation targeting, is supposed to keep inflation between 1% and 3%.

Causes of inflation

There are two main theories about the causes of inflation: supply shock and demand pull. The reality is probably a complex mixture of the two.

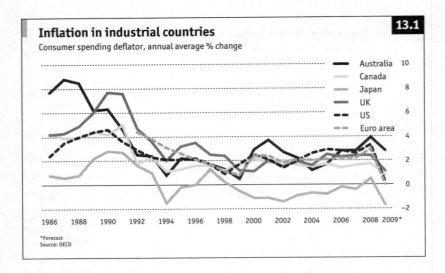

Inflation in industrial countries

Consumer spending deflator, annual average % change

Australia
Canada
Japan
UK
US
Euro area

*Forecast
Source: OECD

Supply shock (or cost push). Prices are pushed up by higher wage and raw materials costs; perhaps owing to trade union power, dearer imports as a result of a weak currency, or a jump in commodity prices.

Demand pull. Prices are pulled up when spending power (demand) is greater than the availability of goods and services. Factors which can boost aggregate demand include tax cuts, higher government spending, wage rises caused by labour shortages and an increase in consumer borrowing.

Recent experiences

Experiences with inflation range from deflation (a fall in prices experienced, for example, during the 1930s depression and by some oil-producing countries in the mid-1980s) to hyperinflation (such as when German wholesale prices rose by about 1.5 trillion % between 1919 and 1923). The most prominent recent example of deflation is Japan, where the consumer price index fell from the late 1990s to 2005. Japan experienced deflation again in 2009. Hyperinflation is frequently associated with rapid increases in the money supply (see Chapter 12).

Industrial countries. Inflation was moderate in the industrial world in the 1960s, averaging about 3% a year. It jumped sharply after the two oil price shocks in the 1970s before falling again in the 1980s. In the fight to

Table 13.1 **Comparative inflation rates, 2008**
% change on previous year

	Compensation per employee*	Consumer prices	Producer prices	— Implicit price deflators —	
				Private consumption	GDP
Australia	5.8	4.4	6.7	3.9	6.4
Austria	2.8	3.2	-3.7	2.8	2.4
Belgium	2.8	4.5	-1.6	4.3	1.7
Canada	4.0	2.4	2.3	1.7	3.9
Denmark	4.4	3.4	-3.7	3.1	4.3
France	2.4	3.2	-0.2	2.8	2.5
Germany	1.8	2.8	-4.2	2.1	1.5
Italy	2.3	3.5	-0.7	3.2	2.8
Japan	-0.1	1.4	0.9	0.5	-0.9
Netherlands	3.4	2.2	-4.2	2.3	2.7
Spain	4.4	4.1	0.4	3.8	3.0
Sweden	0.6	3.4	4.6	3.0	3.4
Switzerland	1.4	2.4	0.5	1.7	2.2
UK	2.0	3.6	4.6	2.4	2.3
US	3.2	3.8	-0.9	3.3	2.2
Euro area	2.4	3.3	-1.2	2.9	2.3
OECD	2.8	na	na	3.2	2.5

*In the private sector.
Source: OECD, national statistics

tame inflation, wage and price controls have generally given way to tight monetary and fiscal policies. Inflation generally stayed low in industrial countries during the 1990s and since, thanks to a combination of weak commodity prices and cautious monetary policies.

Developing countries. Inflation generally accelerated in the developing countries in the 1980s, and reached over 1,000% in some Latin American countries. The early 1990s saw inflation surge in eastern Europe and the former Soviet Union as ex-communist countries struggled to adjust to a market-based economy. Countries in the former Yugoslavia also experienced high inflation after the break-up of the federation.

Since the mid-1990s inflation has moderated in developing countries, falling from 90% in 1994 to 9% in 2008. Inflation slowed especially

Consumer prices

In the 12 months ending in October 2009, the rise in consumer prices in major economies slowed or even reversed into deflation as a result of the world financial crisis. America, the euro area and Japan all saw prices decline over the period. In the United Kingdom, however, inflation remained above 1%, although its retail prices saw a small decline.

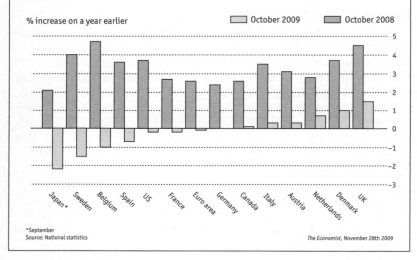

% increase on a year earlier   ☐ October 2009   ☐ October 2008

*September
Source: National statistics

The Economist, November 28th 2009

dramatically in Latin America – in Brazil, it dropped from over 2,000% in 1994 to 3.2% in 1998 – and in central and eastern Europe and the former Soviet Union.

Inflation and the economic cycle

Cycles set in train by supply shocks are evident in Chart 13.1 on page 196. The analysis of inflation is also aided by an understanding of the effects of the economic cycle, where pressures often come through on the demand side. Prices increase less rapidly or even decline during recession when consumer spending is weak. However, at the top of the cycle when personal incomes are buoyant but businesses cannot increase their output, extra demand pulls up prices.

Price indicators

Price indicators measure levels and changes in particular prices or groups of prices. For example, an oil price index covers one set of hydro-carbons while a consumer price index relates to a basket of goods and services purchased by households. In turn, these price series act as leading indicators of cost pressures and also signal movements in current demand.

Price indices are sometimes called deflators when they are used to convert (deflate) figures in current prices into constant price terms.

The composition of price indices

Most price indices are weighted averages of several prices. It is difficult to choose weights for some indicators, such as commodity price indices (see page 205), although often the basis for the weighting is clear. If 20% of an average family's spending goes on food, food has a 20% weight in the index of consumer prices. This can cause problems for interpretation, since there may not be an average family. The average rate of inflation is not experienced by a newly married couple with spending dominated by mortgage payments, nor by a retired person with little expenditure on consumer durables. It also poses problems if spending patterns are changing over time.

- **Base-weighted indices** may be used to measure changes over any period. The weights are the same for each year, so changes in the index reflect changes in prices only. The snag is that the weights may become outdated.
- **Implicit deflators** reflect changes in prices and spending patterns. For example, the American GDP implicit price deflator measures the difference between current and constant price GDP. Since the weights reflect the composition of GDP in each period, changes in the index reflect movements in both prices and the composition of GDP.

The transmission of inflationary pressures

When looking at price indicators, think about their relationship to final prices.

Sequence. The briefs on wages and prices are arranged loosely in the order in which inflationary pressures are transmitted through the economy: from raw materials' prices and wages through producers' selling prices and consumer prices to the GDP deflator. Indicators towards the end of the chapter are also signals of the state of aggregate demand.

Prices in the early stages of production generally fluctuate more than prices at later stages. A 5% change in raw materials prices is generally less worrying than a 5% change in producers' selling prices.

Relationships. The sequence of cost pressures is clear. However, it is not so simple to identify a fixed relationship between any pair of price indicators.

- There are leads and lags. In general, changes in raw materials costs take longer to feed through to retail prices than movements in producers' selling prices.
- The ultimate effect depends on the cost mix. For example, if raw materials prices rise by 10% and account for one-tenth of a manufacturer's costs, and if all other costs are held constant, the effect is a 1% increase in list prices.
- Any movement in output prices will reflect the extent to which higher input costs are absorbed in profits or offset by improved efficiency and productivity.

Indicators to use

Consumer prices are the most rapidly available guides to "national" inflation and they can be used as yardsticks for interpreting other price indicators. For example, wage settlements above the rate of consumer price inflation suggest increasing inflationary pressures (unless they are absorbed by productivity growth – see Unit labour costs, page 217).

Cost pressures are signalled by commodity prices, producer prices and wages and earnings. Surveys of price expectations are valuable leading indicators. The GDP deflator itself may be the best overall guide to inflation and should fluctuate least because it covers so many things, but it is available only after a time lag. Share prices and house prices are useful indicators of asset prices, which influence aggregate demand (see Consumer spending, pages 92–6).

For reviewing particular groups of prices or their effect on certain industries or groups of consumers, select an appropriate indicator. For example, to track the cost of capital equipment purchased by a particular industry, look for a sub-index in the producer prices or the GDP investment deflators.

Cross-references. Just about every economic indicator says something about demand pressures. Capacity use and unemployment are particularly useful, as are indicators of the government's monetary and fiscal stance. See also Balance of payments and, particularly, Exchange rates (Chapters 10 and 11).

Rates of change

Remember to distinguish between a fall in the level of prices and a fall in the rate of increase. If the inflation rate declines but remains positive, prices are still rising.

As a rule of thumb, annual inflation of 0–3% is considered good. Double-digit percentage rises are definitely bad news. Negative inflation, although rarely experienced, is not good either since it signals deflation and – almost certainly – a contracting economy.

Gold price

Measures: Market price of gold.
Significance: Raw material and psychologically important store of wealth.
Presented as: $ per oz.
Focus on: Trends.
Yardstick: Average London spot prices were $294 in 1998, $364 in 2003 and $872 in 2008. In 2009 the price reached over $1,000.
Released: Continuously round the clock.

Influences on the price of gold

The gold price reflects the interaction of supply and demand in a global market with many buyers and sellers and a free flow of information. Supply depends on production and sales from stocks while demand is influenced by gold's dual function as an industrial raw material and the ultimate store of wealth. It provides a security which cannot always be matched by paper money. Speculative demand is the major short-term determinant of price.

Supply. In 2007, China overtook South Africa to become the world's largest gold producer. It maintained that position in 2008, while the United States pushed past South Africa and Australia to become the second-largest producer. Russia and Peru were not far behind. Other countries' production generally edges upwards in the long run in response to higher prices. Sales of gold from stocks are important since stocks are many times greater than annual production. Even though central banks and the IMF sold gold from the 1970s to the 1990s when it fell from favour as a monetary standard, they still hold close to 1 billion oz in their vaults. Uncertainty about what they might do with this may depress prices; and the gold price fell sharply in 1999 after the British government said it planned to sell some of its gold. However, central bankers in developing countries will dent their gold hoards and egos only as a last resort.

Demand. Fabrication demand is mainly for jewellery, electronics and dentistry. Jewellery demand accounts for over three-quarters of industrial and commercial use and is sensitive to price. Electronics demand reflects the fortunes of the industry, decreasing during recession. Use in dentistry is fairly constant, if vulnerable to replacement by man-made materials.

Speculative and investment demand is much harder to predict since flows are large in relation to stocks and output. There tend to be flights into gold which push up its price during rapid inflation, exchange-rate turbulence or political instability worldwide. However, these are less marked now that financial markets offer more sophisticated hedging instruments. Indeed, gold-backed financial instruments, such as gold options, have eroded the lure of holding the metal itself.

Forward sales. Financial engineers have also created a wide range of instruments which allow producers to hedge several years' future output. This was probably the most important influence on prices in 1990. Every time prices rose, they were capped as forward sales pushed more metal into the world market. According to market analysts' GFMS, forward sales increased through the 1990s, peaking in 1999 at 3,080 tonnes of gold. This had fallen to 333 tonnes at the end of 2008.

Currency. Since gold is generally priced in dollars it is important to distinguish between exchange-rate effects and underlying price movements. The easiest way to do this is to convert the price into a basket currency such as the SDR. Surprisingly, not many people do this.

Gold as an indicator of inflation
Many economists, especially Americans, argue that gold is a useful indicator of inflationary pressures, but it is difficult to disentangle all the influences on gold prices. Baskets of commodity prices probably make better leading indicators than gold alone. Moreover, it does not make much difference whether gold is included or excluded from such baskets if they are weighted according to world production levels. If gold is given a greater weight to reflect its psychological importance,

the predictive value of such baskets deteriorates. In other words, a commodity price index is preferable as a leading indicator of inflation.

Oil prices

Measures: Market price of crude petroleum.
Significance: Major energy source essential to every economy; also a chemical feedstock.
Presented as: $ per barrel.
Focus on: Traded crude such as North Sea Brent or West Texas Intermediate.
Yardstick: In 1990 the oil price was around $20 a barrel. In 1999 it dipped to around $10 a barrel before recovering to $25 a barrel before the end of the year. In 2005 it reached $60 dollars a barrel and topped $75 a barrel in 2006. After a brief fall during 2007, it climbed up to $145 in mid-2008, only to fall abruptly to $30 by the end of the year. In 2009 it rose to nearly $80.
Released: Continuously round the clock.

Prices, supply and demand

Oil prices are sensitive to supply and demand, with OPEC exports being the major determinant of short-term price fluctuations.

Demand. There are obvious seasonal variations in oil demand; consumption always decreases during the hot summer months. However, in the short term annual demand is fixed in relation to GDP. Consumption fluctuates with the economic cycle in industrialised countries and rises relentlessly in line with economic growth in less developed countries. (Since 1973 oil intensity – oil consumption per unit of GDP – has fallen owing to conservation and the substitution of other fuels.)

Supply. Oil producers can be divided into three groups: OPEC, the former communist bloc and what the oil industry has traditionally called the free world. Oil output in the free world is price-responsive; it becomes profitable to extract oil from marginal fields only when prices are high. Within such considerations the free world normally produces oil flat out. The gap between demand and supply is therefore filled by OPEC crude. The organisation's attempts to control the world petroleum markets led to oil price rises in 1973 and 1979 and a sharp slump in 1986. In the past, world market sales from producers in the former Eastern bloc did not fluctuate wildly, but are now rising annually.

In the short term OPEC exports reflect the balance between members' collective willingness to restrict output to try to control the world oil

Table 13.2 **The world oil market**
Barrels per day, m

	1995	2000	2005	2006	2007	2008
Demand						
World	69.3	76.1	83.1	83.8	84.9	84.5
North America	21.2	23.5	25.0	24.9	25.0	23.8
South & Central America	4.1	4.9	5.1	5.3	5.7	5.9
Europe & Eurasia	19.6	19.6	20.3	20.5	20.0	20.2
Asia Pacific	18.1	21.1	24.3	24.6	25.3	25.3
Middle East	4.2	4.6	5.6	5.8	6.1	6.4
Africa	2.2	2.4	2.7	2.7	2.8	2.9
OECD	44.5	47.7	49.5	49.3	48.8	47.3
Supply						
World	68.1	74.9	81.1	81.5	81.4	81.8
North America	13.8	13.9	13.7	13.7	13.6	13.1
South & Central America	5.8	6.8	6.9	6.9	6.6	6.7
Europe & Eurasia	13.8	15.0	17.5	17.6	17.8	17.6
Asia Pacific	7.3	7.9	7.8	7.8	7.9	7.9
Middle East	20.3	23.5	25.3	25.5	25.2	26.2
Africa	7.1	7.8	9.8	10.0	10.3	10.3
OECD	20.7	21.5	19.9	19.5	19.1	18.4
OPEC	27.7	32.6	35.7	36.0	35.7	36.7
Prices, $/barrel						
West Texas Intermediate	18.42	30.37	56.59	66.02	72.20	100.06
Brent crude	17.02	28.50	54.52	64.14	72.39	97.26

Source: BP Statistical Review of World Energy

market, their individual need for revenue and the general political situation in the oil-producing countries. More ominously for the longer term, OPEC members are sitting on oil reserves which promise to outlast all other supplies.

Stocks. Whereas almost all the gold ever produced is still in existence (even if some is in orbit or on the sea bed), oil is rapidly consumed. Oil companies and some governments hold working and strategic stocks which help to prevent prices rocketing in times of temporary crisis, such as during the Iraqi invasion of Kuwait in 1990. Stocks of 100 days' forward consumption are about the highest to expect.

Traded crude. OPEC's slippery grip on oil trade means that its official selling prices (OSPs) are not necessarily representative of market pressures. However, whereas nearly all oil was sold on long-term contracts at fixed prices in the past, most is now traded at market prices. Traded crudes such as North Sea Brent blend or West Texas Intermediate are therefore good indicators of market conditions.

Commodity price indices

Measures:	Changes in groups of commodity prices.
Significance:	Advance warning of inflationary pressures.
Presented as:	Index numbers.
Focus on:	Trends.
Yardstick:	Prices fluctuate wildly; hope for level trends.
Released:	Daily by Reuters; weekly by *The Economist*; others monthly.

Significance

Commodities are unprocessed or semi-processed raw materials used for food or in the manufacture of other goods. Commodity prices in general are important lead indicators of cost pressures. Prices of metals and, to a lesser extent, non-food agriculturals are also indicative of the level of demand in the industrialised countries.

Monetarists note with glee the correlation between high commodity prices and liquidity in the late 1980s, and the monetary contraction and commodity price falls of the early 1990s.

Price instability

Analysis by the World Bank shows that price instability for sugar, the least stable commodity price, is over 11 times greater than that for oranges, the most stable. Moreover, commodity price fluctuations have increased sharply since the 1960s. Quite apart from the eightfold increase in the real price of oil during the 1970s, the prices of other commodities moved sharply. For example, food prices fell while timber prices rose in the 1980s. Many economic problems can be traced to these shocks and the policy responses to them.

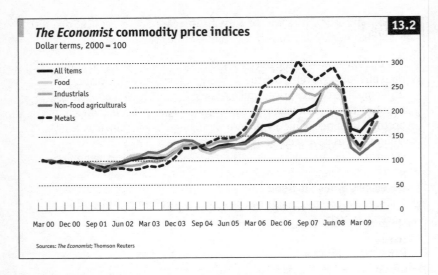

13.2

The Economist commodity price indices

Dollar terms, 2000 = 100

- All items
- Food
- Industrials
- Non-food agriculturals
- Metals

Mar 00 Dec 00 Sep 01 Jun 02 Mar 03 Dec 03 Sep 04 Jun 05 Mar 06 Dec 06 Sep 07 Jun 08 Mar 09

Sources: *The Economist*; Thomson Reuters

Influences on prices

Commodities may be divided into three broad groups depending on whether their prices are influenced mainly by demand, supply, or both.

Demand. The prices of industrial raw materials, such as metals and minerals, fluctuate in response to changes in demand, reflecting mainly economic conditions in industrialised countries. Recession brings lower demand and weaker prices. Supply tends to be more stable and predictable.

Demand for metals declined as the industrial countries introduced materials-saving technology during the 1970s and 1980s. Between 1990 and 1993, *The Economist* commodities dollar index for metals fell by over 30 percentage points. By around mid-1994 it had recovered all that lost ground and more, before it dropped in 1995 to slightly below its 1990 level. By November 2001 it had fallen a further 39%. It then turned up, thanks to Chinese demand, and by June 2007 had soared by 284%, only to fall by 58% by March 2009 amid the world economic downturn.

Supply. Food prices are influenced most heavily by unplanned changes in the supply side. For example, world vegetable oil prices depend significantly on the effects of weather on the American soyabean crop and on policies relating to American stockpiles. Food prices fell in the late 1980s and early 1990s as production and stocks recovered from the 1988 drought in America, which cut output and pushed up prices.

Metals

The ups and downs in the prices of industrial metals since the beginning of 2008 have reflected the fluctuating fortunes of the world economy. The copper price, which peaked in April 2008, had fallen by over two-thirds from that high by December 30th last year, when it hit bottom. The price of nickel fell by a whopping 72.3% from peak to trough. Prices have recovered as growth has returned to most rich countries. Copper is now selling for more than it did at the beginning of last year. The price of zinc has doubled from its low point last December, though it is still 2.9% cheaper than it was at the start of 2008. The nickel price has risen by nearly two-thirds in the year to November 24th.

Metals
Price, January 1st 2008=100

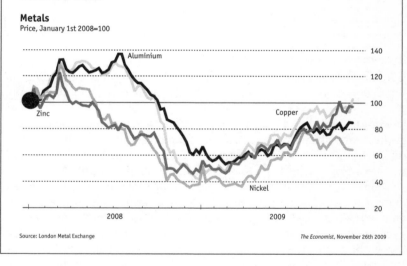

The Economist, November 26th 2009

Supply and demand. Non-food agricultural products such as cotton and rubber are vulnerable to changes in both supply and demand.

Index composition

Creating an ideal commodity price index is intellectually testing because:

- commodities are not comparable – 1 tonne of coffee is quite different from 1 tonne of copper;

207

Creeping up

Food prices are inching up again

World food prices are 2.2% lower now than they were at the beginning of 2008, according to *The Economist*'s food-price index, which has fallen by nearly a quarter since its peak in July last year. The price of wheat, which has the largest weight in the index, is now nearly a third below its January 2008 level. Rice prices, which had risen to over two-and-a-half times their level at the beginning of 2008 by the end of April last year, have now fallen to just over half that level. But rice is still nearly one-and-a-half times as expensive as it was at the beginning of 2008. A steady rise in the price of sugar over the past month means that it is now more expensive than it has been at any point since the beginning of last year.

Food prices
January 1st 2008=100, $ terms

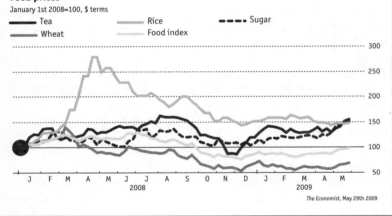

The Economist, May 29th 2009

 they are difficult to value – for example, only 6% of rice production is traded on international markets; and

 relative prices are distorted by large fluctuations in individual commodity prices.

Despite these problems there are many indices combining the prices of several commodities. Apart from *The Economist* commodities price index, the most widely followed indices are prepared by the IMF, the UN, the

World Bank and the American Commodity Research Bureau (CRB). They differ in three main ways.

The basket contents. *The Economist* index includes only commodities which are freely traded on open markets. This excludes items such as iron ore which has a big weight in the other main indices. *The Economist* also omits oil and precious metals such as gold. The two previous briefs suggest that gold and oil are important commodities but they are subject to special factors which may make them less valuable as simple cost indicators.

The basket weights. *The Economist* index is designed to measure cost pressures in industrial countries; its constituents are weighted according to their share in world imports. The UN, IMF and World Bank indicators are intended to monitor the terms of trade in developing countries; the constituents are weighted to reflect shares in developing countries' exports. The CRB index just gives equal weight to all components, which understates the importance of industrial commodities and so makes it less useful as a leading indicator of inflation.

The currency. Commodity prices are most often quoted in dollars. As a result, currency fluctuations will move indices even when there is no underlying change in commodity prices.

Bottom line

The Economist index is hard to beat for tracking the interrelation between cost pressures and inflation; see the weekly table in *The Economist*. A rise in the index may signal higher inflation, but the final outcome depends on monetary conditions and supply and demand in other factor markets such as labour.

A UN, IMF or World Bank index should be used if you are interested in the way that changes in commodity prices affect the external balances of developing countries: a fall in commodity prices implies a deterioration in exporters' trade balances.

Export and import prices; unit values

Measures: Prices of traded goods.

Significance: Helps identify cost pressures, potential exchange-rate problems and changes in competitiveness.

Presented as: Index numbers.

Focus on: Changes in unit values (see text).

Yardstick: A positive rate of increase, as close to zero as possible, is good. Check the ratio between import and export prices (see Terms of trade, page 172).

Released: Monthly with trade figures; quarterly with GDP.

Prices. Import or export price indices, including the deflators released with GDP data, capture changes in both the prices and the composition of a country's external trade.

Unit values. Indices of import or export unit values, which are essentially fixed-weight price indices, highlight changes in prices only. This is useful for reviewing cost and competitive pressures. However, since the weights get out of date when the structure of trade changes – as it inevitably does – unit value indices are best for analysing short-term trends.

Export prices or values. Compare export price indices with domestic price indicators, such as the producer price index for home-produced goods, to get a feel for the way that manufacturers are passing on cost pressures to foreign buyers; or perhaps being constrained from doing so by international competitive pressures.

Import prices or values. Use import price indices to judge external cost pressures. Import prices that are rising faster than domestic prices are a clear warning of imported inflation.

Erratic items. Prices of raw materials can fluctuate widely. It is often sensible to look at price indices which exclude these more erratic items to identify underlying pressures.

Terms of trade. One of the most useful ways of looking at import and export prices is by examining the ratio between them, which is known as the terms of trade (see page 172).

Producer and wholesale prices

Measures: Prices of goods at the factory gate.
Significance: Leading indicator of cost pressures.
Presented as: Monthly index numbers.
Focus on: Percentage changes.
Yardstick: OECD average producer prices rose 3.5% during the period 1990–98 and 3.4% a year during the period 2000–08.
Released: Monthly, at least one month in arrears.

Wholesale price indices (WPIs) cover prices charged at the first stage of bulk distribution and generally include import prices. WPIs were first introduced to measure prices of raw materials.

Producer price indices (PPIs) track prices of home-produced goods at the factory gate. Most PPIs cover output prices of goods, although some countries also prepare input price indices for raw materials purchased by industry. In principle, input prices include transport to the factory and output prices are ex-works, although such prices cannot always be identified neatly.

PPIs shed light on cost pressures affecting domestic production and are more useful than WPIs. Most major countries now produce PPIs. The indices cover manufacturing and, sometimes, construction.

Index construction

The indices are compiled on the basket principle with weights reflecting the output of each contributor relative to the total. For example, if lacemakers account for 1% of total industrial production, lace prices have a 1% weight in the index.

Weights are generally updated at 5–10 year intervals to take account of the changing structure of industry. Data are acquired by surveys, usually of major companies. The Greek index covers 3,000 price series, the British index over 9,000, and the American index over 100,000.

In many cases returns are collected continuously so that the prices are effectively monthly averages rather than those applying on just one date. Even so, changes one month will not be reflected fully until the following month.

Taxes such as VAT are usually excluded. Excise duties such as on tobacco and alcohol are treated as manufacturers' costs and are included, so the index moves if they are changed.

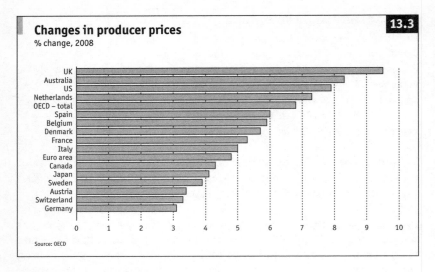

Changes in producer prices 13.3
% change, 2008

Source: OECD

The cycle

Prices are generally order prices with list prices adjusted by government statisticians to allow for "normal" discounts in each industry. This is fine when the economy is stable, but the PPI may overstate cost pressures when above-average discounts are offered during a recession. Conversely, the PPI understates cost pressures when inflation is rapid; deliveries may be at prices which were negotiated perhaps several months earlier and which are much below current order prices scored in the index.

Use

Producer output prices and consumer prices tend to follow the same path, with producer prices fluctuating more widely. However, producer prices generally increase less rapidly than consumer prices (compare Tables 13.4 and 13.7).

Producer input price indices vary more widely than output prices in response to movements in both commodity prices and exchange rates and are a useful guide to raw materials cost pressures. See the comments on pages 199–200 about the way that pressures feed through the system.

Seasonal adjustment. PPIs are rarely seasonally adjusted. Even if they are, the seasonal adjustment can be suspect, especially on the input side, since, for example, exchange rates do not follow a neat seasonal path.

Table 13.3 **Producer prices (manufacturing)**
Annual average % change

	1985–89	1990–94	1995–99	2000–04	2005–08	2008
Australia	6.7	2.3	1.4	3.0	6.1	8.2
Austria	-0.7	0.9	-0.1	2.2	3.1	3.4
Belgium	-0.4	-0.2	0.7	2.5	4.3	5.9
Canada	2.5	1.9	2.1	1.4	2.4	4.3
Denmark	2.2	0.6	1.1	1.8	3.5	4.3
France	2.6	-0.8	-0.2	0.9	3.6	5.3
Germany	0.9	1.2	1.3	1.4	2.5	3.1
Italy	4.0	3.4	0.5	2.5	3.9	5.0
Japan	-1.4	-0.3	2.1	-0.8	2.0	4.2
Netherlands	-1.3	-0.5	-0.9	3.0	5.3	7.3
Spain	3.3	2.3	0.9	2.5	4.8	6.0
Sweden	5.0	2.9	1.8	1.0	3.8	3.9
Switzerland	1.1	0.9	1.4	0.4	2.3	3.3
UK	3.9	4.2	-1.0	1.1	4.9	9.6
US	1.9	1.9	1.6	2.2	5.3	8.0
Euro area	2.0	1.8	1.2	1.9	3.6	4.9
OECD	2.4	2.9	3.2	2.4	4.4	6.7

Source: OECD

Comparisons over 12 months provide a safer guide to trends, while underlying producer price pressures can often be better identified by examining PPIs excluding items such as food prices, which tend to bump around erratically.

Detail. Producer price numbers are usually available at a high level of detail, covering commodity groups (metals, furniture), stages of processing (crude materials, intermediate goods) and industries (farm machinery, capital goods). Watch especially the prices of finished goods in general and of consumer goods.

Special applications. PPIs are frequently used as the basis for price indices for inflation accounting and also for contract price adjustments, often in combination with earnings indices.

Surveys of price expectations

Measures: Manufacturers' perceptions of inflationary pressures.
Significance: Excellent anecdotal warning of potential price changes.
Presented as: Percentage balances (for example, percentage of those expecting to raise prices).
Focus on: Trend in expectations.
Yardstick: An increase of a few points over a few months is a warning of inflationary pressures.
Released: Monthly; not revised.

Coverage and interpretation

Surveys of price expectations provide excellent inflation indicators usually straight from the horses' mouths. Various organisations conduct monthly or quarterly surveys (see Business conditions, page 115) in which respondents are asked questions such as: "Do you intend to raise your prices within the next four months?" The balance of those answering yes over those saying no is presented as, say, +20% or (50 + 20) = 70. If a net 20% of respondents expect to lower prices, the balance would be −20% or (50 − 20) = 30.

The absolute balance may not be a good guide, since there may always be an excess of companies planning price rises even in times of low and stable inflation. As a quick guide, see if the latest numbers are above or below figures for recent months; a change in the trend may suggest a potential increase or decrease in cost pressures. Better still, examine a long run of data so that you can put the latest figure in the context of the economic cycle.

Wages, earnings and labour costs

Measures: Labour costs and influences on consumers' incomes.
Significance: Indicator of both cost and demand pressures.
Presented as: Usually index form, some figures in cash terms.
Focus on: Percentage change over 12 months.
Yardstick: Compare with growth of output and consumer prices. In the OECD, compensation per employee in the business sector rose by 4.5% a year during the period 1990–2007, declining from 7% in 1997 to 3.4% in 2007.
Released: Mainly monthly, at least one month in arrears; revised.

Terminology

Wage rates. Basic pay per period (hour, week, and so on). Manual

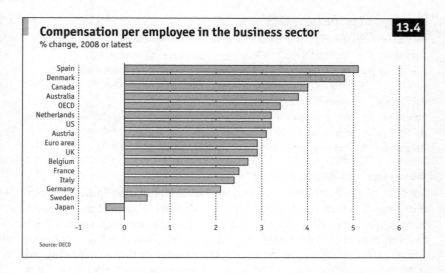

Compensation per employee in the business sector 13.4
% change, 2008 or latest

Source: OECD

workers tend to have wages, white collar workers have salaries (are paid monthly).

Earnings. Basic pay plus overtime and bonuses. These may be quoted before or after tax and other deductions. Take-home pay is earnings after deductions.

Wage drift. The tendency for earnings to rise faster than wage rates, for example, due to overtime and bonuses.

Labour costs. Sometimes called total compensation, these are wages and salaries plus pension contributions, payroll taxes such as social security, free meals and a host of other perks. Non-wage costs are 20–50% of labour costs. (See also page 217.)

The Phillips curve. In the 1950s a New Zealand economist, A.W. Phillips, identified an apparent trade-off between unemployment and the rate of increase in wages. His curve suggested that low annual increases in wages are associated with a high unemployment rate; or, conversely, high wage inflation is associated with a low unemployment rate. (See Unemployment, page 68.)

Table 13.4 **Hourly earnings in manufacturing**
Annual average % change

	1985–89	1990–94	1995–99	2000–04	2008
Australia	7.5	4.1	3.9	5.1	5.7
Austria	4.4	5.3	3.2	2.5	na
Belgium	2.5	3.9	2.3	2.3	2.9
Canada	3.9	4.0	1.7	2.4	1.7
Denmark	6.0	3.6	4.0	3.8	3.2
France	4.0	3.2	2.5	3.6	3.1
Germany	4.1	5.0	2.6	2.1	2.8
Italy	6.9	5.8	3.0	2.3	3.4
Japan	3.3	2.4	1.3	1.0	0.1
Netherlands	2.1	3.2	2.4	3.1	3.8
Spain	8.6	7.5	4.2	4.1	5.4
Sweden	7.9	5.2	4.4	3.1	3.9
UK	8.4	6.7	4.3	3.9	2.9
US	2.7	3.1	2.8	3.1	2.8
Euro area	4.9	5.1	4.2	3.2	4.2
OECD	na	5.1	4.2	3.5	2.7

Source: OECD

Key figures

Cash totals. Many government and private-sector bodies publish money wage rates and earnings in various industries, sometimes including the cash value of perks such as company cars. The figures are interesting for comparisons between industries, sectors and countries. International comparisons, however, are complicated by differences in coverage, tax regimes and by fluctuations in exchange rates.

Time series. Governments also produce indices showing trends in wages and earnings, while various organisations (including those mentioned in Business conditions, page 115) track pay settlements. These are important indicators of both cost pressures and aggregate demand. Personal incomes (see page 90) offer a better guide to potential consumer demand because earnings are usually quoted before tax and other deductions, often cover only part of total employment and may ignore income from self-employment.

At one extreme, American average weekly earnings exclude salary-earners and cover only production and non-supervisory workers. At the other, British average earnings cover both manual and non-manual employees.

Interpretation

Wages and earnings are closely linked to the economic cycle. When aggregate demand begins to recover after a recession, producers respond first by increasing overtime and earnings rise faster than wage rates. Only when higher demand seems more established do employers take on more workers, which then puts upward pressure on wage rates. When the cycle turns and output begins to decline, overtime is cut first and earnings rise less rapidly or fall. Then staff are laid off. The annual increase in wage rates tends to decline as unemployment rises, although usually with a lag.

A change in average earnings can reflect changes in wage rates, total hours, the mix of standard hours and overtime, output (piecework and profit-sharing), and the relative mix of jobs, grades, industry, and so on.

In general, if earnings are rising faster than consumer price inflation, real spending power is growing. It should be noted, however, that earnings data can be distorted by industrial disputes, delays in implementing pay settlements, lump-sum back pay and temporary lay-offs during bad weather.

Unit labour costs

Measures: Labour costs per unit of output.
Significance: Indicator of cost pressures and competitiveness.
Presented as: Index form.
Focus on: Percentage change over 12 months.
Yardstick: OECD average unit labour costs in the whole economy rose by 3.7% a year during the period 1990–99 and by 2.0% during the period 2000–08.
Released: At least one month after the end of the quarter; frequently revised.

Significance

Unit labour costs (ULCs) measure the average cost of producing one unit of output; for example, labour costs divided by GDP. This is a key indicator of the cost efficiency of labour. If unit labour costs fall, the same output can be produced for less expenditure on labour.

Unit labour costs reflect two factors, labour costs and productivity. Britain's rapid increases in unit labour costs in 1989 and 1990 reflected the twin evils of rising wages and falling output, and hence declining productivity.

Table 13.5 **Unit labour costs in the whole economy**
Annual average % change

	1985–89	1990–94	1995–99	2000–04	2008
Australia	5.5	2.0	1.2	2.2	4.1
Austria	2.0	2.6	-0.8	0.4	2.7
Belgium	2.3	4.2	0.6	1.5	3.9
Canada	4.1	1.8	0.8	2.0	4.0
Denmark	4.4	0.8	2.2	2.3	6.4
France	1.9	1.8	0.4	1.9	2.4
Germany	1.5	3.4	0.3	0.2	2.5
Italy	5.7	4.3	1.7	2.5	4.0
Japan	-0.2	1.2	-0.9	-2.8	1.5
Netherlands	0.2	2.3	1.5	2.9	2.9
Spain	5.9	7.2	2.3	2.9	2.7
Sweden	7.0	2.9	1.1	2.0	3.3
UK	6.1	4.5	2.1	2.9	2.6
US	3.3	3.2	1.4	2.1	1.7
Euro area	2.5	3.5	0.7	1.6	3.2
OECD – total	7.1	5.3	3.6	2.2	2.3

Source: OECD

The cycle

Within the economic cycle, the rate of increase in unit labour costs generally peaks 12–18 months after a peak in activity. When output first begins to fall ULCs rise faster because there is less production for the same spending on labour.

Competitiveness

Relative movements in ULCs are important signals of international competitiveness in traded goods. Businesses in a country where ULCs are rising faster than in other countries might temporarily absorb the pressures by cutting profit margins or improving efficiency.

In the longer term deteriorating competitiveness will reduce exports, output and employment and so eventually tame inflation the hard way. Some economists still advocate devaluation to restore price competitiveness, but experience shows that the initial benefit is quickly eroded by faster inflation.

A fixed exchange rate can impose a useful discipline on pay bargaining.

Consumer or retail prices

Measures: Price of a basket of goods and services.
Significance: Indicates inflation as experienced by a "typical" household.
Presented as: Monthly index numbers.
Focus on: Percentage changes.
Yardstick: OECD average consumer prices rose by 9.3% a year during the 1980s and by 2.8% during the period 2000–08.
Released: Monthly, one month in arrears; quarterly in Australia, New Zealand and Ireland; rarely revised.

Composition

The consumer price index (CPI) is the indicator most people use to track inflation. The index is familiar and readily available, but not necessarily accurate. The European Union's statistical agency, Eurostat, publishes a harmonised index of consumer prices (HICP) for the EU member states, which is equivalent to Britain's CPI. Estimates of HICP for individual member states are also published. The European Central Bank's inflation target is defined in terms of HICP for the 16 euro area countries.

Basket contents and weighting. CPIs measure the cost of a basket of goods and services purchased by the average household each month. The basket's composition and weighting are usually based on surveys of household or family expenditure habits.

Some indices cover "essentials" only. By careful selection a consumer price index can be dominated by subsidised commodities and those subject to official price controls. This is how some developing countries keep down their reported consumer price inflation. Most indices, however, cover a fairly full range of discretionary expenditure. Weights are updated annually in Britain and France, but most countries change their weights only every 5–10 years.

Price data. Taxes on expenditure and subsidies are included in CPIs; it would be difficult to exclude them. Other taxes such as those on incomes are excluded, as are savings, life insurance premiums and capital spending.

Prices are usually found by observation, perhaps of over 100,000

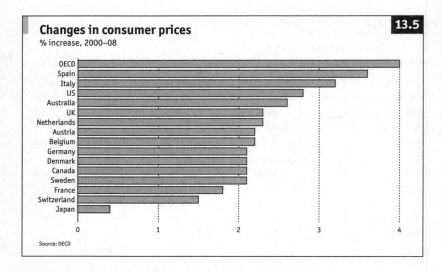

Changes in consumer prices `13.5`
% increase, 2000–08

Source: OECD

items each month. Collection points vary from six state capitals in Australia to over 100 urban centres in France and Germany.

The information is collected by surveys on a particular day so a price change late one month may not be caught in the index until the following month. Indeed, in America, for example, prices of most goods and services other than food and fuel are collected monthly in the five largest geographic areas and every other month in the remaining 80 survey locations. In some other countries major surveys are conducted only every three months.

Housing. The British Retail Price Index and Canada's index exclude the cost of houses and capital repayments on home loans but include mortgage interest payments. As a result, if interest rates are increased in response to inflationary pressures, the index rises automatically, which is exactly the opposite to the desired and underlying effect. Most other countries use a more satisfactory rental equivalent for measuring housing costs. See also "House prices" below.

Variations

Many countries produce more than one CPI. America has two main indices: the CPI-U for urban consumers (about 87% of the population) and the CPI-W for wage earners (32% of the population).

As well as the headline index, CPI, which excludes most housing

Table 13.6 **Consumer prices**
Annual average % change

	1985–89	1990–94	1995–99	2000–04	2008
Australia	7.8	3.0	2.0	3.4	4.4
Austria	2.2	3.4	1.4	2.0	3.2
Belgium	2.4	2.8	1.4	2.1	4.5
Canada	4.3	2.8	1.6	2.4	2.4
Denmark	4.3	2.1	2.1	2.2	3.4
France	3.6	2.5	1.2	1.9	2.8
Germany	1.2	3.8	1.3	1.5	2.6
Italy	6.2	5.3	3.0	2.5	3.3
Japan	1.1	2.0	0.4	-0.5	1.4
Netherlands	0.7	2.8	2.1	2.6	2.5
Spain	6.9	5.6	2.9	3.2	4.1
Sweden	5.6	5.8	0.8	1.5	3.4
Switzerland	2.1	3.9	0.8	0.9	2.4
UK	4.6	4.6	2.0	1.2	3.6
US	3.6	3.6	2.4	2.5	3.8
OECD – total	7.6	5.7	4.9	3.1	3.7

Source: OECD

costs, Britain also publishes an index excluding mortgage-interest payments (RPIX) and an index excluding mortgage-interest payments and indirect taxes (RPIY). The Bank of England's inflation target is now defined in terms of the CPI. If mortgage payments were included in the target, then interest rate increases would have the perverse effect of increasing the target measure of inflation.

Use and abuse

CPIs are the most timely and best understood inflation indicators. They are often used in setting wage demands and in determining index-linked pay, pension or social welfare payments. They are also used to convert wages and prices of consumer goods (including capital items such as houses) into "real" terms.

Consumer expenditure and GDP deflators are often better guides to inflation, but usually they are not available quickly enough.

221

Interpretation

Getting at the underlying rate of inflation may not be easy. CPIs are generally not seasonally adjusted and the necessary 12-month comparison is slow to highlight changes in trends. Looking at movements over the latest few months can be misleading because of erratic and distorting factors such as seasonal variations in food prices, annual price-cutting sales promotions, one-off changes in the rate of sales tax and erratic bumps in oil prices.

It is almost always necessary to make adjustments to highlight the "core" rate of inflation. Many statistical agencies produce helpful sub-indices, usually excluding food and energy prices.

House prices

Measures: Changes in prices of residential property.

Significance: Warning of asset-price bubbles or collapses.

Presented as: Index numbers or average prices.

Focus on: Trends.

Yardstick: Affordability, ie, relationship with incomes.

Released: Mostly monthly, by government, central banks, building societies, private organisations.

Overview

As the asset bubble grew in the 1990s and early 2000s, more attention was drawn to indicators of house prices around the world. Data are in indexed or average value terms and are published by both government and private sources. They can only be a guide as the basket of houses may change or be different in different countries, and the quality and intrinsic value of the same house over time can vary greatly.

You can't keep 'em down

Houses remain overvalued in many countries where prices are now rising

Housing markets continue to strengthen, as The Economist's latest survey of global house prices shows. Our periodic round-up was dominated for nearly a year by countries where house prices were falling year-on-year. But the latest available data show that in half of the 20 countries whose markets we monitor, house prices are higher than they were twelve months earlier.

The Economist house-price indicators
% change

	Latest	Q4 2008	1997-	Under(-)/
	on a year earlier		2010*	over(+) valued†
Hong Kong	27.7	-4.6	-16	49.1
Singapore	24.5	-4.7	9	19.6
Australia	13.6	-4.1	197	56.1
China	10.7	0.5	na	2.7
Britain	9.0	-14.9	180	31.2
South Africa	6.6	0.5	417	na
Switzerland	6.2	3.7	31	-7.1
Sweden	5.8	-2.0	159	37.0
New Zealand	1.1	-8.9	105	na
Canada	0.9	-0.1	68	21.8
United States (Case-Shiller ten-city index)	nil	-19.2	97	3.9
Germany	-0.4	1.1	na	-14.6
Netherlands	-2.0	-5.4	86	20.4
United States (Case-Shiller national index)	-2.5	-18.2	63	-3.7
Belgium	-3.0	2.7	149	30.9
Japan	-4.0	-2.6	-36	-33.7
Italy	-4.1	1.1	96	13.1
France	-4.3	-3.0	133	39.7
United States (FHFA)	-4.7	-4.3	74	13.1
Spain	-6.3	-3.2	166	53.4
Denmark	-13.1	-10.5	91	17.5
Ireland	-18.5	-9.7	142	24.5

*Or most recent available figure   †Against long-run average of price-to-rents ratio
Sources: ABSA; ESRI; Hypoport; Japan Real Estate Institute; Nationwide; Nomisma; NVM; FHFA; Quotable Value; Stadim; Swiss National Bank; Standard & Poor's; Thomson Reuters; government offices; The Economist

The Economist, April 15th 2010

Since these indicators were last published at the end of 2009, house-price inflation has quickened in each of the seven countries where it was already positive. In Hong Kong, prices are more than a quarter above their level a year earlier. With the exception of Ireland, the pace of decline has slowed in countries where the market has yet to turn the corner. In America, two of the three measures we follow show that prices remain below their level a year earlier, but the Case-Shiller index of house prices in ten big cities was at the same level in January as it was a year earlier.

continued on next page

Singapore has gone from being one of the most depressed housing markets in the third quarter of 2009 to being the second-frothiest in the three months to March. This effervescence clearly worries its government, which has made it more difficult for buyers to delay mortgage payments and taken steps to deter speculative purchases. In Canada, another country where house prices are rising again, new rules announced in February make it more expensive to buy an investment property and reduce the amount that existing homeowners can borrow against their houses.

Should other countries consider similar steps? That depends in part on a judgment about whether prices have fallen far enough to erase the excesses of the bubble, or whether houses remain overvalued. One way to get at this is to compare the ratio of house prices to rents in a country to its long-run average, as our measure of fair value in housing does.

In Japan, Switzerland and Germany housing-to-rent ratios are below their long-run average. But even for America, one version of The Economist's fair-value measure suggests that the correction in house prices may have gone far enough. Prices measured using the Case-Shiller national index have fallen enough to make houses there look underpriced. In the big American cities covered by the Case-Shiller ten-city index, the price-to-rent ratio is nearing its historic average. Houses in America are still overvalued by around 13% if prices are measured using the index maintained by the Federal Housing Finance Agency, but this excludes properties financed using subprime mortgages, many of which have been sold at very low prices, and so may understate the extent to which prices have been plummeting.

The story is different in Britain. British house prices had risen by nearly 10% in the year to the end of the first quarter of 2010, but the country's price-to-rent ratio still outstrips its long-term average by nearly a third. This pattern – of prices rising in markets where houses still look overvalued – is also seen in Hong Kong, Singapore, Australia, Sweden and Canada. In France, Italy, Spain and Ireland, houses do appear overpriced relative to their earnings potential, but at least prices there are still falling.

Table 13.7 **Consumer spending deflators**
Annual average % change

	1985–89	1990–94	1995–99	2000–04	2008
Australia	7.3	3.2	1.6	2.5	3.9
Austria	2.1	3.3	1.3	1.7	2.8
Belgium	2.8	2.8	1.2	2.2	4.3
Canada	4.1	2.8	1.5	1.8	1.7
Denmark	4.1	2.1	1.7	2.1	3.1
France	3.8	2.5	0.8	1.6	2.8
Germany	1.1	3.3	0.9	1.4	2.1
Italy	6.2	5.8	3.2	2.9	3.2
Japan	1.1	1.3	0.1	-1.0	0.5
Netherlands	0.9	2.7	1.8	2.8	2.3
Spain	6.9	5.9	3.0	3.2	3.8
Sweden	5.7	6.1	1.5	1.7	3.0
Switzerland	1.5	3.7	0.5	0.9	1.7
UK	5.1	5.1	2.7	1.6	2.4
US	3.6	3.1	1.7	2.1	3.3
Euro area	4.0	4.2	1.7	2.1	2.9
OECD	6.9	4.3	4.0	2.5	3.2

Source: OECD

Consumer or private expenditure deflators

Measures: Price changes affecting total consumers' expenditure.

Significance: A broad indicator of consumer price inflation which is less susceptible to fiddling than consumer price indices.

Presented as: Quarterly and annual index numbers.

Focus on: Percentage changes.

Yardstick: OECD average consumer expenditure deflators rose by 4.6% a year during the period 1990–2008, declining from 6.5% in 1990 to 3.2% in 2008.

Released: Quarterly, at least one month in arrears; frequently revised.

Advantages

Consumer expenditure or private consumption deflators are derived from current and constant price estimates of total consumer expenditure. This reflects actual spending, which is arguably better than the consumer prices basket approach of outlays by an average family. It also avoids a selective approach when specifying what goes in the basket.

In addition, consumer prices data are collected at one point each month, while deflators relate to averages over the period, usually three months at a time. The deflators normally include an imputed figure for house rents, which is less distorting than the interest-rate approach used for the British RPI and the Canadian CPI.

Problems

Deflators are not available as rapidly as consumer price indices and the deflators are revised more often. Movements in implicit price deflators reflect changes in the composition of consumers' expenditure as well as changes in prices (fixed-weight deflators avoid this problem). The personal sector is broader than households; it often also covers unincorporated businesses (such as farms, pension funds and trusts) and private non-profit bodies (such as charities and trade unions).

Bottom line

Consumer expenditure deflators should be used with care. They usually provide a valuable alternative to consumer price indices. If nothing else, they are a useful check on the signals from other inflation indices.

GDP deflators

Measures: Overall national price changes.
Significance: Broadest indicator of inflation.
Presented as: Quarterly and annual index numbers.
Focus on: Percentage changes.
Yardstick: OECD average GDP deflators rose by 8.0% a year during the 1980s and by
               2.7% a year during the period 2000–08.
Released: Quarterly, at least one month in arrears; frequently revised.

Definition

Deflators measure the difference between current and constant price GDP and its components. For example, if GDP increases by 2% in real terms and 5% in nominal terms, the implied economy-wide rate of inflation is 3%.

Deflators can be found at any level of detail from one component of consumer spending or business investment right up to total GDP (see Table 13.1). They are not always published, but they can be readily calculated in index form if current and constant price data are available: for each period divide the current by the constant price data and multiply by 100.

Table 13.8 **GDP deflators**
Annual average % change

	1985–89	1990–94	1995–99	2000–04	2008
Australia	7.1	2.1	1.2	3.6	6.4
Austria	2.4	3.2	0.6	1.5	2.4
Belgium	3.2	3.0	1.0	1.9	1.7
Canada	4.0	2.0	1.3	2.6	3.9
Denmark	4.4	2.1	1.6	2.4	4.3
France	4.0	2.2	1.0	1.8	2.5
Germany	2.2	3.6	0.7	0.8	1.5
Italy	7.3	5.5	3.3	2.8	2.8
Japan	1.3	1.4	-0.3	-1.4	-0.9
Netherlands	0.7	2.3	1.9	3.2	2.7
Spain	7.4	5.9	3.2	4.0	3.0
Sweden	6.4	4.8	1.5	1.5	3.4
Switzerland	2.8	3.2	0.3	0.8	2.2
UK	5.6	4.4	2.7	2.4	2.3
US	3.1	2.8	1.6	2.3	2.2
Euro area	4.7	4.0	1.7	2.1	2.3
OECD	6.9	5.0	4.4	2.9	2.5

Source: OECD

Unless otherwise stated, most deflators are implicit price deflators. These measure changes in the composition of GDP as well as changes in price. Fixed-weight indicators show changes in price only (see page 198).

Use

Deflators are valuable for identifying trends and obtaining advance warning of price changes in many areas.

The consumer expenditure deflator is an important alternative to the consumer prices index (see pages 219–22). The overall GDP deflator (also known as the index of total home costs per unit of home output) is the best indicator of overall economy-wide inflation.

Since deflators cover many items and price movements self-cancel to some extent, deflators do not fluctuate as much as narrower indices such as those covering consumer prices or producer prices.

Appendix Useful websites

Here is a list of some useful websites for official statistics:

International
European Union
Eurostat
www.ec.europa.eu/eurostat
European Central Bank
www.ecb.int

IMF
www.imf.org

OECD
www.oecd.org

United Nations
www.un.org
United Nations Population Fund
www.unfpa.org
United Nations Conference on Trade and Development
www.unctad.org

World Bank
www.worldbank.org

National statistical offices/central banks
Australia
Bureau of Statistics
www.abs.gov.au
Reserve Bank
www.rba.gov.au

Austria
Statistik Austria
www.statistik.at

National Bank
www.oenb.at

Belgium
National Institute of Statistics
www.statbel.fgov.be
National Bank
www.nbb.be

Brazil
Institute of Statistics and Geography
www.ibge.gov.br
Central Bank
www.bcb.gov.br

Canada
Statistics Canada
www.statcan.gc.ca
Bank of Canada
www.bankofcanada.ca

China
National Bureau of Statistics
www.stats.gov.cn
People's Bank of China
www.pbc.gov.cn

Finland
Statistics Finland
www.tilastokeskus.fi
Bank of Finland
www.bof.fi

France
INSEE
www.insee.fr
Bank of France
www.banque-france.fr

Germany
Federal Statistical Office
www.destatis.de
Bundesbank
www.bundesbank.de

India
Ministry of Statistics
www.mospi.nic.in
Reserve Bank
www.rbi.org.in

Ireland
Central Statistics Office
www.cso.ie
Central Bank
www.centralbank.ie

Italy
ISTAT
www.istat.it
Bank of Italy
www.bancaditalia.it

Japan
Statistics Bureau
www.stat.go.jp
Bank of Japan
www.boj.or.jp

Mexico
National Institute of Statistics, Geography and Informatics
www.inegi.org.mx
Bank of Mexico
www.banxico.org.mx

Netherlands
Statistics Netherlands
www.cbs.nl

Netherlands Bank
www.dnb.nl

Russia
Federal State Statistics Services
www.gks.ru
Central Bank
www.cbr.ru

South Korea
Statistics Korea
www.kostat.go.kr
Bank of Korea
www.bok.or.kr

Spain
National Institute of Statistics
www.ine.es
Bank of Spain
www.bde.es

Sweden
Statistics Sweden
www.scb.se
Bank of Sweden
www.riksbank.se

Switzerland
Federal Statistical Office
www.bfs.admin.ch
Swiss National Bank
www.snb.ch

UK
National Statistics
www.ons.gov.uk
Bank of England
www.bankofengland.co.uk

US

FedStats (links to federal government statistics)
www.fedstats.gov
Commerce Department, Bureau of Economic Analysis, US Census
Bureau
www.bea.gov
www.census.gov
US Treasury
www.ustreas.gov
Federal Reserve
www.federalreserve.gov

Links to central banks

Bank for International Settlements
www.bis.org/cbanks.htm

Index